BRITISH
WARSHIPS
& Auxiliaries
1952

HMS Vanguard

First published in the United Kingdom in 2011 by Maritime Books, Lodge Hill, Liskeard, Cornwall, PL14 4EL

CONTENTS

THE DOMINION NAVIES

NAVAL AVIATION

AUTHOR'S NOTES

Maritime Books have produced the annual *British Warships & Auxiliaries* since the first edition appeared in 1979. In the intervening 33 years the Royal Navy has changed dramatically. The Cold War has come and gone and the RN is re-inventing itself to counter the perceived threats of the future. It is smaller and far more technologically advanced than it has ever been before. However, each year we publish the book, there are fewer and fewer warships and the most frequent comment we receive is the inevitable "it wasn't like that in my day".

I have often toyed with the idea of producing a "retro" edition of the book, to see exactly what it was like 'in my day' and the Diamond Jubilee of Her Majesty the Queen in 2012 seemed to be an ideal time to take a look back at the Royal Navy of 1952.

The RN was, much as today, re-inventing itself after the Second World War as it tried to counter the ever increasing threat from the Soviet Communists to the east. There was a massive shipbuilding programme underway as wartime tonnage was updated and new warships built to bring the new technologies of the day into frontline service. A lot of what we know today about these times, and the programmes of the day, benefit from knowledge obtained after the event, sometimes several decades after the event. The idea of this book was to write it as if published in 1952, and therefore a lot of that knowledge had to be ignored as the aim is to present a picture of the RN in the context of the day.

Wherever possible I have stuck to that premise, but there are occasions, where the exact timing of certain decisions is a little grey. Details of the future fleet in particular are a little hazy as to the exact sequence of ordering, naming, renaming, issuing of pennant numbers etc and so for clarity such information has been included, even though it may extend beyond the end of 1952. As far as images are concerned I have also tried to use contemporary images and the majority of the photographs pre-date the end of 1952. There may be the odd one or two which post date the book - it might be that I couldn't source an earlier image, or that the image was incorrectly dated but, as far as is possible, I have tried to stay within the prescribed timeline.

In some entries alongside the dates you will see a few abbreviations (L = Launched; LD = Laid Down; Ordered = Work yet to start). These are included to show how far programmes have progressed or, in some cases, where completion dates are not known (it appears that many of the build programmes recorded launch as the significant date rather than completion).

Although my name appears on the cover of the book, I must acknowledge the extensive help received from two highly regarded naval historians and former Royal Navy

Officers, whose expertise and knowledge of the period have greatly enhanced my appreciation of the period. Firstly my thanks go to Ben Warlow, who tried to frighten me off the project by producing a never ending list of ships and submarines which would have to fit within the covers, but remained supportive throughout and passed final judgement on the finished article prior to printing. Secondly, to David Hobbs, who enthusiastically researched the Naval Aviation aspects of the book which has resulted in a comprehensive review of all things air related. Without their help this volume would have been considerably thinner!

I hope that you find the book of interest, but please bear in mind that this is intended as a handbook to provide an overview of the RN fleet in 1952 and not an academic study of the period.

Steve Bush
Plymouth 2011

THE ROYAL NAVY
1952

After years of post-war neglect, the Royal Navy of 1952 finds itself in the middle of a substantial shipbuilding and conversion programme with well over 100 ships under construction, conversion or planning.

Fanciful post-war visions of war at sea being dominated by large airborne squadrons dropping atomic weapons on warships at sea or huge underwater vessels powered by atomic fission destroying any surface vessel have now somewhat moderated and it is believed that the character of any future naval war is likely to remain pretty much unchanged. There will still be a need to protect large convoys bringing essential supplies to the UK. There will still be a requirement to hunt down and destroy submarines from both the air and the sea. There will still be a need to hunt down and destroy enemy surface vessels from both the sea and air. Advances in technology are likely to make these tasks easier, but the ships and aircraft required to defend our vital supply routes are needed today - and will probably still be needed tomorrow. As Lord Selsdon warned in Parliament, "in spite of atomic bombs and fantastic flights by jet aircraft, this country is still an island and nothing that any scientist could do would prevent it being an island, or eliminate the need for us to obtain food, oil, petrol and other supplies from overseas."

The real threat to our ability to keep this country supplied in the event of war comes from the Communist rise in the east and its growing number of submarines, mines and long range bomber aircraft.

Although numerically the Royal Navy may appear to be strong, the truth is that much of the fleet is in reserve and despite being relatively young, advances in technology with regard to anti-submarine operations and radar means that the destroyers and escorts in the fleet, both reserve and active, are nearing, or indeed have reached, obsolescence.

The danger from submarines and mines today is perceived as being greater than at the beginning of World War II. This being the case, a three year, £4,700 million, re-armament programme was announced in 1949, with the intention of introducing fast anti-submarine ships and modern minesweepers into the fleet. Although the build programme is now underway, the government now realise that the programme is likely to take four years to deliver, rather than three. This is not only due to a shortage of skilled manpower, but also, priority is being given to material and labour required to complete export projects. Added to this is the parlous state of the economy - funding such a project is a huge undertaking in the financially constrained climate and defence projects, with their advances in technology and therefore complexity have significantly increased costs (a destroyer in 1914 would typically cost £150 per ton to build. Today that figure is closer to £700 per ton).

The list of vessels under the course of construction comprise the Fleet Carrier ARK ROYAL together with 7 Light Fleet Carriers whose ocnstruction has been suspended since the end of the war; 3 cruisers (construction suspended); 6 Daring class ships; 9 frigates together with 30 Coastal and 35 Inshore minesweepers. A programme of new Coastal Forces vessels is also underway with construction of at least three classes, including a new type of small vessel, the Seaward Defence Boat, designed to undertake coastal anti-submarine work. Additionally there are to be up to 45 destroyer to frigate conversions undertaken to produce a fleet of fast anti-submarine ships.

At present the emphasis of the naval programme continues to be placed on the building up of the minesweeping and anti-submarine forces. Progress with the new minesweepers is being maintained though there have been some delays arising inevitably from the introduction of a large programme of vessels of a new type embodying novel features and of a considerable size. The first vessels are nearly finished, and by next year a steady stream of these new vessels should enter service.

Although the new frigate programme is underway, a plan that should see 24 new-build frigates introduced to the fleet, these complex vessels are experiencing delays in production, mainly due to shortages in steel and skilled manpower. As a result, the Type 15 (Full Conversion) and Type 16 (Limited Conversion) destroyer to frigate programmes, which, although extensive in the scope of their conversions, can be completed for less money and in a quicker timeframe, will provide a stop-gap capability until the new vessels enter service. Indeed the first of these vessels (VERULAM, VENUS, VIRAGO and ORWELL) have recently entered service. Likewise there is a planned destroyer to frigate Aircraft Direction conversion plan underway as a stop-gap for the planned new AD Frigate programme.

During the year work continued on the fleet carrier ARK ROYAL and on the four light fleet carriers of the Hermes Class. ARK ROYAL should enter service next year and three of the light fleet carriers should be completed within twelve to eighteen months.

Of the Daring class two more, DUCHESS and DEFENDER have now joined the Fleet and DAINTY is about to do so: the remaining three are nearing completion.

Most of the Seaward Defence Boats and Fast Patrol Boats on order should be completed before the end of 1953-54. Two experimental fast patrol boats are due to enter service shortly.

It is expected that the small hospital ship which will, in peacetime, serve as a Royal Yacht for the monarch, will be completed during 1953-54.

Work continues on the fleet carrier VICTORIOUS which is being reconstructed at Portsmouth Dockyard, to enable it to operate the latest types of naval aircraft. The work is extensive and has involved the complete removal of all structure down to the hangar deck. Reconstruction has been delayed, like most other programmes, by lack of steel and suitable manpower. The light fleet carrier WARRIOR is undergoing a less extensive modernisation and should rejoin the fleet shortly.

In respect of Admiralty research and development, there has been steady progress in investigations designed to provide adequate defence against the threat of mines of a number of different types, against modern submarines of high underwater speed and endurance, and against aircraft. Anti-submarine weapons, both shipborne and airborne, far more effective than anything known during the last war are becoming available, and arrangements have been made to enable heavier and faster types of naval aircraft to be handled in, and operated from, fleet carriers.

The efficiency of the propulsion machinery of ships and submarines has been greatly improved from the point of view of generating more power for a given weight of plant, and more power for a given weight of fuel. The introduction of gas turbine propulsion into small coastal forces craft has proved successful and its potential for larger ships such as frigates and destroyers could bring about savings in both space and fuel efficiency. Both these factors are of great importance as, apart from questions of speed and endurance, savings in weight and space achieved in these ways can be applied to the improvement of ships' armaments. The potential of such installations should be proved once HOTHAM has been converted with a gas turbine powerplant and sea trials commenced.

Satisfactory progress is being maintained in naval contributions to the development of guided missiles and in electronics research but, as of yet, there is little concrete sign of such missiles being developed for shipborne use, but it is sure to be a field which will be exploited very rapidly as electronic technology improves and radar and guidance systems become more advanced.

Advances in aircraft carrier operations have also been pioneered by the Royal Navy. A new steam-powered catapult, capable of launching heavier and faster aircraft, has been trialled aboard PERSEUS and is set to replace the older, less capable hydraulic system previously in use. A new flight deck arrangement featuring an angled flight deck is revolutionising how carrier operations are conducted. The new concept allows aircraft to land on the flight deck, angled over the portside, while at the same

9

time take-off operations can be conducted over the bow, or aircraft parked forward without disrupting flying operations. To date the flightdeck angles have been fairly conservative, however, VICTORIOUS will emerge from her refit with a flight deck angled beyond 8 degrees and supported by a sponson extended over the port side of the ship.

This year saw the deployment of a special squadron consisting of HM Ships CAMPANIA, PLYM, TRACKER, NARVIK, and ZEEBRUGGE, to conduct the trials of the British atomic weapon at the Monte Bello Islands off North Western Australia. While most of the ships were there to offer support and logistics to the scientific teams on the island, PLYM was to be used as a target vessel and following detonation of the device she was completely 'vaporised' - not a trace of her was to be found.

Operationally, the Royal Navy continues to have a worldwide presence with vessels stationed in the Mediterranean, Far East, Persian Gulf and Americas and East Indies. Over the past year or two the Royal Navy has been called upon to undertake considerable operational tasks.

The greatest fleet commitment at present has been the continued deployment of warships in support of United Nations operations off Korea. Most of the ships on the Far East Station have been engaged, together with units of the United States Navy, the Royal Canadian, Australian and New Zealand Navies, the French and the Royal Netherlands Navies, all under the command of a British Flag Officer, in blockade and escort duties off the west coast. Ships have also been attached periodically to the American forces operating on the east coast. Naval aircraft have harassed the enemy's land lines of communication and have spotted for ships' bombardments in the face of increasing fighter and anti-aircraft opposition. Cruisers, destroyers and frigates patrolling off the coast have had to contend with a minelaying campaign by the enemy and with strengthened coastal batteries. The threat presented by the United Nations Navies has contained large enemy ground forces.

The following ships of the Royal Navy have taken part in operations in Korean waters during the last twelve months: 2 aircraft carriers, 4 cruisers, 7 destroyers, 10 frigates, 1 aircraft maintenance carrier, 1 headquarters ship and a large number of supporting vessels.

Throughout the year ships of the Mediterranean Fleet have been stationed in the Suez Canal area to safeguard British interests. Within 24 hours of the Egyptian abrogation of the Treaty of 1936, the GAMBIA had arrived and was efficiently berthing and passing through the ships of all nations. The aircraft carriers ILLUSTRIOUS and TRIUMPH were quickly re-roled as troopships to transport the 3rd Infantry Division to Cyprus and the Canal Zone. Until April 1952, RN ship and sailors were required to berth and unberth merchant ships of all nationalities to keep the Canal traffic operating. In April, however, the Egyptian authorities removed the last restriction and the Canal traffic returned to normal; the role of the Royal Navy then reverted to maintaining a watch over our interests.

Further east ships and motor launches have patrolled the coasts of Malaya to prevent gun-running and illegal immigration of bandits. Thirty-nine bombardments by Royal Navy destroyers, frigates, minesweepers and HMMS PELANDOK (Malaya) and five air strikes from British carriers were carried out in support of security forces' operations.

Closer to home progress has been made in improving co-ordination and co-operation with the North Atlantic Treaty Organisation (NATO). Inter-operability and procedures have been practiced through a series of large international exercises which have taken place in both the Atlantic and Mediterranean. Exercise *Castinets* was a maritime defence exercise conducted by Commander-in-Chief, Channel. Exercise *Mainbrace* was a large scale exercise in co-operation between the forces of the Supreme Allied Commander Europe (SACEUR) and the Supreme Allied Commander Atlantic (SACLANT) in the defence of the northern flank of the North Atlantic Treaty Organisation, conducted by Commander-in-Chief North (CINCNORTH). In the Mediterranean Exercise *Beehive II* and Exercise *Longstep* were Mediterranean convoy exercises conducted by Commander-in-Chief, Mediterranean and Commander Allied Naval Forces Southern Europe (COMNAVSOUTH).

Many smaller scale NATO exercises have also been held both in home waters and in the Mediterranean, and Turkish ships took part in a NATO exercise for the first time. Increasingly ships of NATO countries have visited the United Kingdom for anti-submarine training.

The Royal Navy has also maintained its peacetime cycle of deployments around the world, with several high profile visits being achieved. When His Royal Highness the Duke of Edinburgh travelled from Oslo to Helsinki in July 1952, in Trinity House Vessel PATRICIA for the Olympic Games, an escort was provided by the cruiser SWIFTSURE. This was the first visit by one of HM Ships to Finland for some years. The resumption of Fleet visits to Spain took place in September, the most important visit being that to Barcelona by Flag Officer, Flotillas, Mediterranean, in the aircraft carrier HMS GLORY accompanied by three destroyers The cruiser SHEFFIELD visited Valparaiso for the inauguration of President Ibanez on 3 November 1952, and parties from her took part in the ceremonies. The ship itself headed the line of foreign warships at the subsequent Naval Review.

It is obvious that the Royal Navy of today is one that is in transition - at last it is reinventing itself so that it is better able to respond to the requirements of the post war age. Funding has now, at last, been identified and a comprehensive and structured build programme put in place. The Royal Navy that emerges from this regeneration, will be smaller than before, as to be expected, but it will be modern, relevant to the threats of today and as ready as ever to protect our island nation and Dominion territories from those that would do us harm.

11

SHIPS OF THE ROYAL NAVY (Active Fleet)
Pennant Numbers

Penn	Ship Name

Vessels shown in pale italics are yet to complete.

Battleships

B23	VANGUARD

Aircraft Carriers

R05	EAGLE
R09	*ARK ROYAL*
R10	INDEFATIGABLE
R16	TRIUMPH
R31	WARRIOR
R38	VICTORIOUS
R48	CAMPANIA
R49	*HERCULES*
R62	GLORY
R64	THESEUS
R68	OCEAN
R72	UNICORN
R77	*MAJESTIC*
R86	IMPLACABLE
R87	ILLUSTRIOUS
R92	INDOMITABLE
R95	*POWERFUL*
R97	*LEVIATHAN*

Cruisers

C08	SWIFTSURE

Penn	Ship Name
C19	BIRMINGHAM
C33	CLEOPATRA
C21	GLASGOW
C24	SHEFFIELD
C25	SUPERB
C30	CEYLON
C35	BELFAST
C39	DEVONSHIRE
C42	EURYALUS
C48	GAMBIA
C52	BERMUDA
C57	CUMBERLAND
C59	NEWFOUNDLAND
C76	NEWCASTLE

Minelayers

N01	APOLLO
N12	GOSSAMER
N13	MINER III
N14	MINER IV
N15	MINER V
N17	MINER VII
N26	PLOVER
N70	MANXMAN

Submarines

S09	AURIGA
S10	UPSTART
S11	ACHERON

Penn	Ship Name	Penn	Ship Name
S12	TRESPASSER	**Destroyers**	
S14	TACTICIAN		
S18	AMBUSH	D03	CONCORD
S21	TELEMACHUS	D05	DARING
S22	ANCHORITE	D06	MYNGS
S23	ANDREW	D14	ARMADA
S24	THOROUGH	D18	ST KITTS
S26	AUROCHS	D19	ZEPHYR
S27	AENEAS	D20	COMUS
S29	TRADEWIND	D21	CHIVALROUS
S31	TRENCHANT	D22	AISNE
S33	TRUMP	D24	GRAVELINES
S36	UNTIRING	D27	SAVAGE
S37	TALENT	D29	CHARITY
S38	TEREDO	D31	BROADSWORD
S41	ALARIC	D34	COCKADE
S43	AMPHION	D35	DIAMOND
S44	SEA DEVIL	D36	CHIEFTAIN
S47	ASTUTE	D47	GABBARD
S49	ARTEMIS	D48	CONTEST
S51	SUBTLE	D51	CHEVRON
S52	TOTEM	D55	FINISTERRE
S55	THERMOPYLAE	D57	COSSACK
S56	SENTINEL	D60	SLUYS
S58	SCORCHER	D61	CHEQUERS
S59	SIDON	D64	SCORPION
S64	SPRINGER	D65	ST JAMES
S66	SANGUINE	D66	ZAMBESI
S73	SENESCHAL	D68	BARROSA
S77	TIRELESS	D71	CONSTANCE
S87	TALLY-HO	D76	CONSORT
S89	SERAPH	D79	CADIZ
S96	ARTFUL	D82	CREOLE
S126	TUDOR	D83	ULSTER
S137	SCYTHIAN	D86	AGINCOURT
S143	SCOTSMAN	D90	CHEVIOT
S153	SEA SCOUT	D96	CROSSBOW

Penn	Ship Name	Penn	Ship Name
D97	CORUNNA	F82	MAGPIE
D106	DECOY	F93	VIGILANT
D108	DAINTY	F96	PEACOCK
D114	DEFENDER	F98	ORWELL
D118	BATTLEAXE	F123	CRANE
D119	DELIGHT	F138	RAPID
D126	DIANA	F141	UNDINE
D139	OBDURATE	F142	BROCKLESBY
D154	DUCHESS	F156	TUSCAN
D168	CRISPIN	F157	WRANGLER
D180	OPPORTUNE	F159	WAKEFUL
D231	VIGO	F185	RELENTLESS
D248	OBEDIENT	F187	WHIRLWIND
		F189	TERMAGANT
		F193	ROCKET
Frigates		F195	ROEBUCK
		F196	URCHIN
F06	BIGBURY BAY	F197	GRENVILLE
F07	ACTAEON	F253	HELMSDALE
F18	FLAMINGO	F362	PORTCHESTER CASTLE
F20	SNIPE	F379	CARISBROOKE CASTLE
F28	WREN	F383	FLINT CASTLE
F29	VERULAM	F384	LEEDS CASTLE
F33	OPOSSUM	F386	HEDINGHAM CASTLE
F35	ENARD BAY	F389	KNARESBOROUGH CASTLE
F38	CYGNET	F390	LOCH FADA
F41	VOLAGE	F397	LAUNCESTON CASTLE
F42	MODESTE	F399	TINTAGEL CASTLE
F44	TENACIOUS	F423	LARGO BAY
F45	WILD GOOSE	F428	LOCH ALVIE
F47	FLEETWOOD	F429	LOCH FYNE
F50	VENUS	F433	LOCH INSH
F53	UNDAUNTED	F434	LOCH QUOICH
F64	NEREIDE	F436	SURPRISE
F67	TYRIAN	F600	ST. BRIDES BAY
F71	SPARROW	F609	LOCH CRAGGIE
F76	VIRAGO	F615	WIDEMOUTH BAY

Penn	Ship Name	Penn	Ship Name
F619	LOCH GLENDHU	M380	MARINER
F622	BURGHEAD BAY	M385	WAVE
F624	MORECAMBE BAY	M386	WELCOME
F627	MOUNTS BAY	M387	CHAMELEON
F628	LOCH KILLISPORT	M390	JEWEL
F630	CARDIGAN BAY	M427	SURSAY
F633	WHITESAND BAY	M443	MARVEL
F634	ST. AUSTELL BAY	M444	MICHAEL
F639	LOCH MORE	M449	ROMOLA
F645	LOCH RUTHVEN	M452	TAHAY
F647	ALERT		
F651	VERYAN BAY		
F655	LOCH TRALAIG		

Light Forces & Minor Vessels

Penn	Ship Name
F658	LOCH VEYATIE
F690	CAISTOR CASTLE
P10	SIGNET
P16	BARCOMBE
P19	FALCONET
P27	MAGNET
P47	SONNET

Minesweepers

Penn	Ship Name	Penn	Ship Name
M11	BRAMBLE	P50	PLANET
M29	COCKATRICE	P58	WOODBRIDGE HAVEN
M46	PLUTO	P63	PLANTAGENET
M53	FIERCE	P82	NIGHTINGALE
M88	CHEERFUL	P83	VESUVIUS
M163	SKYE	P200	BARFOSS
M214	CIRCE	P201	BARBAIN
M225	RINALDO	P202	BARFOOT
M289	MELITA	P203	BARBROOK
M292	SHEPPEY	P204	BARHILL
M294	PINCHER	P207	BARCLIFF
M295	PLUCKY	P209	BARCASTLE
M297	RATTLESNAKE	P211	BARHOLM
M299	RIFLEMAN	P212	BARCROFT
M303	TRUELOVE	P214	BARBECUE
M350	COQUETTE	P215	BARNDALE
M356	WELFARE	P216	BARGLOW
M379	LYSANDER	P217	BARILLA

Penn	Ship Name	Penn	Ship Name
P218	BARLEYCORN	P276	BARBASTEL
P219	BARMOUTH	P277	BARCOCK
P222	BARBRIDGE	P280	BOWNET
P224	BARSPEAR	P281	BARKING
P227	BARKIS	P282	BARFOAM
P232	BARMOND	P283	DRAGONET
P233	BURGONET	P284	MOORSMAN
P234	BAROVA	P287	BARCAROLE
P235	BARTHORPE	P288	GATESHEAD
P237	BARNABY	P289	BARSOUND
P238	BARNEHURST	P290	BARFOUNT
P239	BARLAKE	P292	BARSTOKE
P240	BARRHEAD	P293	BARRYMORE
P241	BARNARD	P294	BARFOIL
P242	BARBETTE	P295	BARDELL
P243	BARBICAN	P296	BARRICADE
P244	BARFIELD	P297	BARNESTONE
P245	BARNEATH	P298	BARRIER
P246	BARNWELL	P299	BARFORD
P247	BARONIA	P342	FOULNESS
P248	BARLANE	P387	GORREGAN
P251	BARITONE		
P252	BARCOTE		
P254	BARRAGE		**Auxiliaries**
P257	BARBERRY		
P258	BARWIND	A121	BULAWAYO
P259	BARRINGTON	A122	ROC
P260	BARLOW	A146	PROTECTOR
P261	BARTIZAN	A176	BULLFINCH
P262	BARON	A185	MAIDSTONE
P265	BARRANCA	A187	FORTH
P267	BARMILL	A188	MONTCLARE
P269	BARBOUR	A194	TYNE
P270	BARBORNE	A197	PERSEUS
P271	BARDOLF	A206	RIPON
P274	BARCLOSE	A217	SKUA
P275	BARSING	A223	MOORPOUT

Penn	Ship Name	Penn	Ship Name
A231	RECLAIM	A332	CALDY
A232	KINGARTH	A333	COLL
A234	SALVAGE DUKE	A336	FETLAR
A239	RANPURA	A337	FLATHOLM
A251	BLACKBURN	A339	LINDISFARNE
A259	ST. MARGARETS	A340	LUNDY
A262	DISPENSER	A344	SKOMER
A267	MOORBURN	A345	STEEPHOLM
A268	MOORMYRTLE	A346	SWITHA
A269	MOORCOCK	A347	TIREE
A270	MOORSIDE	A348	TRONDRA
A271	MOORESS	A352	MEDA
A272	MOORFIRE	A381	DWARF
A273	MOORFOWL	A394	BOXER
A274	MOORGRIEVE	A482	KINLOSS
A276	LASSO	A489	MOORHEN
A281	KINBRACE	A491	MOORLAND
A290	KING SALVOR	A492	OCEAN SALVOR
A291	SEA SALVOR	A494	SALVALOUR
A292	PRINCE SALVOR	A497	SALVEDA
A301	CHALLENGER	A499	SALVESTOR
A302	DALRYMPLE	A500	SALVICTOR
A303	DAMPIER	A501	SALVIGIL
A304	FRANKLIN	A502	SALVIOLA
A307	COOK	A505	SUCCOUR
A308	SCOTT	A506	SWIN
A310	SHARPSHOOTER	A507	UPLIFTER
A311	OWEN		
A322	SML 2		
A323	SML 3	**Landing Ship Tank**	
A324	SML 4		
A325	SML 5	L3001	FREDERICK GLOVER
A326	SML 6	L3003	ANZIO
A327	SML 7	L3006	TROMSO
A328	ANNET	L3009	REGINALD KERR
A330	BARDSEY	L3010	ATTACKER
A331	BERN	L3012	BEN NEVIS

Penn	Ship Name	Penn	Ship Name
L3013	BEN LOMOND	L3044	NARVIK
L3015	BATTLER	L3504	PURSUER
L3016	DIEPPE	L3505	RAVAGER
L3019	VAAGSO	L3509	HUMPHREY GALE
L3021	CHARLES MCLEOD	L3510	SLINGER
L3024	MAXWELL BRANDER	L3511	REGGIO
L3025	BRUISER	L3513	SALERNO
L3026	CHARGER	L3515	STALKER
L3027	LOFOTEN	L3516	STRIKER
L3028	SNOWDEN SMITH	L3517	ST. NAZAIRE
L3029	CHASER	L3518	SUVLA
L3031	*UN-NAMED*	L3520	THRUSTER
L3033	*UN-NAMED*	L3522	TRACKER
L3036	PUNCHER	L3523	TROUNCER
L3037	EVAN GIBB	L3524	TRUMPETER
L3038	FIGHTER	L3525	WALCHEREN
L3042	HUNTER	L3532	ZEEBRUGGE
L3043	MESSINA		

HMS Vanguard

BATTLESHIPS
VANGUARD CLASS

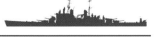

Ship	Completed	Builder
VANGUARD	25.04.46	J. Brown & Co (Clydebank)

Displacement 44,500 tons (51,420 tons FL) Dimensions 814ft 6in x 108ft 6in x 28ft
Machinery Parsons SR Geared Turbines, 8 Admiralty 3-drum boilers, 4 shafts,
130,000 shp Speed 28 knots Armament 8 x 15in, 16 x 5.25in, 60 x 40mm
Complement 1,893

Notes

The largest warship ever built in Great Britain she was finished too late to see service
during World War II. The ship has had a long association with the Royal Family, having
taken King George VI on a tour of South Africa in 1947. A similar tour was proposed in
1948 to New Zealand, but this was cancelled due to the King's ill health. Towards the end
of 1951 Buckingham Palace announced that King George VI was planning to take a short
cruise for his health aboard VANGUARD, which meant that her Admiral's suite had to be
modified to accommodate him and his staff, but the King died on 6 February 1952 before
before preparations were complete. On completion of the refit in spring, VANGUARD
became the Flagship of the Home Fleet, flying the flag of Admiral Sir Geogre Creasy
KCB. She had, prior to her refit, spent four months as flagship of the Training Squadron.
This role has now been assumed by the aircraft carrier INDEFATIGABLE.

19

HMS Eagle

AIRCRAFT CARRIERS
AUDACIOUS CLASS

Ship	Completed	Builder
EAGLE	01.10.51	Harland & Wolff (Belfast)
ARK ROYAL	03.05.50(L)	Cammell Laird (Birkenhead)

Displacement 41,200 tons (49,950 tons FL) Dimensions 803ft 9in x 112ft 9in x 35ft 7in Machinery Parsons SR geared turbines, 8 Admiralty 3-drum boilers, 4 shafts, 152,000 shp Speed 31½ knots Armament 16 x 4.5in, 58 x 40mm, 80-110 aircraft Complement 2,750

Notes

The largest aircraft carrier ever completed for the RN, EAGLE was accepted into service on 1 March 1952 and conducted sea trials off Portsmouth. She has been completed to her original 1942 design with a straight flight deck, though it is thought that she will get an angled flight deck during her first refit. ARK ROYAL is under construction at Cammell Laird's and is scheduled to complete in 1955.

HMS Powerful

MAJESTIC CLASS

Ship	Completed	Builder
HERCULES	22.09.45(L)	Vickers-Armstrong (Walker)
LEVIATHAN	07.06.45(L)	Swan Hunter & Wigham Richardson
MAJESTIC	28.02.45(L)	Vickers-Armstrong (Barrow)
POWERFUL	27.02.45(L)	Harland & Wolff (Belfast)

Displacement 14,000 tons (19,000 tons FL) Dimensions 695ft x 80ft x 24ft
Machinery Parsons SR geared turbines, 2 shafts, 42,000 shp Speed 24½ knots
Armament 30 x 40mm (6 x twin, 8 x single), 35 aircraft Complement 1,100 approx

Notes

A follow-on to the Colossus class taking into account the need to operate heavier aircraft at higher speeds. With the end of the war, building work on all six carriers was suspended pending a review of carrier requirements. Two vessels, TERRIBLE and MAGNIFI-CENT were completed for Australia and Canada respecitvely becoming HMAS SYDNEY and HMCS MAGNIFICENT. Construction work on MAJESTIC was restarted in 1949 following purchase by Australia. Similarly, construction work on POWERFUL resumed in July 1952 to a modified design for completion and transfer to Canada. Work on LEVIATHAN and HERCULES stopped in May 1946 and they remain laid up at Portsmouth and the Gareloch respectively.

21

HMS Triumph

COLOSSUS CLASS

Ship	Completed	Builder
GLORY	02.04.45	Harland & Wolff (Belfast)
OCEAN	30.06.45	A. Stephen & Sons Ltd (Linthouse)
THESEUS	09.01.46	Fairfield SB & Eng Co (Govan)
TRIUMPH	09.04.46	Hawthorn Leslie (Hebburn)
WARRIOR	24.01.46	Harland & Wolff (Belfast)

Displacement 13,190 tons (18,040 tons FL)   Dimensions 693ft x 80ft x 21ft 6in   Machinery Parsons SR geared turbines, 4 Admiralty 3-drum boilers, 2 shafts, 42,000 shp   Speed 25 knots   Armament 24 x 2pdr, 19 x 40mm, 35 aircraft   Complement 1,076 (1,300 war)

Notes

In the past years GLORY, OCEAN and THESEUS have conducted combat operations off the coast of Korea. GLORY was relieved by OCEAN. Since April 1951 GLORY had

22

conducted 4,000 operational sorties during 12 patrols. GLORY will now rejoin the Mediterranean Fleet, which in turn means that THESEUS, which had deployed to the Mediterranean to fill the gap while OCEAN sailed to Korea, can return to the Home Fleet.

TRIUMPH has been conducting trials to assess the suitability of an angled deck layout. With a 3 degree offset centreline painted on the flightdeck, several different types of aircraft were used to fly approaches to the carrier.

WARRIOR, as the last of the class to complete, has been built to a more modern standard than her sisters, incorporating an angled flight deck and mirror landing sight. In April she started a limited modernisation at Devonport. External differences include an extended bridge and a new lattice mast to replace the old tripod structure. She is scheduled to rejoin the fleet towards the end of 1953.

HMS Indefatigable

IMPLACABLE CLASS

Ship	Completed	Builder
IMPLACABLE	28.08.44	Fairfield SB & Eng Co (Govan)
INDEFATIGABLE	03.05.44	J. Brown & Co (Clydebank)

Displacement 26,000 tons (32,850 tons FL) Dimensions 766ft x 95ft x 29ft 9in
Machinery Parsons SR geared turbines, 8 Admiralty 3-drum boilers, 4 shafts, 148,000
shp Speed 32½ knots Armament 16 x 4.5in, 12 x 40mm, 9 x 20mm, 52 x 2pdr
Complement 1,785 (2,200 war)

Notes

A follow on to the Indomitable design, this pair of ships incorporate, two hangars, one
above the other. However, this restricted the hangar height to a mere 14ft and although
relatively modern ships, their inability to accommodate modern aircraft has curtailed their
operational effectiveness. In 1949 INDEFATIGABLE was taken in hand for conversion to
a training ship, with accommodation and classrooms built into the former hangars and
facilities for boat stowage and handling on the flight deck. She commissioned for service
with the Home Fleet Training Squadron in 1950. IMPLACABLE underwent a similar conversion in 1950 and recommissioned in January 1952. In the Spring INDEFATIGABLE
became the Flagship of the Training Squadron.

HMS Indomitable

ILLUSTRIOUS CLASS

Ship	Completed	Builder
ILLUSTRIOUS	25.05.40	Vickers Armstrong (Barrow)
VICTORIOUS	15.04.41	Vickers Armstrong (Walker)
INDOMITABLE	10.10.41	Vickers Armstrong (Barrow)

Displacement 23,207 tons (28,619 tons FL), INDOMITABLE 24,680 tons (29,730 tons FL) Dimensions 753ft x 95ft x 29ft 6in (INDOMITABLE 754ft x 95ft 9in x 29ft 6in) Machinery Parsons SR geared turbines, 6 Admiralty 3-drum boilers, 3 shafts, 110,000 shp Speed 31 knots (INDOMITABLE 30½ knots) Armament 16 x 4.5in, 21 x 40mm, 12 x 20mm, 40 x 2pdr, 54 aircraft (INDOMITABLE 16 x 4.5in, 12 x 40mm, 34 x 20mm, 48 x 2pdr, 65 aircraft) Complement 1,600-1,785

Notes

ILLUSTRIOUS has operated as a trials and training carrier since 1948 carrying out trials with both jet and turboprop aircraft. INDOMITABLE, completed to an improved design during the war, became flagship, Heavy Squadron, Home Fleet in May 1952. VICTORI-OUS was taken in hand for a major modernisation at Portsmouth in March 1950. She is being extensively rebuilt and is expected to emerge as one of the most modern aircraft carriers in the world, incorporating brand new flight deck, landing aids and steam cata-pults. However, the programme is already suffering from delays due to shortages of both material and skilled manpower.

25

HMS Campania

CAMPANIA CLASS

Ship	Completed	Builder
CAMPANIA	07.03.44	Harland & Wolff (Belfast)

Displacement 12,450 tons (15,970 tons FL)   Dimensions 540ft x 70ft x 19ft
Machinery Burmeister & Wain diesels, 2 shafts, 11,000 bhp   Speed 17 knots
Armament 2 x 4in, 16 x 2pdr, 8 x 40mm, 16 x 20mm, 20 aircraft   Complement 700
(as Escort Carrier)

Notes

Refitted as a ferry carrier after the war. Loaned by the Admiralty to the Festival of Britain
in 1951 and converted by Cammell Laird (Birkenhead) as a mobile exhibition. Refitted for
further service in the Special Squadron as a transport for scientific staff for atomic
weapons tests off Monte Bello island, northwest of Australia. To return to the UK at the
end of 1952.

HMS Unicorn

UNICORN CLASS

Ship	Completed	Builder
UNICORN	12.03.43	Harland & Wolff (Belfast)

Displacement 16,510 tons (20,300 tons FL) **Dimensions** 640ft x 90ft x 19ft
Machinery Parsons SR geared turbines, 4 Admiralty 3-drum boilers, 2 shafts, 40,000
shp **Speed** 24 knots **Armament** 8 x 4in, 16 x 2pdr, 16 x 20mm, 35 aircraft
Complement 1,200

Notes

Designed as an Aircraft Repair Ship, she has a comprehensive range of engine, radio,
electrical and airframe workshops together with an extensive stores complex. Her hangar
deck is open at the after end allowing aircraft engine runs to be conducted. Since 1950
has been based in the Far East where she has been providing support to the carriers
and their aircraft engaged in combat operations off Korea.

27

HMS Superb

CRUISERS
MINOTAUR CLASS

Ship	Completed	Builder
SWIFTSURE	22.06.44	Vickers Armstrong (Walker)
SUPERB	16.11.45	Swan Hunter & Wigham Richardson

Displacement 8,000 tons (11,560 tons FL) Dimensions 555ft 6in x 63ft x 16ft 6in (SUPERB 555ft 6in x 64ft x 21ft) Machinery Parsons SR geared turbines, 4 Admiralty 3-drum boilers, 4 shafts, 72,500 shp Speed 31½ knots Armament 9 x 6in, 10 x 4in, 16 x 2pdr, 9 x 40mm, 6 x TT (SUPERB 9 x 6in, 10 x 4in, 18 x 2pdr, 4 x 40mm, 14 x 20mm, 6 x TT) Complement 876 (1,000 war)

Notes

The most modern cruisers in the RN, both are serving with the Home Fleet, SWIFTSURE as flagship of the 2nd Cruiser Squadron and SUPERB as Flag Officer Flotillas.

HMS Gambia

FIJI CLASS

Ship	Completed	Builder
BERMUDA	21.08.42	J. Brown & Co (Clydebank)
CEYLON	13.07.43	A Stephen & Sons Ltd (Linthouse)
GAMBIA	21.02.42	Swan Hunter & Wigham Richardson
KENYA	27.09.40	A Stephen & Sons Ltd (Linthouse)
NEWFOUNDLAND	20.01.43	Swan Hunter & Wigham Richardson

Displacement 8,000 tons (10,354 tons FL) Dimensions 555ft 6in x 62ft x 16ft 6in
Machinery Parsons SR geared turbines, 4 Admiralty 3-drum boilers, 4 shafts, 72,500
shp Speed 31½ knots Armament 9 x 6in, 8 x 4in, 2-16 x 40mm, 4-12 x 20mm, 8-24
x 2-pdr, 6 x TT (CEYLON; NEWFOUNDLAND: 9 x 6in, 8 x 4in, 10 x 40mm, 12 x 20mm,
6 x TT) Complement 750, 766 (CEYLON), 808 (NEWFOUNDLAND)

Notes

CEYLON and KENYA have deployed to the Far East and conducted operations off Korea
although KENYA is now in the Mediterranean. BERMUDA had been in reserve at
Chatham since 1947, however, she re-commissioned at Devonport in October 1950 for
service in the South Atlantic. GAMBIA was brought forward from reserve at Devonport in
1950 and is deployed in the Mediterranean as Flagship of the 1st Cruiser Squadron.
NEWFOUNDLAND completed a modernisation refit at Devonport in October, comprising a new outfit of radar and close range gun directors. On completion of sea trials she
is scheduled to join the Mediterranean Fleet.

HMS Euryalus

DIDO CLASS

Ship	Completed	Builder
CLEOPATRA	05.12.41	Hawthorn Leslie (Hebburn)
EURYALUS	30.06.41	HM Dockyard (Chatham)

Displacement 5,770 tons (7,120-7,515 tons FL) Dimensions 512ft x 50ft 6in x 14ft Machinery Parsons SR geared turbines, 4 Admiralty 3-drum boilers, 4 shafts, 64,000 shp Speed 32¼ knots Armament 8 x 5.25in, 12 x 2pdr, 2 x 40 mm, 4-13 x 20mm, 6 x TT Complement 550-620

Notes

Following service with the 2nd Cruiser Squadron, Home Fleet, CLEOPATRA was reduced to reserve in 1951, but following a short refit she recommissioned for service with the 1st Cruiser Squadron in the Mediterranean. EURYALUS was nominally assigned to the Mediterranean Fleet but spent several spells of duty in the Persian Gulf. After the nationalisation of the Anglo-Persian Oil Company, Iran, EURYALUS was sent to the Persian Gulf from 5 May to 7 June 1951. She left the Mediterranean again in July 1951 with 42 Lancashire Fusiliers to become Abadan guard ship until September. In August 1952 she returned to Devonport and again recommissioned for the Mediterranean.

HMS Belfast

TOWN CLASS (3rd Group)

Ship	Completed	Builder
BELFAST	03.08.39	Harland & Wolff (Belfast)

Displacement 11,550 tons (15,000 tons FL) **Dimensions** 613ft 6in x 66ft 6in x 17ft **Machinery** Parsons SR geared turbines, 4 Admiralty 3-drum boilers, 4 shafts, 80,000 shp **Speed** 32½ knots **Armament** 12 x 6in, 8 x 4in, 4 x 2pdr, 7 x 40mm, 2 x 20mm, 6 x TT **Complement** 710

Notes

Deployed on operations off Korea since January 1951 and involved in both blockading duties and shore bombardment operations. She was relieved by BIRMINGHAM and began her return passage to the UK in September 1952.

HMS Birmingham

SOUTHAMPTON CLASS

Ship	Completed	Builder
BIRMINGHAM	18.11.37	HM Dockyard (Devonport)
GLASGOW	09.09.37	Scotts SB & Eng Co (Greenock)
NEWCASTLE	05.03.37	Vickers Armstrong (Walker)
SHEFFIELD	25.08.37	Vickers Armstrong (Walker)

Displacement 9,100 tons (12,860 tons FL) Dimensions 591ft 6in x 61ft 8in x 17ft Machinery Parsons SR geared turbines, 4 Admiralty 3-drum boilers, 4 shafts, 75,000 shp Speed 32 knots Armament 9 x 6in, 8 x 4in, 8-24 x 2pdr, 6-24 x 40mm, 4-17 x 20mm, 6 x TT Complement 850

Notes

NEWCASTLE has emerged from refit with a lattice foremast and a reshaped, more rounded, bridge front. She sailed to Malta in May for a work-up prior to proceeding to the Far East in June for operations off Korea. BIRMINGHAM underwent a similar refit at Portsmouth and by October was also operating off Korea. It is likely that most of the class will undergo such a modernisation refit. Structurally the refit involves removal of the hangars, reduction in superstructure and bridgework and alterations to the secondary armament. Lattice masts are to replace the tripod masts. GLASGOW is Flagship C-in-C Mediterranean Fleet and SHEFFIELD is now Flagship Heavy Squadron, Home Fleet having returned from the Americas and West Indies station.

HMS Devonshire

KENT CLASS

Ship	Completed	Builder
CUMBERLAND	23.01.28	Vickers Armstrong (Barrow)
DEVONSHIRE	18.03.29	HM Dockyard (Devonport)

Displacement 9,850 tons (13,315 tons FL), CUMBERLAND 10,800 tons (14,450 tons FL) Dimensions 630ft x 66ft x 17ft (CUMBERLAND 630ft x 68ft 6in x 16ft 3in) Machinery Parsons SR geared turbines, 8 Admiralty 3-drum boilers, 4 shafts, 40,000 shp (CUMBERLAND 80,000 shp) Speed 21 knots (CUMBERLAND 31½ knots) Armament 2 x 8in, 4 x 4in, 4 x 2pdr, 1 x 40mm, 3 x 20mm (CUMBERLAND: Armament as required for trials) Complement 679

Notes

CUMBERLAND underwent a conversion refit at Devonport, emerging in May 1951 as a dedicated trials platform for guns, torpedoes and other equipment prior to their introduction to the fleet. DEVONSHIRE is operated as a Cadet Training Ship. She was converted at Devonport in September 1946. Work included the removal of her main armament, with the exception of her forward twin 8-inch turret, and extensive internal changes to provide accommodation and instructional facilities. The ship recommissioned in April 1947.

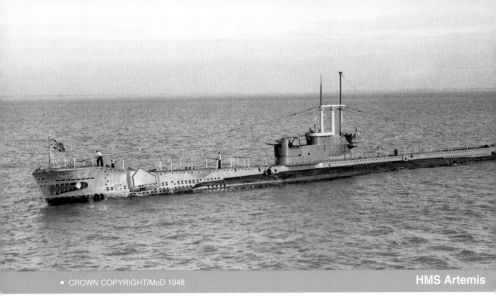

HMS Artemis

SUBMARINES
'A' CLASS

Ship	Completed	Builder
ACHERON	17.04.48	HM Dockyard (Chatham)
AENEAS	31.07.46	Cammell Laird (Birkenhead)
ALARIC	11.12.46	Cammell Laird (Birkenhead)
AMBUSH	22.07.47	Vickers Armstrong (Barrow)
AMPHION	27.03.45	Vickers Armstrong (Barrow)
ANCHORITE	18.11.47	Vickers Armstrong (Barrow)
ANDREW	16.03.48	Vickers Armstrong (Barrow)
ARTEMIS	15.08.47	Scott's SB & Eng Co (Greenock)
ARTFUL	02.02.48	Scott's SB & Eng Co (Greenock)
ASTUTE	30.06.45	Vickers Armstrong (Barrow)
AURIGA	12.01.46	Vickers Armstrong (Barrow)
AUROCHS	07.02.47	Vickers Armstrong (Barrow)

Displacement 1,120 tons (1,443 tons FL); 1,610 tons dived Dimensions 279ft 9in x 22ft 3in x 18ft 1in Machinery Supercharged diesel engines (4300 bhp); Electric motors (1250 bhp); 2 shafts Speed 19 knots (surfaced); 10 knots (dived) Armament

34

10 x 21-in TT (6 bow, 4 stern) up to 16 torpedoes or 26 mines; 1 x 4in deck gun in some

Complement 60

Notes

Large patrol submarines designed for operations in the Pacific during World War II, the submarines were completed too late to see war service. It is likely that these submarine will eventually undergo a modernisation programme similar to the streamlined T Class.

On 16 April 1951 AFFRAY sailed from Portsmouth and disappeared without a trace and the Admiralty suspended all A class operations pending an investigation. The wreck of AFFRAY was found on 14 June 1951 in 278 ft of water about 30 miles north of Guernsey. Initial investigations reveal that the snort tube had snapped off just above deck level.

Cancelled Names

With the end of World War II only 16 of the class were completed. The following submarines were all cancelled on 29 October 1945:

ABELARD, ACASTA, ACE, ACHATES, ADEPT, ADMIRABLE, ADVERSARY, AGATE, AGGRESSOR, AGILE, ALADDIN, ALCESTIS, ANDROMACHE, ANSWER, ANTAEUS, ANTAGONIST, ANZAC, APHRODITE, APPROACH, ARCADIAN, ARDENT, ARGOSY, ASGARD, ASPERITY, ASSURANCE, ASTARTE, ATLANTIS, AUSTERE, AWAKE and AZTEC.

HMS Untiring

'U' CLASS (SECOND GROUP)

Ship	Completed	Builder
UPSTART (ex-P65)	03.04.43	Vickers Armstrong (Barrow)
UNTIRING (ex-P59)	09.06.43	Vickers Armstrong (Walker)

Displacement 545 tons (658 FL); 740 tons dived Dimensions 196ft 10in x 16ft x 14ft 6in Machinery Diesel engines (615 bhp); Electric motors (825 bhp); 2 shafts Speed 11.25 knots (surfaced); 9 knots (dived) Armament 4 x 21-in TT (8 torpedoes or 6 mines) Complement 33

Notes

The sole remaining U class in RN service. They were operated by the Hellenic Navy as AMFITRITI (UPSTART) and XIFIAS (UNTIRING) between 1945 and 1952 when they were returned to the Royal Navy. They are now used in a training role. P52 was lent to the Royal Danish Navy in 1946 where she remains in service as SPRINGEREN.

Several similar V class submarines are also on loan to overseas navies. Denmark operates VULPINE and VORTEX as SAELEN and STOREN respectively. VIRULENT, VENGEFUL, VELDT and VOLATILE are operated by the Hellenic Navy as ARGONAFTIC, DELPHIN, PIPINOS and TRIAINA respectively.

HMS Tireless

'T' CLASS

Ship	Completed	Builder
TACTICIAN (ex-P94)	29.11.42	Vickers Armstrong (Barrow)
TALENT	04.12.43	Vickers Armstrong (Barrow)
TALLY-HO (ex-P97)	12.04.43	Vickers Armstrong (Barrow)
TELEMACHUS	25.10.43	Vickers Armstrong (Barrow)
TEREDO	13.04.46	Vickers Armstrong (Barrow)
THERMOPYLAE	05.12.45	HM Dockyard (Chatham)
THOROUGH	01.03.44	Vickers Armstrong (Barrow)
TIRELESS	18.04.45	HM Dockyard (Portsmouth)
TOKEN	15.12.45	HM Dockyard (Portsmouth)
TOTEM	09.01.45	HM Dockyard (Devonport)
TRADEWIND	18.10.43	HM Dockyard (Chatham)
TRENCHANT	26.02.44	HM Dockyard (Chatham)
TRESPASSER (ex-P92)	25.09.42	Vickers Armstrong (Barrow)
TRUMP	08.07.44	Vickers Armstrong (Barrow)
TUDOR	16.01.44	HM Dockyard (Devonport)

Displacement 1,090 tons (1,442 FL); 1,571 tons dived Dimensions 273ft 3in x 26ft 7in x 15ft 10in Machinery Admiralty pattern diesel engines (2500 bhp); Electric motors (1450 bhp); 2 shafts Speed 15¼ knots (surfaced); 8¾ knots (dived) Armament 11 x 21in TT (8 bow, 3 stern) up to 17 torpedoes or 12 mines; 1 x 4in deck gun in some Complement 63-68

Notes

The specifications above apply to those submarines that remain in their original configuration. Since the end of World War II this class has undergone a multitude of individual modifications, to such an extent that it is difficult to provide a baseline class statistic.

The class is to undergo extensive modernisation and as individual submarines are surveyed their suitability for the modernisation programme will be assessed. In a programme initiated in 1949 eight of the class (TABARD, TIPTOE, TRUMP, TRUNCHEON, THERMOPYLAE, TOTEM, TURPIN and TACITURN) are to be reconstructed along the lines of the German Type XXI U-boats. The pressure hull will be extended by up to 20 feet to allow installation of more batteries and a further pair of electric motors. The gun armament will be removed as will all external torpedo tubes, leaving six in the bow. The original pressure hull casing and conning tower structure will be streamlined.

TACTICIAN, THOROUGH and TELEMACHUS are based in Australia. TAURUS and TAPIR are on loan to the Dutch Navy as DOLFIJN and ZEEHOND.

HMS Seneschal

'S' CLASS

Ship	Completed	Builder
SANGUINE	13.05.45	Cammell Laird (Birkenhead)
SCORCHER	16.03.45	Cammell Laird (Birkenhead)
SCOTSMAN	09.12.44	Scott's SB & Eng Co (Greenock)
SCYTHIAN	11.08.44	Scott's SB & Eng Co (Greenock)
SEA DEVIL	12.05.45	Scott's SB & Eng Co (Greenock)
SEA SCOUT	19.06.44	Cammell Laird (Birkenhead)
SENESCHAL	06.09.45	Scott's SB & Eng Co (Greenock)
SENTINEL	28.12.45	Scott's SB & Eng Co (Greenock)
SERAPH (ex-P69)	10.06.42	Vickers Armstrong (Barrow)
SIDON	23.11.44	Cammell Laird (Birkenhead)
SPRINGER	02.08.45	Cammell Laird (Birkenhead)
SUBTLE	16.04.44	Cammell Laird (Birkenhead)

Displacement 715 tons (854 FL); 990 tons dived Dimensions 217ft x 23ft 9in x 14ft 6in
Machinery Admiralty diesel engines (1900 bhp); Electric motors (1300 bhp); 2 shafts
Speed 14¾ knots (surfaced); 9 knots (dived) Armament 6-7 x 21in TT (6 bow, 1 stern)
up to 12-13 torpedoes or 12 mines; 1 x 3in or 1 x 4in deck gun Complement 48

Again, as in the earlier 'T' class, the extended build programme during World War II and subsequent piecemeal modifications after the war, results in a class where it is difficult to establish baseline data for the entire class, the specifications above reflecting original build state.

SATYR, SCEPTRE and SERAPH, during the war, and SCOTSMAN, SELENE, SLEUTH, SOLENT and STATESMAN post-war, were converted into high speed target submarines to help Allied anti-submarine forces develop tactics against the latest developments of German U-boat. The conversion comprised removal of upperdeck armament and streamlining of the casing in addition to greater battery output for increased underwater speed. SCOTSMAN has undergone several further reconstructions to investigate underwater streamlining.

Four vessels, SATYR, SPITEFUL, SPORTSMAN and STATESMAN, are on loan to France where they are operated as SAPHIR, SIRENE, SIBYLLE and SULTANE respectively. Tragically, SIBYLLE was lost with all hands off Toulon on 24 September. The reason for her loss is not yet known.

XE 7

'XE' CRAFT

Ship	Completed	Builder
XE7	06.11.44	Broadbent (Huddersfield)
XE9	12.11.44	Marshall (Gainsborough)
XE12	15.12.44	Markham (Chesterfield)

Displacement 30 tons (surfaced), 34 tons (dived)   Dimensions 53ft x 5ft 9in
Machinery Diesel engine 42 bhp; Electric motor 30 bhp   Speed 6½ knots (surfaced)
6 knots (dived)   Armament 2 x side charges (4,000lb each)   Complement 5

Notes

Twelve XE-class midget submarines (HMS XE1 to XE12) were built for the RN during
the latter years of the war. They are an improved version of the X Class midgets used
in the attack on the German battleship TIRPITZ, incorporating air conditioning for operations in the Far East. It is believed that XE12 is non-operational and being used as a
source of spares to keep the remaining pair operational. With the recent announcement
of a new class of midget submarines, these may soon be withdrawn from service. In
addition to anti-ship operations they can also be used for clandestine operations close to
shore.

HMS Daring

DESTROYERS
DARING CLASS

Ship	Completed	Builder
DARING	08.03.52	Swan Hunter & Wigham Richardson
DIAMOND	21.02.52	J. Brown & Co (Clydebank)
DUCHESS	23.10.52	J.I. Thornycroft & Co (Woolston)
DEFENDER	05.12.52	A Stephen & Sons Ltd (Linthouse)
DECOY	29.03.49(L)	Yarrow (Scotstoun)
DAINTY	16.08.50(L)	J.S. White & Co (Cowes)
DELIGHT	21.12.50(L)	Fairfield SB & Eng Co (Govan)
DIANA	08.05.52(L)	Yarrow (Scotstoun)

Displacement 2,950 tons (3,580 tons FL)　Dimensions 390ft x 43ft x 12ft 6in
Machinery Parsons double reduction geared turbines (English Electric Co design in
DECOY), 2 Foster-Wheeler boilers (Babcock & Wilcox DARING), 2 shafts, 54,000 shp
Speed 34¾ knots　Armament 6 x 4.5in, 6 x 40mm, 10 x TT, 1 Squid　Complement
278-308

42

Ordered under the 1944 construction programme, there were originally to have been 16 ships in the class. They are intended to perform the anti-submarine or anti-ship role though their slow pace of construction has meant that anti-submarine technology has somewhat overtaken the original design and the ships rather weak A/S weapon fit, comprising a single triple Squid mount might make them somewhat ineffective in that role. However, they incorporate a heavy gun armament comprising three twin 4.5-inch turrets of a new type, fully automated and radar controlled together with a heavy torpedo armament.

Like the earlier Weapon class, these ships have their boiler rooms and engine rooms alternated to increase survivability. This practice results in widely-spaced funnels which in this class comprise a forward funnel trunked up through the lattice foremast and a smaller 'stump' funnel amidships.

Such are their size, the largest destroyers built for the RN, that they are to be known in service as Daring class ships rather than destroyers. All are to be fitted as leaders.

Ships Names

Due to the cancellation of half of the class in December 1945, there was a shuffle of names in order to perpetuate those of the D class destroyers of the 1930s. DELIGHT was previously DISDAIN and prior to that YPRES. DIANA was previously DRUID; DEFENDER was DOGSTAR and DECOY was DRAGON.

Those ships cancelled in 1945 comprised DANAE, DEMON, DERVISH, DECOY, DELIGHT, DESPERATE, DESIRE and DIANA.

HMS Broadsword

WEAPON CLASS

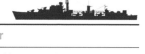

Ship	Completed	Builder
BATTLEAXE	23.10.47	Yarrow (Scotstoun)
BROADSWORD	04.10.48	Yarrow (Scotstoun)
CROSSBOW	04.03.48	J.I. Thornycroft & Co (Woolston)
SCORPION	17.09.47	J.S. White & Co (Cowes)

Displacement 1,980 tons (2,840 tons FL) Dimensions 365ft x 38ft x 12ft 6in
Machinery Parsons geared turbines, 2 Foster Wheeler boilers, 2 shafts, 40,000 shp
Speed 31 knots Armament 4 x 4in, 6 x 40mm, 10 x TT, 2 Squid (SCORPION 2 Limbo)
Complement 234

Notes

Designed and equipped as Fleet A/S escorts. In CROSSBOW and SCORPION the 4-inch
guns are mounted in A and B positions forward of the bridge. In the remaining pair the guns
are mounted forward and aft with the Squid in B position. There are two engine rooms and
two boilers rooms arranged alternately en echelon to help survivability. SCORPION was to
have been named TOMAHAWK. They comprise the 6th Destroyer Squadron, Home Fleet.
Fifteen more of this class were cancelled at the end of the war (CARRONADE, CLAY-
MORE, CULVERIN, CUTLASS, DAGGER, DIRK, GRENADE, HALBERD, HOWITZER,
LONGBOW, MUSKET, POINARD, RIFLE, SPEAR and SWORD).

44

HMS Aisne

LATER BATTLE CLASS

Ship	Completed	Builder
AGINCOURT	25.06.47	Hawthorn Leslie (Hebburn)
AISNE	20.03.47	Vickers Armstrong (Walker)
BARROSA	14.02.47	J. Brown & Co (Clydebank)
CORUNNA	06.06.47	Swan Hunter & Wigham Richardson

Displacement 2,380 tons (3,375 tons FL) Dimensions 379ft x 40ft 6in x 12ft 6in
Machinery Parsons geared turbines, 2 Admiralty 3-drum boilers, 2 shafts, 50,000 shp
Speed 31 knots Armament 5 x 4.5in, 8 x40mm, 10 x TT, 1 x Squid Complement
232-268 (337 in war)

Notes

Apart from a heavier armament this later group can be distinguished from the early Battle
class by the large director tower of US pattern sited just ahead of the mainmast. The
ships also carry an additional 4.5-inch gun in a single mount just aft of the funnel. BAR-
ROSA recommissioned for service with the 4th Destroyer Squadron in May following a
period in reserve at Portsmouth. AGINCOURT was involved in a collision with CADIZ in
July causing minor damage to both ships.

HMS Finisterre

BATTLE CLASS

Ship	Completed	Builder
ARMADA	02.07.45	Hawthorn Leslie (Hebburn)
CADIZ	12.04.46	Fairfield SB & Eng Co (Govan)
FINISTERRE	11.09.45	Fairfield SB & Eng Co (Govan)
GABBARD	10.12.46	Swan Hunter & Wigham Richardson
GRAVELINES	14.06.46	Cammell Laird (Birkenhead)
ST JAMES	12.07.46	Fairfield SB & Eng Co (Govan)
ST KITTS	21.01.46	Swan Hunter & Wigham Richardson
SAINTES	27.09.46	Hawthorn Leslie (Hebburn)
SLUYS	30.09.46	Cammell Laird (Birkenhead)
SOLEBAY	11.10.45	Hawthorn Leslie (Hebburn)
VIGO	09.12.46	Fairfield SB & Eng Co (Govan)

Displacement 2,315 tons (3,235-3,300 tons FL) Dimensions 379ft x 40ft 3in x 12ft 9in Machinery Parsons geared turbines, 2 Admiralty 3-drum boilers, 2 shafts, 50,000 shp **Speed** 32 knots **Armament** 4 x 4.5in, 10 x 40mm, 8-10 x TT **Complement** 247-308

These ships were designed for operations in the Pacific theatre towards the end of World War II, with an emphasis on anti-aircraft armament. As completed some ships carried a single 4-inch gun aft of the funnel. These have now been replaced by single 40mm mounts in all ships. ARMADA, SAINTES, ST JAMES, SOLEBAY and VIGO are fitted as leaders. It is intended that CADIZ, GABBARD, ST JAMES, ST KITTS and SOLEBAY will be fitted with Squid which will necessitate an extension to the after superstructure and the removal of at least one of the 40mm mountings.

ARMADA, GRAVELINES, SAINTES and VIGO operate as the 3rd Destroyer Squadron in the Mediterranean. GABBARD, ST JAMES, ST KITTS and SOLEBAY form the 5th Destroyer Squadron, Home Fleet. FINISTERRE operates as a Gunnery Firing Ship and has had her 40mm mountings removed.

HMS Crispin

'CR' CLASS

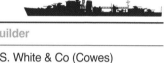

Ship	Completed	Builder
CREOLE	14.10.46	J.S. White & Co (Cowes)
CRISPIN	10.07.46	J.S. White & Co (Cowes)

Displacement 1,865 tons (2,515 tons FL) Dimensions 362ft 9in x 35ft 9in x 10ft
Machinery Parsons SR geared turbines, 2 Admiralty 3-drum boilers, 2 shafts, 40,000
shp Speed 33 knots Armament 3 x 4.5in, 4 x 40mm, 2-6 x 20mm/2pdr, 4 x TT
Complement 186-222

Notes

Both ships have a W/T cabin in place of B turret. CRISPIN has a large AA position amidships with a light director as per the Battle class. Both operate as part of the 3rd Training
Flotilla at Londonderry.

CROMWELL, CROWN, CROZIERS and CRYSTAL were purchased by Norway in 1946
and renamed STAVANGER, OSLO, BERGEN and TRONDHEIM respectively.

HMS Contest

'CO' CLASS

Ship	Completed	Builder
COCKADE	29.09.45	Yarrow (Scotstoun)
COMUS	08.07.46	J.I. Thornycroft & Co (Woolston)
CONCORD	20.12.46	J.I. Thornycroft & Co (Woolston)
CONSORT	19.03.46	A Stephen & Sons Ltd (Linthouse)
CONSTANCE	31.12.45	Vickers Armstrong (Walker)
CONTEST	09.11.45	J.S. White & Co (Cowes)
COSSACK	04.09.45	Vickers Armstrong (Walker)

Displacement 1,865 tons (2,515 tons FL) Dimensions 362ft 9in x 35ft 9in x 10ft
Machinery Parsons SR geared turbines, 2 Admiralty 3-drum boilers, 2 shafts, 40,000
shp Speed 33 knots Armament 3-4 x 4.5in, 4 x 40mm, 2-6 x 20mm/2-pdr, 4 x TT
Complement 186-222

Notes

'X' turret has been removed from all but COCKADE, CONSORT and CONTEST and
replaced by two Squid launchers in the first two. CONTEST is operating as a submarine
target ship from Portsmouth. The remaining ships form the 8th Destroyer Squadron and
are operating off Korea. In April COCKADE entered drydock at Singapore to commence
an interim modification refit.

49

HMS Chequers

'CH' CLASS

Ship	Completed	Builder
CHARITY	19.11.45	J.I. Thornycroft & Co (Woolston)
CHEQUERS	28.09.45	Scott's SB & Eng Co (Greenock)
CHEVIOT	11.12.45	A Stephen & Sons Ltd (Linthouse)
CHEVRON	23.08.45	A Stephen & Sons Ltd (Linthouse)
CHIEFTAIN	07.03.46	Scott's SB & Eng Co (Greenock)
CHIVALROUS	13.05.46	Wm Denny & Bros (Dumbarton)

Displacement 1,885 tons (2,545 tons FL) Dimensions 362ft 9in x 35ft 9in x 10ft
Machinery Parsons SR geared turbines, 2 Admiralty 3-drum boilers, 2 shafts, 40,000
shp Speed 33 knots Armament 3-4 x 4.5in, 4 x 40mm, 2-6 x 20mm/2pdr, 4 x TT
Complement 186-222

Notes

'X' turret has been removed from all but CHARITY. CHEQUERS, CHEVIOT and CHIEF-
TAIN now mount two Squid launchers in place of 'X' turret. Most are based in the
Mediterranean, though CHARITY has been operating off Korea. CHEQUERS has under-
gone a partial modification refit at Malta. ALL form the 1st Destroyer Squadron,
Mediterranean, with the exception of CHARITY which is part of the 8th Destroyer
Squadron in the Far East.

HMS Zephyr

'Z' CLASS

Ship	Completed	Builder
MYNGS	23.06.44	Vickers Armstrong (Walker)
ZAMBESI	18.07.44	Cammell Laird (Birkenhead)
ZEPHYR	06.09.44	Vickers Armstrong (Walker)

Displacement 1,710 tons (2,530 tons FL) MYNGS and ZEPHYR 1,730 tons (2,575 tons FL) Dimensions 362ft 9in x 35ft 9in x 16ft Machinery Parsons SR geared turbines, 2 Admiralty 3-drum boilers, 2 shafts, 40,000 shp Speed 33 knots Armament 3-4 x 4.5in, 6 x 40mm, 8 x TT (4 x TT MYNGS and ZEPHYR) Complement 186

Notes

MYNGS has been allocated to the Type 62 Aircraft Direction frigate conversion programme. The conversion will include the installation of Types 293Q, 969, 974, 982 and 983 radar. In February however she was in collision with the Diving Ship RECLAIM and was holed on the starboard side. ZAMBESI replaced TENACIOUS as a submarine target ship with 3rd Submarine Squadron, though she is expected to reduce to reserve by the end of the year. ZEPHYR operates as a training ship with the 2nd Training Flotilla.

51

HMS Ulster

'U' CLASS

Ship	Completed	Builder
ULSTER	30.06.43	Swan Hunter & Wigham Richardson

Displacement 1,777 tons (2,508 tons FL) Dimensions 362ft 9in x 35ft 9in x 16ft
Machinery Parsons SR geared turbines, 2 Admiralty 3-drum boilers, 2 shafts, 40,000
shp Speed 34 knots Armament 4 x 4.7in, 4 x 40mm, 4 x 20mm, 8 x TT Complement
180

Notes

ULSTER is operating as an Air Target Training ship but is expected to reduce to reserve
by the end of the year.

HMS Savage

'S' CLASS

Ship	Completed	Builder
SAVAGE	08.06.43	Hawthorn Leslie (Hebburn)

Displacement 1,730 tons (2,515 tons FL) **Dimensions** 362ft 9in x 35ft 9in x 16ft
Machinery Parsons SR geared turbines, 2 Admiralty 3-drum boilers, 2 shafts, 40,000
shp **Speed** 32 knots **Armament** 4 x 4.5in (1 x twin, 2 x single), 12 x 20mm, 8 x TT
Complement 230

Notes

Her main armament differed from other ships of the class comprising a trial installation
of the twin 4.5in mounting proposed for the Battle class destroyers. Since 1950 she has
been undertaking noise reduction trials with five-bladed propellers. Since October 1952
she has also been employed as an Air Target Ship. Was allocated to join the Type 62 AD
conversion programme, but was unable to mount the Type 982 and Type 983 radar. Now
scheduled to join the Fast A/S frigate conversion programme.

HMS Obdurate

'O' CLASS

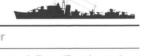

Ship	Completed	Builder
OBDURATE	03.09.42	Wm Denny & Bros (Dumbarton)
OBEDIENT	30.10.42	Wm Denny & Bros (Dumbarton)
OPPORTUNE	14.08.42	J.I. Thornycroft & Co (Woolston)

Displacement 1,610 tons (2,270 tons FL) Dimensions 345ft x 35ft x 15ft 9in Machinery Parsons SR geared turbines, 2 Admiralty 3-drum boilers, 2 shafts, 36,000 shp Speed 31 knots Armament 4 x 4in, 4 x 2pdr, 6 x 20mm Complement 175

Notes

All have been converted to be able to carry and lay mines in an emergency. They can carry up to 60 mines which can be laid via rails over the stern to both port and starboard.

OBEDIENT replaced ZEST as an Air Target ship in October 1952 having been withdrawn from the Type 16 conversion programme. OBDURATE and OPPORTUNE were expected to enter the Type 16 frigate A/S conversion programme. OPPORTUNE had been operating as an Air Target Ship since 1950 and entered refit in 1952, but work was suspended in October.

In 1949 OFFA and ONSLOW were transferred to Pakistan becoming TARIQ and TIPPU SULTAN. In 1952 ONSLAUGHT was also transferred being renamed TUGHRIL.

HMS Verulam

FRIGATES

TYPE 15 CLASS

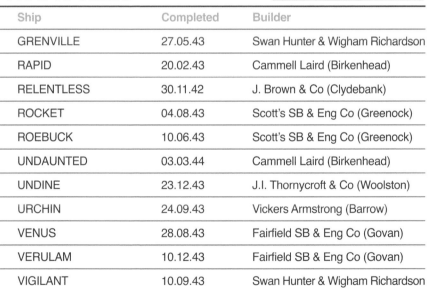

Ship	Completed	Builder
GRENVILLE	27.05.43	Swan Hunter & Wigham Richardson
RAPID	20.02.43	Cammell Laird (Birkenhead)
RELENTLESS	30.11.42	J. Brown & Co (Clydebank)
ROCKET	04.08.43	Scott's SB & Eng Co (Greenock)
ROEBUCK	10.06.43	Scott's SB & Eng Co (Greenock)
UNDAUNTED	03.03.44	Cammell Laird (Birkenhead)
UNDINE	23.12.43	J.I. Thornycroft & Co (Woolston)
URCHIN	24.09.43	Vickers Armstrong (Barrow)
VENUS	28.08.43	Fairfield SB & Eng Co (Govan)
VERULAM	10.12.43	Fairfield SB & Eng Co (Govan)
VIGILANT	10.09.43	Swan Hunter & Wigham Richardson

Displacement 2,300 tons (2,700 tons FL) Dimensions 358/362ft 6in x 35ft 9in x 14ft 6in Machinery Parsons SR geared turbines, 2 Admiralty 3-drum boilers, 2 shafts, 40,000 shp Speed 31 knots Armament 2 x 4in (1 x twin), 2 x 40mm (1 x twin), 2 x Squid/Limbo AS mortars, 2 x TT (RELENTLESS) Complement 174

Notes

In an effort to counter the growing threat from advances in submarine technology and to bridge the gap between the current slow A/S escorts and the arrival of the newer high speed, technologically advanced types (Type 12 and Type 14) now under construction, a programme is now underway to utilise some of the young, but fast, wartime destroyers into fast A/S frigates, the Type 15. Some 47 such destroyers are available from both active and reserve fleets. Conversion involves removing all superstructure, weapons, masts and equipment down to upper deck level. The opportunity is also taken to overhaul all machinery. Structurally the forecastle deck was extended aft to leave only a small quarterdeck, providing much improved accommodation. The superstructure is 'ironed out' to present a minimum resistance to atomic blast and designed so that virtually all the ship's company will be under cover when the ship is at action, and so screened from atomic radiation. This has meant the elimination of the traditional bridge, the ship being fought from an operations room, with a periscope arrangement to permit the captain all round vision. Two lattice masts are provided to carry the range of radars, HF/DF and communications aerilas that are now an essential part of the modern warship. Armament comprises a pair of Limbo A/S mortars on the quarterdeck (ROCKET and RELENTLESS have been completed with the prototype Limbo, following ships will receive Squid in the interim until Limbo becomes available). They will carry a new anti-submarine weapon, the Mark 20E torpedo, in a pair of trainable tubes on each beam. For self defence, a twin 4-inch Mk XIX gun is carried aft, and behind the bridge is a twin 40 mm MkV Bofors gun. RELENTLESS and ROCKET are attached to the 3rd Training Squadron at Londonderry whereas the V class conversions so far completed are attached to the 6th Frigate Squadron.

Type Numbering

In July 1950, to try and remedy confusion over the many new classes of vessel entering service, a series of Type numbers was introduced to differentiate between various designs and roles. All ocean-going escorts, including converted destroyers, are to be known as frigates. These are then classed by role using a system of type numbers. Anti-Submarine frigates are to be numbered from Type 11 onwards; Anti-Aircraft frigates from Type 41 onwards and Aircraft Direction frigates from Type 61.

Conversions Underway

Ship	Shipyard	Start	Completion
RAPID	A. Stephen & Sons Ltd (Linthouse)	1950	Ongoing
RELENTLESS	H M Dockyard (Portsmouth)	1949	1951
ROCKET	H M Dockyard (Devonport)	1949	1951
ROEBUCK	H M Dockyard (Devonport)	1951	Ongoing
GRENVILLE	H M Dockyard (Chatham)	1952	Ongoing
UNDAUNTED	J.S. White & Co (Cowes)	1951	Ongoing
UNDINE	A. Stephen & Sons Ltd (Linthouse)	1951	Ongoing
URCHIN	Barclay Curle & Co Ltd (Glasgow)	1952	Ongoing
VENUS	H M Dockyard (Devonport)	1950	1952
VERULAM	H M Dockyard (Portsmouth)	1950	1952
VIGILANT	J.I Thornycroft & Co (Woolston)	1951	Ongoing
VIRAGO	H M Dockyard (Chatham)	1951	1952
VOLAGE	J.S. White & Co (Cowes)	1951	Ongoing
WAKEFUL	Scott's SB & Eng Co (Greenock)	1951	Ongoing
WHIRLWIND	Palmers SB & Iron Co Ltd (Jarrow)	1951	Ongoing
WRANGLER	Harland & Wolff (Birkenhead)	1951	Ongoing

HMS Tenacious

TYPE 16 CLASS

Ship	Completed	Builder
ORWELL	17.10.42	J.I. Thornycroft & Co (Woolston)
TENACIOUS	30.10.43	Cammell Laird (Birkenhead)
TERMAGANT	18.12.43	Wm Denny & Bros (Dumbarton)
TUSCAN	11.03.43	Swan Hunter & Wigham Richardson
TYRIAN	08.04.43	Swan Hunter & Wigham Richardson

Displacement 1,800 tons (2,300 tons FL) Dimensions 362ft 9in x 35ft 9in x 15ft 6in Machinery Parsons SR geared turbines, 2 Admiralty 3-drum boilers, 2 shafts, 40,000 shp Speed 31 knots Armament 2 x 4in (1 x twin), 7 x 40mm (1 x twin, 5 x single), 4 x TT, 2 x Squid AS mortars Complement 175

Notes

Concurrently with the Type 15 conversions, a programme was instigated in 1951 for the conversion, on a limited scale, of further war construction standard destroyers to specialist A/S ships, with TENACIOUS as the prototype. The Type 16 will be much less elaborate and involves very little structural alteration, as a result the ships retain their tradi-

58

tional destroyer appearance. All existing armament is landed and a twin 4-in Mk XVI is fitted in 'B' position on the forward shelter deck. A twin 40mm Bofors is fitted amidships and the after quad 21-in torpedo tubes refitted. A deckhouse now occupies the space vacated by the forward torpedo tubes. Two Squid A/S mortars are fitted on the after shelter deck in 'X' position with a bomb handling room built at the end of the deck. ORWELL, on completion of her conversion, is expected to retain her emergency minelaying capability.

TENACIOUS recommissioned as the first Type 16 frigate in January and operates with the 3rd Training Squadron at Londonderry. TERMAGANT was towed to Liverpool in August 1951 to begin her conversion which is scheduled to complete in 1953, as are those of TYRIAN, TUSCAN and ORWELL.

Conversions Underway

Ship	Shipyard	Start	Completion
ORWELL	HM Dockyard (Rosyth)	1952	Ongoing
TENACIOUS	HM Dockyard (Rosyth)	1951	1952
TERMAGANT	Grayson Rollo (Liverpool)	1951	Ongoing
TUSCAN	Mount Stuart Dry Dock (Cardiff)	1952	Ongoing
TYRIAN	Harland & Wolff (Birkenhead)	1951	Ongoing

HMS Sparrow

MODIFIED BLACK SWAN CLASS

Ship	Completed	Builder
ACTAEON	24.07.46	J.I. Thornycroft & Co (Woolston)
CRANE	10.05.43	Wm Denny & Bros (Dumbarton)
CYGNET	01.12.42	Cammell Laird (Birkenhead)
MAGPIE	30.08.43	J.I. Thornycroft & Co (Woolston)
MERMAID	12.05.44	Wm Denny & Bros (Dumbarton)
MODESTE	03.09.45	HM Dockyard (Chatham)
NEREIDE	06.05.46	HM Dockyard (Chatham)
OPOSSUM	16.06.45	Wm Denny & Bros (Dumbarton)
PEACOCK	10.05.44	J.I. Thornycroft & Co (Woolston)
SNIPE	09.09.46	Wm Denny & Bros (Dumbarton)
SPARROW	16.12.46	Wm Denny & Bros (Dumbarton)

Displacement 1,475 tons (1,925 tons FL) Dimensions 299ft 6in x 38ft 6in x 8ft 9in Machinery Parsons SR geared turbines, 2 Admiralty 3-drum boilers, 2 shafts, 4,300 shp Speed 19¾ knots Armament 6 x 4in, 6 x 40mm, Hedgehog Complement 192

60

Although not really suited for upgrading to modern standards with regard to weapons and radar due to their hull size and limited space, these vessels remain effective in terms of operating costs and continue to prove themselves useful as guardships on overseas stations.

SNIPE and SPARROW returned to the UK in mid-1952 following extended service on the Americas and West Indies Station. By late 1952, following refit, SPARROW recommissioned for service in the Far East. MAGPIE, MERMAID and PEACOCK are serving with the Mediterranean Fleet and OPOSSUM joined the 3rd Frigate Squadron in the Autumn for service in the Far East. CRANE recommissioned in late 1951 and will replace HART in the Far East. NEREIDE has, since 1946, been deployed on the South Atlantic Station. CYGNET, which since 1948 had been operating with the Fishery Protection Squadron, has been refitted for further service in the Mediterranean with the 5th Frigate Flotilla. MODESTE had been used as an accommodation ship at Portsmouth as part of Vernon II. This year she has been brought forward from reserve for refit and further service with the Far East Fleet.

HMS Wild Goose

BLACK SWAN CLASS

Ship	Completed	Builder
ERNE	26.04.41	Furness SB Co Ltd (Haverton)
FLAMINGO	03.11.39	Yarrow (Scotstoun)
WILD GOOSE	11.03.43	Yarrow (Scotstoun)
WREN	04.02.43	Wm Denny & Bros (Dumbarton)

Displacement 1,300 tons (1,750 tons FL) Dimensions 299ft 6in x 37ft 6in x 8ft 6in
Machinery Parsons SR geared turbines, 2 Admiralty 3-drum boilers, 2 shafts, 4,300
shp Speed 19¾ knots Armament 6 x 4in, 4 x 40mm, Hedgehog Complement 180

Notes

WREN was refitted at Malta in 1949. Her A/S gear was removed and replaced by two
deckhouses on the quarterdeck containing accommodation for the captain. All except
ERNE are operating in the Persian Gulf. In 1950 ERNE, which has been in reserve
since 1946, was selected for refitting as a stationary RNVR drill ship. She was refitted
at Portsmouth where she was stripped of all armament and radar, save for an instructional set, and took up her new duties as Solent Division Drill Ship at Southampton in
May. In her new role she has been renamed WESSEX.

HMS Morecambe Bay

BAY CLASS

Ship	Completed	Builder
BIGBURY BAY	10.07.45	Hall Russell (Aberdeen)
BURGHEAD BAY	20.09.45	Charles Hill & Sons (Bristol)
CARDIGAN BAY	25.06.45	Henry Robb (Leith)
ENARD BAY	04.01.46	Smith's Dock (Middlesborough)
LARGO BAY	26.01.46	W Pickersgill & Sons (Sunderland)
MORECAMBE BAY	22.02.49	W Pickersgill & Sons (Sunderland)
MOUNTS BAY	11.08.49	W Pickersgill & Sons (Sunderland)
ST AUSTELL BAY	29.05.45	Harland & Wolff (Belfast)
ST BRIDES BAY	15.06.45	Harland & Wolff (Belfast)
VERYAN BAY	13.05.45	Charles Hill & Sons (Bristol)
WIDEMOUTH BAY	13.04.45	Harland & Wolff (Belfast)
WHITESAND BAY	30.07.45	Harland & Wolff (Belfast)

Displacement 1,580 tons (2,420 tons FL) **Dimensions** 307ft 6in x 38ft 6in x 12ft 9in
Machinery Triple expansion, 2 Admiralty 3-drum boilers, 2 shafts, 5,500 ihp **Speed**
19½ knots **Armament** 4 x 4in, 6 x 40mm, 2 x 20mm, Hedgehog **Complement** 157

Notes

Unlike the Loch class, which were designed and completed for A/S work, as the tempo
of the Second World War shifted, so the need for Anti-aircraft vessels increased. The
Bay class, therefore, were completed, primarily, for AA escort duties.

CARDIGAN BAY, MORECAMBE BAY, MOUNTS BAY, ST BRIDES BAY and WHITE-
SAND BAY are all operating off Korea in support of the Untied Nations operations.

BURGHEAD BAY, following a refit at Devonport, has replaced BIGBURY BAY on the
Americas and West Indies station. She was ordered from Port Stanley in the Falkland
Islands to Graham Land where a stores party from the research vessel JOHN
BRISCOE were stopped by armed Argentineans.

Former Loch Class Names

BIGBURY BAY (ex-LOCH CARLOWAY); BURGHEAD BAY (ex-LOCH HARPORT);
CARDIGAN BAY (ex-LOCH LAXFORD); CARNARVON BAY (ex-LOCH MADDY);
CAWSAND BAY (ex-LOCH ROAN); ENARD BAY (ex-LOCH BRACADALE); LARGO
BAY (ex-LOCH FOIN); MORECAMBE BAY (ex-LOCH HEILEN); MOUNTS BAY (ex-
LOCH KILBERNIE); PADSTOW BAY (ex-LOCH COULSIDE); PORLOCK BAY (ex-
LOCH SEAFORTH (II), ex-LOCH MUICK); ST AUSTELL BAY (ex-LOCH LYDDOCH);
ST BRIDES BAY (ex-LOCH ACHILITY); START BAY (ex-LOCH ARKLET); TREMADOC
BAY (ex-LOCH ARNISH); VERYAN BAY (ex-LOCH SWANNAY); WHITESAND BAY (ex-
LOCH LUBNAIG); WIDEMOUTH BAY (ex-LOCH FRISA); WIGTOWN BAY (ex-LOCH
GARASDALE).

HMS Loch Veyatie

LOCH CLASS

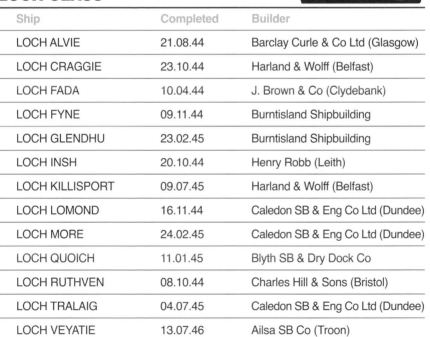

Ship	Completed	Builder
LOCH ALVIE	21.08.44	Barclay Curle & Co Ltd (Glasgow)
LOCH CRAGGIE	23.10.44	Harland & Wolff (Belfast)
LOCH FADA	10.04.44	J. Brown & Co (Clydebank)
LOCH FYNE	09.11.44	Burntisland Shipbuilding
LOCH GLENDHU	23.02.45	Burntisland Shipbuilding
LOCH INSH	20.10.44	Henry Robb (Leith)
LOCH KILLISPORT	09.07.45	Harland & Wolff (Belfast)
LOCH LOMOND	16.11.44	Caledon SB & Eng Co Ltd (Dundee)
LOCH MORE	24.02.45	Caledon SB & Eng Co Ltd (Dundee)
LOCH QUOICH	11.01.45	Blyth SB & Dry Dock Co
LOCH RUTHVEN	08.10.44	Charles Hill & Sons (Bristol)
LOCH TRALAIG	04.07.45	Caledon SB & Eng Co Ltd (Dundee)
LOCH VEYATIE	13.07.46	Ailsa SB Co (Troon)

65

Displacement 1,435 tons (2,260 tons FL) Dimensions 307ft x 38ft 6in x 12ft
Machinery Triple expansion (Double reduction geared turbines in LOCH ARKAIG and
LOCH TRALAIG), 2 Admiralty 3-drum boilers, 2 shafts, 5,500 ihp Speed 19½ knots
Armament 1 x 4in, 4 x 2pdr, 10 x 20mm, 2 x Squid Complement 103

Notes

Designed for A/S escort duties during World War II, 110 ships were ordered. In the event,
26 were re-armed as Bay class frigates optimised for AA duties and 56 were cancelled.

The class are to undergo a modernisation programme with LOCH INSH and LOCH
RUTHVEN entering refit at Devonport and LOCH ALVIE and LOCH FADA similarly at
Portsmouth. The modernisation will involve replacing the single 4in gun with a Mk XIX
twin mounting. Secondary armament will be increased to six 40mm guns comprising a
single twin MkV mounting and four single MkVII mountings. A new Type 277 radar is also
to be installed. LOCH FYNE has been placed in care and maintenance at Sheerness as
she awaits a similar refit. LOCH LOMOND is awaiting refit having paid off in April.

LOCH CRAGGIE and LOCH MORE are attached to the 5th Frigate Flotilla in the
Mediterranean. LOCH KILLISPORT is a part of the 6th Frigate Squadron, Home Fleet,
while LOCH GLENDHU and LOCH QUOICH are operating on the East Indies station.
LOCH TRALAIG and LOCH VEYATIE are attached to the A/S Training Squadron operating from Londonderry and Rosyth.

Cancelled Ships

LOCH AFFRIC, LOCH AWE, LOCH BADCALL, LOCH CAROY, LOCH CLUNIE, LOCH
COULSIDE, LOCH CRERAN, LOCH DOINE, LOCH EARN, LOCH ENOCH, LOCH
ERICHT, LOCH ERISORT, LOCH EYE, LOCH EYNORT, LOCH FANNICH, LOCH
GARVE, LOCH GLASHAN, LOCH GOIL, LOCH GRIAM, LOCH HARPORT, LOCH
HARRAY, LOCH HOURNE, LOCH INCHARD, LOCH KEN, LOCH KIRBISTER, LOCH
KIRKAIG, LOCH KISHORN, LOCH KNOCKIE, LOCH LARO, LOCH LINFERN, LOCH
LINNHE, LOCH LURGAIN, LOCH LYON, LOCH MABERRY, LOCH MINNICK, LOCH
NELL, LOCH ODAIRN, LOCH OSSIAN, LOCH RONALD, LOCH RYAN, LOCH
SCRIDAIN, LOCH SEAFORTH, LOCH SHEALLAG, LOCH SHIEL, LOCH SKAIG,
LOCH SKERROW, LOCH STEMSTER, LOCH STENNES, LOCH STRIVEN, LOCH
SUNART, LOCH SWIN, LOCH TANNA, LOCH TILT, LOCH TUMMELL, LOCH URIGILL,
LOCH VANAVIE, LOCH VENNACHER and LOCH WATTEN.

HMS Helmsdale

RIVER CLASS

Ship	Completed	Builder
HELMSDALE	15.10.43	A & J Inglis (Glasgow)
MEON	31.12.43	A & J Inglis (Glasgow)

Displacement 1,370 tons (1,830 tons FL) Dimensions 301ft 6in x 36ft 9in x 14ft
Machinery Triple expansion, 2 Admiralty 3-drum boilers, 2 shafts, 5,500 ihp Speed 20
knots Armament 2 x 4in, 10 x 20mm, Hedgehog Complement 140

Notes

Originally designed as A/S frigates, HELMSDALE is now disarmed and used as a training and experimental ship. In 1945 MEON was converted at Southampton to a Landing
Ship Headquarters (Small), a conversion which entailed the removal of her A/S equipment and the installation of extra communications and accommodation. Following periods in reserve, she recommissioned in 1951 to join Plymouth Command for Combined
Operations training. In May this year she was transferred to Portsmouth Command to
join the Amphibious Warfare Training Squadron. In July she left Portsmouth to serve as
the Afloat HQ of the Amphibious Warfare Squadron (Gulf).

HMS Portchester Castle

CASTLE CLASS

Ship	Completed	Builder
CAISTOR CASTLE	29.09.44	J. Lewis (Aberdeen)
CARISBROOKE CASTLE	17.11.43	Caledon SB & Eng Co Ltd (Dundee)
FLINT CASTLE	31.12.43	Henry Robb (Leith)
HEDINGHAM CASTLE (II)	12.05.45	J. Crown & Sons Ltd (Sunderland)
KNARESBOROUGH CASTLE	05.04.44	Blyth SB & Dry Dock Co
LAUNCESTON CASTLE	20.06.44	Blyth SB & Dry Dock Co
LEEDS CASTLE	15.02.44	Wm Pickersgill & Sons (Sunderland)
PORTCHESTER CASTLE	08.11.43	Swan Hunter & Wigham Richardson
TINTAGEL CASTLE	07.04.44	Ailsa SB Co (Troon)

Displacement 1,060 tons (1,510 tons FL) Dimensions 252ft x 36ft 8in x 13ft 6in
Machinery Triple expansion, 2 Admiralty 3-drum boilers, 2,880 ihp Speed 16½ knots
Armament 1 x 4in, 6 x 20mm, 1 x Squid Complement 99

During World War II, as some shipbuilders could not cope with the longer hull of a frigate, an improved type of corvette was introduced to keep the national shipbuilding capacity fully extended. 96 were ordered, including 12 for the Royal Canadian Navy, but 51 were later cancelled. They were rated as corvettes until 1947 when they were officially reclassified as A/S frigates. All are attached to the 2nd Training Squadron and operate from Portland.

Cancelled Names

ALTON CASTLE, APPLEBY CASTLE, AYDON CASTLE, BARNWELL CASTLE, BEESTON CASTLE, BERE CASTLE, BODIAM CASTLE, BOLTON CASTLE, BOWES CASTLE, BRAMBER CASTLE, BRIDGNORTH CASTLE, BROUGH CASTLE, CALDECOT CASTLE, CALSHOT CASTLE, CANTERBURY CASTLE, CAREW CASTLE, CHEPSTOW CASTLE, CHESTER CASTLE, CHRISTCHURCH CASTLE, CLARE CASTLE, CLAVERING CASTLE, CLITHEROE CASTLE, CLUN CASTLE, COLCHESTER CASTLE, CORFE CASTLE, CORNET CASTLE, COWES CASTLE, COWLING CASTLE, CRICCIETH CASTLE, CROMER CASTLE, DEVIZES CASTLE, DHYFE CASTLE, DOVER CASTLE, DUDLEY CASTLE, DUNSTER CASTLE, EGREMONT CASTLE, FOTHERINGAY CASTLE, HELMSLEY CASTLE, MALLING CASTLE, MALMESBURY CASTLE, NORWICH CASTLE, OSWESTRY CASTLE, PENDENNIS CASTLE, RABY CASTLE, RHUDDLAN CASTLE, THORNBURY CASTLE, TONBRIDGE CASTLE, TREMATON CASTLE, TUTBURY CASTLE, WARKWORTH CASTLE and WIGMORE CASTLE,

HMS Apollo

FAST MINELAYERS
ARIADNE CLASS

Ship	Completed	Builder
APOLLO	12.02.44	Hawthorn Leslie (Hebburn)
MANXMAN	20.06.41	A Stephen & Sons Ltd (Linthouse)

Displacement 2,650 tons (3,475 tons FL, 3,415 tons FL MANXMAN) Dimensions 418ft x 40ft x 11ft 3in Machinery Parsons SR geared turbines, 4 Admiralty 3-drum boilers, two shafts, 72,000 shp Speed 35+ knots Armament 4-6 x 4in, 10 x 40mm, 2 x 20mm, 100 mines Complement 246

Notes

Both ships spent their later war career, using their speed to transport essential supplies, or vast stores carrying capacity to help with repatriation duties in the Pacific following VJ Day. In 1946 both ships returned to the UK and reduced to reserve, MANXMAN at Sheerness and APOLLO at Chatham. In 1951 MANXMAN returned to operational use and following a refit joined the Mediterranean Fleet in September that year. Also in 1951, as part of the coningency plans taken after the outbreak of war in Korea, APOLLO was also returned to service.

HMS Plover

COASTAL MINELAYERS
PLOVER CLASS

Ship	Completed	Builder
PLOVER	24.09.37	Wm Denny & Bros (Dumbarton)

Displacement 805 tons (1,020 tons FL) Dimensions 195ft 3in x 37ft 6in x 8ft 6in
Machinery Triple Expansion, 2 water boilers, 2 shafts, 1400 Ihp Speed 14¾ knots
Complement 69

Notes

Built to lay minefields in the approaches to UK harbours. She is employed as a minelaying tender to the Torpedo and Anit-Submarine School, HMS Vernon.

HMS Miner IV

CONTROLLED MINELAYERS
MINER CLASS

Ship	Completed	Builder
GOSSAMER (ex-MINER II)	19.01.40	Philip & Son (Dartmouth)
MINER III	16.03.40	Philip & Son (Dartmouth)
MINER IV	12.11.40	Philip & Son (Dartmouth)
MINER V	26.06.41	Philip & Son (Dartmouth)
MINER VII	31.03.44	Philip & Son (Dartmouth)

Displacement 300 tons (346-350 tons FL)　Dimensions 110ft 3in x 26ft 5in x 8ft
Machinery Ruston and Hornby diesels, 2 shafts, 360 bhp　Speed 10 knots
Complement 32

Notes

Controlled minelayers are designed to lay minefields in the approaches to harbours which they could then activate or deactivate. GOSSAMER is employed as a mine location vessel. MINER V and MINER VII are tenders to HMS Defiance, Torpedo, Anti-Submarine and Electrical School Devonport. MINER III and MINER IV have black hull, red waterline and light grey upper works with their respective numbers painted on the funnels.

72

HMS Cheerful

MINESWEEPERS
ALGERINE CLASS

Ship	Completed	Builder
Turbine Group		
BRAVE	03.08.44	Blyth SB & Dry Dock Co
CHAMELEON	14.09.44	Harland & Wolff (Belfast)
CHEERFUL	13.10.44	Harland & Wolff (Belfast)
CIRCE	16.10.42	Harland & Wolff (Belfast)
JEWEL	09.12.44	Harland & Wolff (Belfast)
PINCHER	12.11.43	Harland & Wolff (Belfast)
PLUCKY	10.12.43	Harland & Wolff (Belfast)
RIFLEMAN	11.02.44	Harland & Wolff (Belfast)
RINALDO	18.06.43	Harland & Wolff (Belfast)
Reciprocating Group		
BRAMBLE (II)	28.06.45	Lobnitz & Co Ltd (Renfrew)
COCKATRICE	10.04.43	Fleming & Ferguson (Paisley)
COQUETTE	13.07.44	Redfern (Toronto)

73

Ship	Completed	Builder
FIERCE	28.11.45	Lobnitz & Co Ltd (Renfrew)
LYSANDER	21.11.44	Port Arthur Shipbuilding
MARINER	23.05.45	Port Arthur Shipbuilding
MARVEL	02.04.45	Redfern (Toronto)
MELITA	20.12.43	Toronto Drydock
MICHAEL	20.05.45	Redfern (Toronto)
PLUTO	04.10.45	Port Arthur Shipbuilding
RATTLESNAKE	23.06.43	Lobnitz & Co Ltd (Renfrew)
ROMOLA	03.05.45	Port Arthur Shipbuilding
TRUELOVE	03.04.44	Redfern (Toronto)
WAVE	14.11.44	Lobnitz & Co Ltd (Renfrew)
WELCOME	20.01.45	Lobnitz & Co Ltd (Renfrew)
WELFARE	04.04.44	Redfern (Toronto)

Displacement Turbine Group: 850 tons (1,125 tons FL), Reciprocating Group: 1,010 tons (1,305 tons FL) Dimensions 235ft x 35ft 6in x 10ft 6in Machinery Turbine Group: Parsons SR geared turbines, 2 Admiralty 3-drum boilers, 2 shafts, 2,000 shp, Reciprocating Group: Reciprocating triple expansion steam, 2 Admiralty 3-drum boilers, 2 shafts, 2,400 shp Speed 16½ knots Armament 1 x 4in, 4-6 x 20mm Complement 85

Notes

Built between 1942 and 1945, the Algerines were the most efficient of all RN Fleet sweepers during World War II. They were designed to cope with the varied demands of magnetic, contact and acoustic minesweeping. However, their large size and armament comprising, 4-inch gun, 20mm cannon and depth charges made them ideal for escort work. Post war, once the mine clearance operations were completed, many ships found themselves in reserve, while others operated in secondary patrol tasks. They are to be eventually replaced by the new Coastal Minesweepers, which will have a lower magnetic signature and be far more effective in countering the modern influence mine.

MARVEL is operating with 1MSF attached to HMS Vernon, Portsmouth. CHAMELEON, PLUCKY, RIFLEMAN are based at Malta with 2 MSF. CHEERFUL, COCKATRICE and

PINCHER, are attached to 4 MSF, although CHEERFUL was temporarily assigned to the Fishery Protection Squadron (FPS) in October. COQUETTE, MARINER, ROMOLA, TRUELOVE and WELCOME are also assigned to the FPS. BRAMBLE, RINALDO and RATTLESNAKE are operating out of Harwich based on the maintenance ship MULL OF GALLOWAY. Both PLUTO and WELFARE are assigned to trials, the latter as an experimental minesweeper at Lochinvar. CIRCE is the RNVR drill ship for Dundee Division and JEWEL is similarly assigned to Tay Division. MELITA had been assigned to Tyne Division RNVR between 1948-51 (renamed SATELLITE) but has now reverted to her original name and is refitting prior to being reduced to reserve. She has been replaced by BRAVE (now renamed SATELITTE). LYSANDER had been at Hong Kong (1950-51) as RNVR CORNFLOWER but has now reverted to her original name and operating with 6 MSF as is LYSANDER. MICHAEL had been in reserve at Singapore but in 1950 was recommissioned for the Malayan patrol.

WAVE had been operating with the FPS but on 30 September 1951 was blown ashore, off St, Ives, Cornwall, during a gale. She was holed in the starboard side and suffered a flooded engine room. She was successfully refloated two days later and docked at Devonport for repairs. On completion of repairs it is not known whether she will return to the FPS or be reduced to reserve.

In a programme agreed in 1949 six Algerines have been acquired by Belgium. LIBERTY, renamed ADRIEN de GERLACHE, was transferred in 1949; CADMUS renamed GEORGES LECOINTE was transferred in 1950; Both FANCY and READY were handed over in 1951 and renamed A.F. DUFOUR and JAN VAN HAVERBECKE respectively. The final pair ROSARIO and SPANKER are scheduled to transfer this year and will be renamed DE MOOR and DE BROUWER. ROSAMUND and PELORUS were transferred to South Africa in 1947 and renamed BLOEMFONTEIN and PIETERMARITZBURG while Thailand took delivery of MINSTREL (now PHOSAMTON). FLY (renamed PALANG) was transferred to Iran in 1948 and FLYNG FISH (now VIJAYA) to Ceylon in 1949.

MMS 1783

MOTOR MINESWEEPERS
105 FT CLASS

Ship	Completed	Builder
1532	1941	Macduff Eng. & Ship Builders Co.
1534	1941	J. Noble (Fraserburgh)
1535	1941	Wilson Noble (Fraserburgh)
1536	1941	Wivenhoe Shipyard Ltd
1546	1941	J. L. Bolson (Poole)
1548	1941	J. W. & A. Upham (Brixham)
1550	1941	Clapson & Sons (Barton on Humber)
1553	1941	Herd & Mackenzie (Buckie)

Ship	Completed	Builder
1556	1941	J. Noble (Fraserburgh)
1557	1942	J. Noble (Fraserburgh)
1558	1942	J. L. Bolson (Poole)
1569	1942	Richards Ironworks (Lowestoft)
1579	1941	G. Forbes (Peterhead)
1584	1942	Wivenhoe Shipyard Ltd
1586	1942	Wivenhoe Shipyard Ltd
1587	1942	Wivenhoe Shipyard Ltd
1599	1942	Wagstaff & Hatfield (Canada)
1600	1942	Wagstaff & Hatfield (Canada)
1602	1942	Wagstaff & Hatfield (Canada)
1603	1942	Shelburne Company (Nova Scotia)
1604	1942	Clare Shipbuilding Co (Metaghan)
1605	1942	Clare Shipbuilding Co (Metaghan)
1606	1942	Clare Shipbuilding Co (Metaghan)
1609	1942	J. Morris (Gosport)
1610	1942	J. Morris (Gosport)
1635	1942	Clapson & Sons (Barton on Humber)
1644	1944	Colombo Port Commissioners
1667	1942	F. Curtis (Par)
1672	1942	F. Curtis (Totnes)
1681	1942	Clapson & Sons (Barton on Humber)
1685	1942	G. Forbes (Peterhead)
1687	1942	R. Irvin (Peterhead)
1688	1942	J. Noble (Fraserburgh)
1689	1942	Wilson Noble (Fraserburgh)
1691	1942	Macduff Eng. & Ship Builders Co.

Ship	Completed	Builder
1693	1942	Herd & Mackenzie (Buckie)
1717	1942	W. Reekie (St Monance)
1722	1946	Belmont Dock (Kingston, Jamaica)
1724	1942	F. Curtis (Par)
1728	1942	F. Curtis (Par)
1733 (ST DAVID)	1942	J. L. Bolson (Poole)
1736	1942	Wivenhoe Shipyard Ltd
1761 (VENTURER)	1942	R. Irvin (Peterhead)
1763	1943	Clapson & Sons (Barton on Humber)
1771	1943	F. Curtis (Par)
1772	1943	J. W. & A. Upham (Brixham)
1775	1943	Macduff Eng. & Ship Builders Co.
1783	1943	J. W. & A. Upham (Brixham)
1785 (ISIS)	1943	F. Curtis (Par)
1786	1943	F. Curtis (Par)
1789 (THAMES)	1943	J. Morris (Gosport)
1790	1943	F. Curtis (Totnes)
1791	1943	F. Curtis (Totnes)
1796	1943	F. Curtis (Par)
1797	1943	F. Curtis (Par)
1801	1943	Wilson Noble (Fraserburgh)
1807	1943	Wilson Noble (Fraserburgh)
1810	1945	Abdul Wahbad (Beirut)
1813	1945	Abdul Wahbad (Beirut)

Displacement 225 tons (295 tons FL) Dimensions 119ft x 23ft x 9ft 6in Machinery Diesel engine, one shaft, 500 bhp Speed 10 knots Armament 2 x 20mm Complement 20

Built between 1940-1944 these vessels were of wooden construction, which was considered a safer vessel to deal with magnetic mines, than the older steel hulled trawlers, but their towing capacity was poor. An acoustic sweeping capability was added by the addition of an acoustic hammer box which could be deployed over the bow on an 'A' frame. Most remain un-named, but 1500 was added to the original numbers in 1947 (MMS 1534 was originally MMS 34 etc). Those vessels which show names after their number are assigned to RNR Divisions. Many have been transferred to foreign navies and six are on loan to Belgium.

MMS 1044

126 FT CLASS

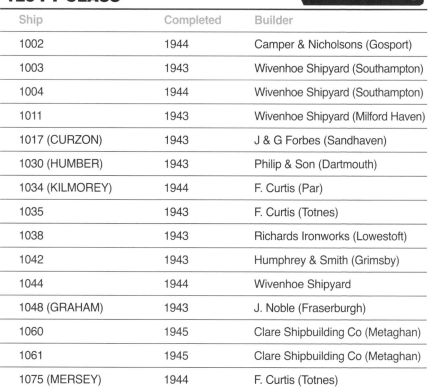

Ship	Completed	Builder
1002	1944	Camper & Nicholsons (Gosport)
1003	1943	Wivenhoe Shipyard (Southampton)
1004	1944	Wivenhoe Shipyard (Southampton)
1011	1943	Wivenhoe Shipyard (Milford Haven)
1017 (CURZON)	1943	J & G Forbes (Sandhaven)
1030 (HUMBER)	1943	Philip & Son (Dartmouth)
1034 (KILMOREY)	1944	F. Curtis (Par)
1035	1943	F. Curtis (Totnes)
1038	1943	Richards Ironworks (Lowestoft)
1042	1943	Humphrey & Smith (Grimsby)
1044	1944	Wivenhoe Shipyard
1048 (GRAHAM)	1943	J. Noble (Fraserburgh)
1060	1945	Clare Shipbuilding Co (Metaghan)
1061	1945	Clare Shipbuilding Co (Metaghan)
1075 (MERSEY)	1944	F. Curtis (Totnes)

Ship	Completed	Builder
1077 (MONTROSE)	1944	F. Curtis (Looe)
1089 (KILLIECRANKIE)	1945	East Anglian Constructors (Oulton)
1090 (BERNICIA)	1945	Philip & Son (Dartmouth)

Displacement 360 tons (430 tons FL) Dimensions 139ft 9in x 26ft x 10ft 6in Machinery Diesel engine, single shaft, 500 bhp Speed 10 knots Armament 2 x 20mm Complement 21

Notes

A larger and more powerful design than the previous class of MMS they entered service between 1943-45. MMS 1002, 1003, 1004 and 1011 operate under the Blue Ensign and are employed as mobile wiping and deperming vessels. Those vessels which show names after their number are assigned to RNVR Divisions. MMS 1035 is operated as a trials vessel. A large number are in service with foreign navies. One vessel is on loan to Belgium. A number of these craft will be found in reserve.

HMS Sursay

TRAWLERS
ISLES CLASS

Ship	Completed	Builder
Minesweepers		
FOULNESS	30.06.43	J. Lewis (Aberdeen)
GATESHEAD	11.05.43	G.T. Davie (Lauzon)
GORREGAN	16.06.43	Ardrossan Shipbuilding
SKYE	22.07.42	Henry Robb (Leith)
STEEPHOLM	01.12.43	J. Lewis (Aberdeen)
Danlayers		
SURSAY	26.02.45	Cook, Welton & Gemmell
TAHAY	25.03.45	Cook, Welton & Gemmell
Wreck Dispersal & Diving Vessels		
ANNET	19.06.43	Cook, Welton & Gemmell

Ship	Completed	Builder
BERN	30.09.42	Cook, Welton & Gemmell
FETLAR	09.01.42	Cochrane Shipbuilders (Selby)
FLATHOLM	20.08.43	Cook, Welton & Gemmell
LINDESFARNE	17.09.43	Cook, Welton & Gemmell
LUNDY	15.01.43	Cook, Welton & Gemmell
SKOMER	04.11.43	J. Lewis (Aberdeen)
TIREE	12.01.42	Goole Shipbuilding
TRONDRA	16.01.42	J. Lewis (Aberdeen)

Naval Servicing Craft

Ship	Completed	Builder
BARDSEY	18.09.43	Fleming & Ferguson (Paisley)
CALDY	07.01.44	J. Lewis (Aberdeen)
COLL	05.09.42	Ardrossan Dockyard
SWITHA	15.06.42	A & J Inglis (Glasgow)

Displacement 545 tons (735 tons FL) Dimensions 164ft x 27ft 6in x 14ft Machinery Triple expansion, one cylindrical boiler, 1 shaft, 850 ihp Speed 12 knots Armament 1 x 12pdr, 3 x 20mm Complement 40

Notes

Just a handful of this once numerous class of trawlers remain in service, but few in their original minesweeping or anti-submarine roles. After the war there was a huge require-ment for Wreck Dispersal Vessels - ships that could operate around the ports and coasts of the UK to disperse the many hundreds of wrecks that were cluttering the sea lanes and harbour approaches. The Isles class were ideal due to their large working decks and their capacity to carry a large amount of depth charges - the preferred weapon for destroying the wrecks. As this requirement has started to die down some of the ships have been further converted as Naval Servicing Craft, operating as tank cleaning ves-sels. It is reported that GATESHEAD is used as a depot ship for XE craft, midget sub-marines.

MFV 1204

MOTOR FISHING VESSELS
MFV CLASS

Ship	Completed	Builder
SQUIRREL (MFV 1151)	00.05.45	Herd & McKenzie
WATCHFUL (MFV 1080)	00.06.44	J. Noble (Fraserburgh)

Displacement 114 tons Dimensions 75ft 6in x 19ft 9in x 12ft Machinery Diesel engine, 1 shaft, 160 bhp Speed 8½ knots Complement 9

Notes

There are over 250 such vessels in service of four basic designs - 45 ft, 61.5 ft, 75 ft or 90 ft in length. They are employed around the world on naval service replacing drifters for various secondline duties in both the fleet and dockyards. SQUIRREL (ex MFV 1151) and WATCHFUL (ex MFV 1080) employed as Fishery Protection Gunboats. Some have adopted unofficial names (1204 - ESCORT; 1051 - ANTHONY and 1179 - DUCKLING).

FPB 5516

COASTAL FORCES
MGB CLASS

Ship	Completed	Builder
FPB 5511 (ex-MTB 2011)	08.07.44	Camper & Nicholson (Gosport)
FPB 5512 (ex-MTB 2012)	27.10.44	Camper & Nicholson (Gosport)
FPB 5513 (ex-MTB 2013)	22.01.45	Camper & Nicholson (Gosport)
FPB 5514 (ex-MTB 2014)	09.04.45	Camper & Nicholson (Gosport)
FPB 5515 (ex-MTB 2015)	15.06.45	Camper & Nicholson (Gosport)
FPB 5516 (ex-MTB 2016)	00.07.45	Camper & Nicholson (Gosport)
FPB 5517 (ex-MTB 2017)	31.01.46	Camper & Nicholson (Gosport)
FPB 5518 (ex-MTB 2018)	16.07.46	Camper & Nicholson (Gosport)

Displacement 93 tons (113 tons FL) Dimensions 117ft x 22ft 3in x 4ft 3in Machinery Three V12 Packard supercharged engines, 3 Shafts, 4,050 bhp Speed 31 knots Armament 2 x 6pdr, 6 x 20mm, 4 x 18in TT (5516 has 2 x 20mm amidships) Complement 30

Notes

MGB 5514, 5516 and 5517 are believed to be operational with the remaining vessels being in reserve or under refit.

MTB 5008

FAIRMILE 'D' MGB/MTB CLASS

Ship	Completed	Builder
FPB 5001 (ex-MTB 780)	11.01.45	Kris Cruisers Ltd (Isleworth)
FPB 5002 (ex-MTB 5002)	00.12.44	Wallasea Bay Yacht Station Ltd
FPB 5003 (ex-MTB 790)	00.07.45	Boat Construction Co. Ltd (Falmouth)
FPB 5008 (ex-MTB 5008)	00.06.45	William King (Burnham on Crouch)
FPB 5009 (ex-MTB 5009)	05.04.45	Lady Bee Ltd (Shoreham by Sea)
FPB 5015 (ex-MTB 5015)	00.03.45	Cardnell Brothers (Chelmsford)
FPB 5020 (ex-MTB 5020)	00.12.44	William Osbourne (Littlehampton)
FPB 5031 (ex-MTB 758)	00.10.44	Alex Robertson Ltd (Sandbank)
FPB 5032 (ex-MTB 779)	16.10.44	Herbert Woods (Great Yarmouth)
FPB 5033 (ex-MTB 785)	12.03.45	Brooke Marine Ltd (Lowestoft)
FPB 5035 (ex-MTB 793)	05.03.45	Alex Robertson Ltd (Sandbank)
FPB 5036 (ex-MTB 794)	22.12.44	Herbert Woods (Great Yarmouth)
FPB 5037 (ex-MTB 795)	00.08.44	William Osbourne (Littlehampton)

Displacement 102 tons (118 tons FL) Dimensions 115ft x 21ft 3in x 5ft Machinery Four Packard engines, 4 Shafts, 5,000 bhp Speed 30 knots Armament 2 x 6pdr, 2 x 20mm, 8 x MG and 4 x 18in TT (ex-5000 series - 2 x 6pdr, 2 x 20mm, 1 or 2 Rocket Projectors (single 4.5in in 5008), 2 x 21in TT) Complement 30

Notes

Six vessels are thought to be operational (5001, 5008, 5020, 5032, 5035 and 5036) with the remainder being in reserve.

Several dozen Fairmile D class MGBs can still be seen around the country at various coastal ports as they were given to the Sea Cadet Corps for use as unit HQ vessels. Those still believed to be in existence include: MGB 602, MGB 609, MGB 610, MGB 616, MGB 617, MGB 621, MGB 624, MGB 668, MGB 701, MGB 714, MGB 718, MGB 724, MGB 730, MGB 733, MGB 738, MGB 740, MGB 741, MGB 742, MGB 746, MGB 747, MGB 748, MGB 751, MGB 752, MGB 753, MGB 754, MGB 755, MGB 756, MGB 757, MGB 759, MGB 760, MGB 761, MGB 763, MGB 765, MGB 766, MGB 768, MGB 769, MGB 770. MGB 771, MGB 772, MGB 775, MGB 777, MGB 781, MGB 788, MGB 796 and MGB 5004.

SDB 3002

FAIRMILE 'D' MASB CLASS

Ship	Completed	Builder
SDB 3001 (ex-MTB 731)	00.07.44	Alex Robertson (Sandbank)
SDB 3002 (ex-MTB 750)	00.05.44	A M Dicke & Sons (Bangor)
SDB 3050 (ex-MTB 5010)	00.01.45	A M Dicke & Sons (Bangor)
SDB 3053 (ex-MTB 5013)	00.03.45	Risdon Beazley Ltd (Southampton)

Displacement 102 tons (118 tons FL) Dimensions 115ft x 21ft 3in x 5ft Machinery Four Packard engines, 4 Shafts, 5,000 bhp Speed 29 knots Armament 32 Depth Charges (3050/3053 have Hedgehog), 3053 has Depth Charge throwers and a 40mm Bofors aft Complement 30

Notes

3001/3002 are used for anti-submarine training. The remaining pair are used for special service trials of prototype anti-submarine equipment.

MTB 529

MTB VOSPER SHORT HULL CLASS

Ship	Completed	Builder
1002 (ex-MTB 392)	11.11.44	Vosper (Wivenhoe)
1024(ex-MTB 524)	01.12.46	Vosper (Portchester)
1025 (ex-MTB 525)	31.10.45	Vosper (Portchester)
1026 (ex-MTB 526)	02.01.46	Vosper (Portchester)
1027 (ex-MTB 527)	28.02.46	Vosper (Portchester)
1029 (ex-MTB 529)	23.05.46	Vosper (Portchester)
1032 (ex-MTB 532)	13.02.46	Vosper (Wivenhoe)
1033 (ex-MTB 533)	05.12.45	Vosper (Wivenhoe)

Displacement 48.75 tons Dimensions 73ft x 19ft 6in x 5ft 6in Machinery Packard petrol engines, 3 shafts, 4,050 bhp Speed 40 knots Armament 1 x 6pdr, 2 x 20mm (1 x twin), 4 x 303 MG, 2 x 21in TT Complement 13

Notes

MTBs 1024, 1025, 1027, 1029 and 1032 are currently active with the reminder in refit or reserve. It is thought that at least 17 vessels remain laid up in reserve around various ports.

FPB 5208

EX-SCHNELLBOOTE CLASS

Ship	Completed	Builder
FPB 5208 (ex-S208)	28.09.44	Lurssen (Vegesack)
FPB 5212 (ex-S212)	11.10.44	Lurssen (Vegesack)
FPB 5230 (ex-S130)	21.10.43	Schlichting (Travemunde)

Displacement 100 tons Dimensions 92ft 6in x 16ft 9in x 4ft 9in Machinery 3 x Mercedes-Benz MB511 20 cylinder V-banked diesel engines, 3 shafts, 7,500 bhp Speed 41 knots Armament Now unarmed Complement 21

Notes

Recovered on surrender of Germany after the Second World War. Returned to the UK and used for experimental purposes. FPB 5208 and FPB 5230 are reported to operate in the Baltic assigned to the British Baltic Fishery Protection Squadron. In Spring 1951 a contract was awarded to the German company Lurssen (Bremen) to modify and upgrade FPB 5208. A similar contract was awarded in 1952 for FPB 5230.

FPB 1601

VOSPER EXPERIMENTAL TYPE

Ship	Completed	Builder
FPB 1601 (ex-MTB 538)	27.08.48	Vosper (Portsmouth)

Displacement 36 tons (45 tons FL) Dimensions 74ft 2in x 20ft 3in x 6ft Machinery Packard petrol engines, 3 shafts, 4,050 bhp Speed 40 knots Armament 2 x 20mm (1 x twin), 4 x 18in TT Complement 15

Notes

Although designed late in the war, she was not completed by Vosper until 1948. Powered by three packard petrol engines, she is of conventional wooden construction and is capable of 40 knots. As an MTB she mounts 4-18 inch torpedo tubes & twin 20 mm Oerlikons as an MGB, she has a short 4.5 in gun & twin 20 mm Oerlikons.

FPB 1602

SAUNDERS-ROE EXPERIMENTAL TYPE

Ship	Completed	Builder
FPB 1602 (ex-MTB 539)	21.03.50	Saunders-Roe (Beaumaris)

Displacement 43 tons (50 tons FL) Dimensions 75ft 3in x 19ft 9in x 5ft 6in Machinery Packard petrol engines, 3 shafts, 4,050 bhp Speed 42 knots Armament 2 x 20mm (1 x twin), 4 x 18in TT Complement 16

Notes

An experimental design built by Sauders-Roe incorporating an aluminium alloy hull. At some time in 1951 the boat suffered a gearbox explosion and was taken to the south coast for repairs. On removal of the gearbox and engine, the damage was such that it ws deemed necessary to return the boat to Saunders-Roe for repair. The old gearbox and engine were loosely replaced inside the machinery space and the vessel taken under tow for the journey north. In the Irish Sea the vessel encountered a storm and broke free from the tug. In the violent motion of the sea, the machinery broke loose and punctured the hull and the vessel foundered on 31.01.52.

ML 2196

FAIRMILE 'B' ML CLASS

Ship	Completed	Builder
2154 (ex-ML 154)	05.11.40	Jas Silver (Rosneath & D'barton)
2155 (ex-ML 155)	11.12.40	Woodnutt (Bembridge Isle of Wight)
2196 (ex-ML 196)	01.02.41	Jas Miller (St Monance)
2217 (ex-ML 217)	00.05.41	Dickie (Bangor & Tarbert)
2220 (ex-ML 220)	00.02.41	Tough Brothers (Teddington)
2221 (ex-ML 221)	24.02.41	William King (Burnham on Crouch)
2222 (ex-ML 222)	20.04.41	Doig (Grimsby)
2223 (ex-ML 223)	00.05.41	Alexander Robertson (Sandbank)
2248 (ex-ML 248)	00.04.41	Brooke Marine (Lowestoft)
2250 (ex-ML 250)	11.07.41	F Curtis (Looe)
2337 (ex-ML 337)	18.11.41	Dickie (Bangor & Tarbert)
2342 (ex-ML 342)	10.10.41	Johnson & Jago (Leigh on Sea)
2357 (ex-ML 357)	01.08.42	Anglo-American Nile Tourist Co (Cairo)
2360 (ex-ML 360)	00.12.42	Anglo-American Nile Tourist Co (Cairo)
2461 (ex-ML 361)	20.11.41	Cardnel L (Maylandsea)

Ship	Completed	Builder
2462 (ex-ML 462)	15.12.41	Dorset Yacht (Hamworthy)
2489 (ex-ML 489)	01.03.42	Jas Miller (St Monance)
2491 (ex-ML 491)	00.05.42	Boat Construction Co (Falmouth)
2493 (ex-ML 493)	00.05.42	Curtis (Looe)
2564 (ex-ML 564)	14.11.42	Johnson & Jago (Leigh on Sea)
2567 (ex-ML 567)	12.04.43	H J Percival (Horning)
2568 (ex-ML 568)	00.02.43	F Curtis (Looe)
2569 (ex-ML 569)	15.01.43	Collins (Lowestoft)
2571 (ex-ML 571)	19.02.43	Jas Taylor (Chertsey)
2575 (ex-ML 575)	02.02.34	Johnson & Jago (Leigh on Sea)
2576 (ex-ML 576)	13.07.43	Jas Taylor (Chertsey)
2577 (ex-ML 577)	05.03.43	Johnson & Jago (Leigh on Sea)
2581 (ex-ML 581)	00.05.43	Johnson & Jago (Leigh on Sea)
2583 (ex-ML 583)	12.10.43	F Curtis (Looe)
2585 (ex-ML 585)	19.07.43	Jas Miller (St Monance)
2586 (ex-ML 586)	31.08.43	Jas Miller (St Monance)
2592 (ex-ML 592)	15.11.43	Jas Miller (St Monance)
2593 (ex-ML 593)	19.10.43	Johnson & Jago (Leigh on Sea)
2595 (ex-ML 595)	16.06.46	Curtis (Looe)
2840 (ex-ML 840)	15.06.44	Anglo-American Nile Tourist Co (Cairo)
2866 (ex-ML 866)	27.06.44	Thomas Cook (Cairo)
2882 (ex-ML 882)	30.03.45	Anglo-American Nile Tourist Co (Cairo)
2886 (ex-ML 886)	09.08.45	Anglo-American Nile Tourist Co (Cairo)
2889 (ex-ML 889)	14.04.45	Thomas Cook (Cairo)
2901 (ex-ML 901)	31.12.43	Johnson & Jago (Leigh on Sea)
2912 (ex-ML 912)	22.07.44	William Weatherhead (Cairo)

Ship	Completed	Builder
2919 (ex-ML 919)	09.10.44	Jas Miller (St Monance)
2921 (ex-ML 921)	22.11.44	William Weatherhead (Cockenzie)

Displacement 85 tons **Dimensions** 112ft x 18ft 3in x 5ft **Machinery** 2 x Hall-Scott Defender engines, 1,200 bhp **Speed** 15½ knots **Armament** 1 x 40mm (single) or 2 x 20mm (1 x twin) **Complement** 16-18

Notes

A large quantity of this class was built during World War II for coastal operations, protecting coastal convoys, port approaches and coastal waters against submarines. A feature of the boats was that they could be reconfigured for different roles with 48 hours notice. To meet this requirement the boats were fitted with steel strips, with tapped holes. Armament was bolted to the strips dependant upon role - including torpedo tubes, mines, depth charges, various guns and other specialist gear. Later in the war some were modified for use as minesweepers.

Many of the vessels remaining in service today undertake the minesweeping role, but these are likely to be replaced by the new programme of Inshore Minesweepers currently under production. The remainder conduct secondary patrol and training functions. Not all vessels are in the active fleet at anyone time.

ML 2582 was lost on 5 June, together with 12 of her crew when a Royal Netherlands Air Force Thunderjet struck her mast and crashed on deck while making a mock attack.

ML 6034

EX- GERMAN ASR LAUNCH

Displacement 65 tons **Dimensions** 91ft x 16ft 3in x 5ft 3in **Machinery** MWM Engines
Speed 16½ knots **Armament** 3 x 20mm **Complement** 16-18

Notes

At least six of these vessles are in service (MLs 6009 - 6014). All are ex-German Air/Sea
Rescue launches which constitute the Rhine Flotilla, based on HMS ROYAL PRINCE at
Krefeld. The unit is responsible for the safe and secure passage of all waterborne traffic
along the River Rhine between the Dutch border and the French Zone south of Bonn.
The unit is equipped with fast patrol boats and a number of Landing Craft crewed by both
Royal Navy and Royal Marine personnel.

SDML 3515

FAIRMILE SDML CLASS

Ship	Completed	Builder
SDML 3502 (ex-1105)	03.03.43	Africa Marine (Mombasa)
SDML 3503 (ex-1280)	25.04.44	Bute Slip (Clyde)
SDML 3505 (ex-1333)	15.09.44	Nichol (Durban, South Africa)
SDML 3506 (ex-1334)	16.10.44	Nichol (Durban, South Africa)
SDML 3507 (ex-1335)	02.01.45	Nichol (Durban, South Africa)
SDML 3508 (ex-1385)	00.08.43	Newman (Hamworthy, Dorset)
SDML 3510 (ex-1420)	28.04.44	Woods (Potter Heigham)
SDML 3511 (ex-1279)	24.11.43	Bute Slip (Clyde)
SDML 3512 (ex-1295)	12.11.43	Sussex Shipbuilding Co (Shoreham)
SDML 3513 (ex-1378)	11.10.43	Blackmore (Bideford)
SDML 3514 (ex-1402)	16.07.44	Hillyard (Littlehampton)
SDML 3515 (ex-1391)	00.11.43	Berthon Boat (Lymington)
SDML 3516 (ex-1387)	29.12.43	Newman (Hamworthy, Dorset)

Displacement 46 tons (54 tons FL) Dimensions 72ft x 15ft 10in x 5ft 6in Machinery
Two Gardner Diesels, 2 Shafts, 260/320 bhp Speed 11-12 knots Armament 1 x 3pdr
or 40mm; 1 x 20mm Complement 14

HDMLs were originally intended for the defence of estuarial and local waters against submarines during World War II, but they proved such a versatile and seaworthy design that they were retained after the war. After the war HDMLs (reclassified as SDMLs in 1948) continued to operate in defence of ports and local waters, while some were allocated to RNVR units to provide valuable seagoing training. A small number were converted for survey duties (see page 115).

Many of these craft have found further service in overseas navies, being particularly suited to patrol work in the waters of the Malayan peninsula. From 1949 a handful of these SDMLs, formerly from the RN's 200th Patrol Squadron in Singapore, have been progressively transferred to the Malayan Naval Force (SDML 3502 and SDML 3509 in 1949; SDML 3501 in 1951; SDML 3506, SDML 3507 and SDML 3508 in 1950).

CT 8102

CONTROL TARGET BOATS
J.S. WHITE TYPE

Ship	Completed	Builder
CT 8101 (ex-CT 101)	11.11.47	J.S. White & Co (Cowes)
CT 8102 (ex-CT 102)	27.02.48	J.S. White & Co (Cowes)
CT 8103 (ex-CT 103)	09.04.48	J.S. White & Co (Cowes)
CT 8104 (ex-CT 104)	19.04.48	J.S. White & Co (Cowes)

Displacement 44 tons Dimensions 77ft x 19ft 9in x 5ft 6in Machinery 3 x Packard engines, 3,370 bhp Speed 35 knots

Notes

These vessels are designed to tow targets at speed and also to control remotely operated target boats (Radio Control Boats (RCB)). The majority of such vessels were conversions of surplus MTB/MGBs but these were new build and designed for the purpose.

CT 8044

VOSPER TYPE II

Ship	Completed	Builder
CT 8044 (ex-CT 44)	23.09.47	Vosper
CT 8045 (ex-CT 45)	00.12.45	Vosper

Displacement 48.75 tons Dimensions 72ft 6in x 19ft 6in x 5ft 6in Machinery Packard petrol engines, 3 shafts, 4,050 bhp Speed 40 knots Complement 13

Notes

With the end of the war this pair of Vosper 73ft Type II MTBs, MTB 531 and MTB 537, were altered and modified for conversion to Control Target Boats CT 44 and CT 45 respectively. They were stripped of all armament and equipped with a petrol driven winch aft.

RCB 8201

RADIO CONTROL BOATS

Ship	Completed	Builder
RCB 8201	15.01.44	British Power Boat (Hythe)
RCB 8202	01.03.45	British Power Boat (Hythe)
RCB 8203	01.11.46	British Power Boat (Hythe)
RCB 8204	31.04.45	British Power Boat (Hythe)
RCB 8205	06.09.44	British Power Boat (Hythe)

Displacement 37 tons Dimensions 71ft 9in x 20ft 6in x 5ft 9in Machinery Packard 12 cylinder petrol engine, 3 shafts, 4,050 bhp Speed 42 knots Complement 12

Notes

Former MTB/MGBs converted for use as Radio Control Target Boats. They are crewed during transit between operating base and target areas, but operated un-manned and controlled by Control Target Boats once in exercise area.

Previous Identities

RCB 8201 (ex-CT 8201, ex-RCB 1, ex-MTB 457, ex-MGB 138)
RCB 8202 (ex-CT 8046, ex-RCB 2, ex-CT 46, ex-MTB 499)
RCB 8203 (ex-CT 8203, ex-RCB 3, ex-MTB 1521, ex-MTB 521)
RCB 8204 (ex-CT 8204, ex-RCB 4, ex-MTB 1580, ex-MTB 480, ex-MGB 161)
RCB 8205 (ex-CT 8205, ex-RCB 5, ex-MTB 1588, ex-MTB 488, ex-MGB 169)

HMS Messina

AMPHIBIOUS CRAFT
LST 3 CLASS

Ship	Completed	Builder
LST (C)		
MESSINA (3043)	00.00.45	Scott's SB & Eng Co (Greenock)
NARVIK (3044)	04.04.46	Vickers Armstrong (Barrow)
LST (3)		
ATTACKER (3010)	05.04.45	Fairfield SB & Eng Co (Govan)
BRUISER (3025)	27.06.45	Smith's Dock (Middlesborough)
CHARGER (3026)	16.06.45	Blyth SB & Dry Dock Co
DIEPPE (3016)	00.00.45	Hawthorn Leslie (Hebburn)
FIGHTER (3038)	27.07.45	Fairfield SB & Eng Co (Govan)
HUNTER (3042)	16.11.45	Harland & Wolff (Govan)
LOFOTEN (3027)	24.10.45	Blyth SB & Dry Dock Co
REGGIO (3511)	14.09.45	Davie Shipbuilding (Lauzon)
SALERNO (3513)	31.08.45	Davie Shipbuilding (Lauzon)
STALKER (3515)	05.06.45	Yarrow (Esquimalt)
STRIKER (3516)	10.07.45	Yarrow (Esquimalt)

102

Ship	Completed	Builder
SUVLA (3518)	09.08.45	Canadian Vickers (Montreal)
TRACKER (3522)	30.09.45	Davie Shipbuilding (Lauzon)
TROUNCER (3523)	00.10.45	Davie Shipbuilding (Lauzon)
TRUMPETER (3524)	06.11.45	Davie Shipbuilding (Lauzon)
WALCHEREN (3525)	13.11.45	Davie Shipbuilding (Lauzon)
ZEEBRUGGE (3532)	03.11.45	Marine Industries (Sorel)

LST (A)

ANZIO (3003)	30.11.45	Vickers Armstrong (Walker)
BATTLER (3015)	21.09.45	Barclay Curle & Co Ltd (Glasgow)
CHASER (3029)	29.08.45	A. Stephen & Sons Ltd (Linthouse)
PUNCHER (3036)	05.05.45	Ailsa SB Co (Troon)
PURSUER (3504)	25.05.45	Canadian Vickers (Montreal)
RAVAGER (3505)	20.06.45	Canadian Vickers (Montreal)
ST NAZAIRE (3517)	08.09.45	Yarrow (Esquimalt)
SLINGER (3510)	17.07.45	Davie Shipbuilding (Lauzon)
THRUSTER (3520)	25.10.45	Canadian Vickers (Montreal)
TROMSO (3006)	29.03.45	Harland & Wolff (Belfast)
VAAGSO (3019)	30.12.44	Swan Hunter & Wigham Richardson

LST(Q)

BEN LOMOND (3013)	24.11.45	Fairfield SB & Eng Co (Govan)
BEN NEVIS (3012)	25.09.45	Fairfield SB & Eng Co (Govan)

AA Firing Ships

3031	11.07.45	C. Connell & Co (Scotstoun)
3033	19.07.45	Wm Pickersgill & Sons (Sunderland)

Royal Army Service Corps

CHARLES MCLEOD (3021)	20.04.45	Wm Lithgow (Port Glasgow)

Ship	Completed	Builder
EVAN GIBB (3037)	31.05.45	Fairfield SB & Eng Co (Govan)
FREDERICK GLOVER (3001)	29.06.45	Vickers Armstrong (Walker)
HUMPHREY GALE (3509)	22.06.45	Davie Shipbuilding (Lauzon)
MAXWELL BRANDER (3024)	15.03.45	Smith's Dock (Middlesborough)
REGINAL KERR (3009)	11.05.45	Harland & Wolff (Belfast)
SNOWDEN SMITH (3028)	19.05.45	A Stephen & Sons Ltd (Linthouse)

Displacement 2,256 tons Dimensions 345ft 9in x 54ft x 11ft 6in (aft); 4ft 7in (forward)
Machinery Steam reciprocating engine, Admiralty three-drum boiler, 2 shafts, 5,500 shp
Speed 13 knots Armament 10 x 20mm Complement 104

BEN LOMOND, BEN NEVIS
Displacement 1,625 tons Dimensions 347ft 6in x 55ft 3in x 12ft 6in Machinery
Steam reciprocating engine, Admiralty three-drum boiler, 2 shafts, 5,500 shp Speed
13½ knots Armament 4 x 40mm, 16 x 20mm Complement 100

Notes

Many of the class are in reserve. In 1946 Ministry of Transport chartered four vessels to the Atlantic Steam Navigation Company for commmercial Ro-Ro services, though they were to be available for recall in an emergency. The ships concerned were LST 3507, 3519, 3534 and 3512 . They were renamed EMPIRE GAELIC, EMPIRE BALTIC, EMPIRE CEDRIC and EMPIRE CELTIC respectively. These were joined in 1948 by LST 3041 (renamed EMPIRE DORIC).

Seven vessels were transferred to the Royal Army Service Corps in 1946 to help with the postwar redistribution of stores and equipment and were renamed as above. In 1952 the operation of these vessels was handed over to the Atlantic Steam Navigation Company.

Six vessels were transferred on loan to the Royal Hellenic Navy in 1947 where they are still in operation. The vessels are LSTs 3002 (renamed ALIAKMON), 3007 (renamed AXIOS), 3020 (renamed ALFIOS), 3502 (renamed STRYMON), 3503 (renamed ACHE-LOOS) and 3506 (renamed PINHOS).

LST(Q)s acted as mother ships. They had two huts erected on the main deck to accommodate 40 officers and berths on the tank deck to accommodate an extra 196 men. A bakery and extra refridgeration spaces were provided, as were four extra distilling units which provided fresh water, which was stored in the ballast tanks which were converted for the task.

LCT 407

LCT 4 CLASS

Ship	Completed	Builder
403 (1220)	1945	Stockton Construction (Thornaby)
404 (1221)	1945	Stockton Construction (Thornaby)
405 (523)	1943	A Findlay (Old Kilpatrick)
406 (941)	1943	Teeside Bridge (Middlesborough)
407 (1186)	1944	Lagan (Belfast)
408 (1202)	1944	Warrenpoint Shipyard

Displacement 350 tons (586 tons FL) Dimensions 187ft 3in x 33ft 9in x 4ft 6in
Machinery Davey Paxman 12 cylinder diesels, 2 shafts, 920 bhp Speed 10 knots
Armament 2 x 20mm Complement 12

Notes

Designed during World War II to meet the requirement for a shallow draught tank land-ing craft capable of making cross-Channel trips. Capacity to carry 6-9 tanks or up to 12 3-ton lorries. Operated by the Rhine Flotilla (see page 109).

LCT 4001

LCT 8 CLASS

Ship	Completed	Builder
4001	1945	Stockton Construction (Thornaby)
4002	1945	Stockton Construction (Thornaby)
4025	1945	Tees-Side Bridge (Middlesborough)
4037	1945	Arrol (Alloa)
4038	1945	Arrol (Alloa)
4039	1945	Arrol (Alloa)
4040	1945	Arrol (Alloa)
4041	1945	Arrol (Alloa)
4042	1945	Arrol (Alloa)
4043	1945	Arrol (Alloa)
4044	1945	Arrol (Alloa)
4045	1945	Arrol (Alloa)
4049	1945	A Findlay (Old Kilpatrick)
4050	1945	A Findlay (Old Kilpatrick)
4061	1946	Redpath Brown (Meadowside)

Ship	Completed	Builder
4062	1946	Redpath Brown (Meadowside)
4063	1946	Redpath Brown (Meadowside)
4064	1946	Arrol (Alloa)
4073	1946	MacLellan (Bo'ness)
4074	1946	MacLellan (Bo'ness)
4085	1946	Motherwell Bridge (Meadowside)
4086	1946	Motherwell Bridge (Meadowside)
4097	1946	Fairfield (Chepstow)
4098	1946	Fairfield (Chepstow)
4099	1946	Fairfield (Chepstow)
4128	1946	J.S. White & Co (Cowes)
4148	1946	Warren Point Shipyard
4156	1946	Lagan (Belfast)
4164	1947	A Findlay (Old Kilpatrick)
4165	1947	A Findlay (Old Kilpatrick)

Displacement 657 tons (895 to 1017 full load) Dimensions 225ft x 39ft x 5ft (aft) 3ft 2in (forward) Machinery 4 x Paxman diesel engines; 2 shafts; bhp 1840 Speed 12 knots Complement 25

Notes

This is an improved version of the LCT designed for operation in the Far East where increased capacity and range were required. Accommodation is provided for both crew and embarked vehicle crews. 157 were completed and of those, 6 remain in service in Germany, 4 in the Mediterranean and 24 are in reserve.

There remain several earlier variants of the LCT in reserve around the country. These include LCT(R)(3) 419, 434 and 440, which are rocket armed conversions of the standard LCT design. There is also LCT(E) 413, an engineering variant of the LCT.

L 243

LCI(L) CLASS

Ship	Completed	Builder
243	1942	Todd, Eyrie & Barber (NY)

Displacement 384 tons **Dimensions** 158ft 6in x 23ft 8in x 6ft 6in **Machinery** Two General Motors diesels, 2 shafts, 1,440 bhp **Speed** 14 knots **Armament** 4 x 20mm **Complement** 24

Notes

More than 540 of these Landing Craft Infantry (Large) were built during the war, though this is the sole remaining LCI(L) in service. Designed to carry large numbers of infantry on 'raids' across the channel these vessels could transport 200 fully equipped troops.

There are several hundred smaller amphibious craft in service and in reserve at locations around the world, but to list them all would require a volume by itself. For completeness the basic details of class, type and numbers remaining are listed below.

The Rhine Flotilla

Based on HMS ROYAL PRINCE (above) at Krefeld and, in cooperation with the US Navy's Rhine River Patrol at Karslruhe and the French Forces Maritimes du Rhin based at Koblenz, are responsible for the safe and secure passage of all waterborne traffic along the River Rhine between the Dutch border and the French Zone south of Bonn. The unit is also required to maintain military expertise in the planning and execution of major river crossings in the event of any projected attack by Russian Forces. As such the unit is equipped with fast patrol boats (see page 96) and a number of Landing Craft.

LCM CLASS

Displacement 28 tons (63 tons FL) Dimensions 60ft 3in x 16ft x 3ft 8iin Machinery Petrol engines, 2 shafts, 290 bhp Speed 9 knots Armament 2 x MG Complement 4

Notes

Designed for the transportation of vehicles and small tanks, the Landing Craft Mechanised was produced in several variants, most of those now remaining being the

109

LCM (7) type. When production stopped at the end of the war at least 140 had been built. There are currently 13 in service in Germany, 7 in the Mediterranean and 16 in reserve.

LCA CLASS

Displacement 9 -13½ tons Dimensions 38ft 9in x 10ft x 7ft 9in Machinery Two Ford V8 or Kermath engines, 2 shafts, 60 hp Speed 10 knots Armament Position for a Bren gun or MG Complement 2

Notes

The LCA is the principal means of ship-to-shore transfer of troops and is carried in davits on a parent ship (such as an LST(3)). During the war many hundreds were built, and such was the demand that construction was sub-contracted to Public Works Departments and even furniture manufacturers. of the 1,929 built, 11 remain in service in Germany, 30 in the Mediterranean and at least 229 are in reserve.

LCP CLASS

Displacement 7-11 tons Dimensions 36ft x 10ft 6in x 2ft Machinery Hall-Scott Petrol engine or Gray diesel Speed 7½ knots Armament 1 x 0.303in MG Complement 3

Notes

Throughout the Second World War there were many variants of small landing craft developed and brought into service for the rapid transportation of troops and their delivery to the landing site. These developed from rudimentary vessels with no ramp, armour or shelter for the helmsman through the LCP (Large) and finaly the more sophisticated LCVPs which were large enough to carry a light vehicle and had a ramp to disembark both personnel and equipment. The majority of those vessels left in service comprise the latter.

HMS Owen

SURVEY SHIPS
COOK CLASS

Ship	Completed	Builder
COOK	20.07.50	Wm Pickersgill & Sons (Sunderland)
DALRYMPLE	10.02.49	Wm Pickersgill & Sons (Sunderland)
DAMPIER	06.03.48	Smith's Dock (Middlesborough)
OWEN	23.09.49	Hall Russell (Aberdeen)

Displacement 1,640 tons (2,280 tons FL) Dimensions 307ft x 38ft 6in x 12ft 6in
Machinery Two 4-cylinder triple expansion engines, 2 Admiralty 3-drum boilers, 2 shafts, 5,500 ihp Speed 19½ knots Complement 160 (158 COOK)

Notes

All are conversions of Bay class frigates whose contracts were terminated at launch in 1944. The ships were redesigned and were completed as Survey Ships. Both DAL-RYMPLE and COOK were towed to HM Dockyard Devonport for conversion with DAL-RYMPLE completing in February 1949 and COOK in July 1950. DAMPIER and OWEN were converted at HM Dockyard Chatham completing in March 1948 and September 1949. The conversion involved the deletion of all armament and provision of additional accommodation and office space for hydrographic work. More boats and associated handling facilities were fitted together with Type 972 radar suitable for survey work . The ships are all named after notable British hydrographers.

111

COOK has been engaged on surveys in Home waters, while DALRYMPLE and OWEN have been surveying the Persian Gulf and Mediterranean. DAMPIER has been in the Far East surveying areas around the Malay Peninsula.

Previous Names

COOK (ex PEGWELL BAY, ex LOCH MOCHRUM), DAMPIER (ex HERNE BAY, ex LOCH EIL), DALRYMPLE (ex LUCE BAY, ex LOCH GLASS), OWEN (ex THURSO BAY, ex LOCH MUICK).

HMS Challenger

CHALLENGER CLASS

Ship	Completed	Builder
CHALLENGER	13.03.32	HM Dockyard (Chatham)

Displacement 1,140 tons (1,705 tons FL) Dimensions 220ft x 36ft x 12ft 6in
Machinery Triple expansion steam engine, 2 Admiralty 3-drum boilers, single shaft, 1,200 ihp Speed 12½ knots Complement 84

Notes

She was laid down in 1930 at HM Dockyard Chatham and built in a dry dock. After that, the ship was moved to Portsmouth for completion and commissioned on 15 March 1932.

The ship is on an extended 'World tour' surveying the Pacific Ocean. She left Chatham in 1950 and is expected to return to the UK in 1953. It was during this deployment, in 1951, that the ship surveyed the Mariana Trench near Guam, identifying the deepest known point in the oceans, 10,911 metres (35,797 ft) deep at its maximum. This point has been named the Challenger Deep as a result of the survey.

HMS Scott

HALCYON CLASS

Ship	Completed	Builder
FRANKLIN	04.07.38	Ailsa SB Co Ltd (Troon)
SCOTT	23.02.39	Caledon SB & Eng Co Ltd (Dundee)
SHARPSHOOTER	17.12.37	HM Dockyard (Devonport)

Displacement 830 tons (1,330 tons FL) Dimensions 245ft x 33ft 6in x 7ft Machinery Parsons geared turbines, 2 Admiralty 3-drum boilers, 1,750 shp Speed 17 knots Complement 80

Notes

Although all nominally Halcyon class minesweeping sloops FRANKLIN and SCOTT were ordered to be used exclusively as Survey Ships without armament (a further pair, JASON and GLEANER were converted pre-war for survey operations). A large chartroom was built at the after end of the forecastle deck, and the bridge was enlarged. A large derrick was fitted for handling survey beacons. Post-war SHARPSHOOTER was converted at HM Dockyard Chatham in July 1948 to replace JASON and GLEANER which, following the war, never returned to surveying duties. After a period of operations in the Far East she returned to the UK in 1949. Following a refit she resumed survey operations in Home Waters joining FRANKLIN and SCOTT.

HMS Meda

SML CLASS

Ship	Completed	Builder
MEDA (ex-ML 1301)	06.04.43	Blackmore (Bideford)
SML 322 (ex-ML 1053)	12.07.41	Morgan Giles (Teignmouth)
SML 323 (ex-ML 1081)	19.09.41	Bolson (Poole)
SML 324 (ex-ML 1085)	16.09.41	Sussex Shipbuilding Co (Shoreham)
SML 325 (ex-ML 1091)	16.07.42	Ranalah Yacht Yard (Wooton)
SML 326 (ex-ML 1393)	10.02.44	Berthon Boat (Lymington)
SML 327 (ex-ML 1411)	02.05.44	Blackmore (Bideford)

Displacement 46 tons (54 tons FL) **Dimensions** 72ft x 15ft 10in x 5ft 6in **Machinery** Two Gardner Diesels; 2 Shafts; 260/320 bhp **Speed** 11-12 knots **Complement** 14

Notes

Former Harbour Defence Motor Launches, they have been converted to conduct survey operations in inshore and coastal waters.

HMS Alert

DESPATCH VESSELS
ALERT CLASS

Ship	Completed	Builder
ALERT	24.10.46	Blyth Dry Dock & SB Co. Ltd
SURPRISE	09.09.46	Smith's Dock (Middlesborough)

Displacement 1,590 tons (2,440 tons FL) Dimensions 307ft 6in x 38ft 6in x 12ft 9in
Machinery Triple expansion steam engine, 2 Admiralty 3-drum boilers, 5,500 ihp
Speed 19½ knots Armament 2 x 4in, 2 x 40mm Complement 160

Notes

To have been completed as frigates, but with the end of the war it was decided to complete them as Despatch Vessels. SURPRISE is based in the Mediterranean and ALERT in the Far East. In November SURPRISE returned to the UK for a refit at Portsmouth, where she is to be converted to serve as a Royal Yacht for Coronation celebrations in 1953.

Previous Names

ALERT (ex-DUNDRUM BAY, ex-LOCH SCAMADALE), SURPRISE (ex-GERRANS BAY, ex-LOCH CARRON)

HMS Redpole

TRIALS & TRAINING SHIPS
MODIFIED BLACK SWAN CLASS

Ship	Completed	Builder
REDPOLE	24.06.43	Yarrow (Scotstoun)
STARLING	01.04.43	Fairfield SB & Eng Co (Govan)

Displacement 1,470 tons (1,925 tons FL) Dimensions 299ft 6in x 38ft 6in x 11ft
Machinery Parsons geared turbines, 2 Admiralty 3-drum boilers, 2 shafts, 4,300 shp
Speed 19½ knots Complement 192

Notes

Formerly Sloops (re-rated frigates in 1947). Armament removed and lattice mainmasts
for radar fitted. Now serving a Navigation School training ships. REDPOLE retains a tripod foremast whereas STARLING has lattice masts.

117

HMS Fleetwood

GRIMSBY CLASS

Ship	Completed	Builder
FLEETWOOD	19.11.36	HM Dockyard (Devonport)

Displacement 990 tons   Dimensions 266ft x 36ft x 7ft 6in   Machinery Parsons geared turbines, 2 Admiralty 3-drum boilers, 2 shafts, 2,000 shp   Speed 16½ knots

Notes

Operated as a Radio Trials Ship by the Admiralty Signal and Radar Establishment (ASRE). All armament removed and bridge extended to provide extra accommodation. Underwent a refit and partial hull reconstruction in 1950 to extend her service life for a further five years.

118

HMS Brocklesby

HUNT CLASS (Type II)

Ship	Completed	Builder
BROCKLESBY	09.04.41	Cammell Laird (Birkenhead)

Displacement 1,050 tons (1,430 tons FL)   Dimensions 280ft x 31ft 6in x 7ft 9in
Machinery Two Admiralty 3-drum boilers, Parsons SR geared turbines, 2 shafts, 19,000 shp   Speed 25 knots   Complement 146

Notes

BROCKLESBY was refitted as a trials ship at Devonport between 1951-52. She has been disarmed and will operate with the 2nd Training Squadron at Portland.

HMS Hotham

CAPTAIN CLASS

Ship	Completed	Builder
HOTHAM	08.02.44	Bethlehem-Hingham (Lynn)

Displacement 1,400 tons (1,740 tons FL)   Dimensions 306ft x 36ft 9in x 14ft
Machinery Gas Turbine Armament 4 x 20mm Speed Unknown Complement 220

Notes

In dockyard hands to have original geared steam turbines with electric drive replaced by experimental gas turbine machinery. The new machinery, built by English Electric, was acquired in 1951 and scheduled to be fitted this year, but it is reported that work has been suspended pending the availability of a more advanced plant.

HMS Boxer

LST (1) CLASS

Ship	Completed	Builder
BOXER	10.04.43	Harland & Wolff (Belfast)

Displacement 4,250 tons (6,240 tons FL)   Dimensions 400ft x 49ft x 17ft 6in
Machinery Parsons geared turbines, Foster Wheeler 'D' type boiler, 7,000 shp Speed
16 knots Complement 17 officers, 220 ratings plus 50-80 under training

Notes

Originally built as a Landing Ship Tank, she was converted in 1944 to operate as a
Fighter Direction ship, for use during the Normandy landings. Post war she was further
converted as a Radar Personnel Training Ship.

HMS Deepwater

WAR PRIZE CLASS

Ship	Completed	Builder
DEEPWATER	1940	Norderwerft Koser & Meyer

Displacement 1,200 tons Dimensions 260ft x 38ft x 11ft 6in Machinery 2 x Sulzer Diesels; 1,750 bhp Speed 17 knots Complement 61

Notes

Commissioned into the Kreigsmarine as WALTER HOLTZAPFEL in August 1940 becoming attached to the Institute for Torpedo Experiments. Acquired by the UK in 1946 as a war prize and renamed DEEPWATER. Employed as a Diving Tender from 1947 based at the Diver Training School, HMS VERNON.

HMS Maidstone

SUBMARINE DEPOT SHIPS
FORTH CLASS

Ship	Completed	Builder
FORTH	12.05.39	J. Brown & Co (Clydebank)
MAIDSTONE	05.05.38	J. Brown & Co (Clydebank)

Displacement 8,900 tons (11,815 tons FL)   Dimensions 531ft x 73ft x 20ft 2in
Machinery Brown Curtis geared turbines (Parsons in MAIDSTONE), 4 Admiralty 3-drum boilers, 2 shafts, 7,000 shp   Speed 17 knots   Armament 8 x 4.5in, 8 x 2pdr
Complement 1,167

Notes

These vessels are equipped with a foundry, coppersmiths, plumbers and carpenter's shops. There are heavy and light machine shops and facilities for electrical and torpedo repairs. They are also able to recharge submarine batteries. In addition they also provide hotels services, such as laundry, cinema and hospital facilities together with accommodation for up to nine submarines at a time. In their holds they can carry up to 100 torpedoes or mines to supply to her submarines. These large ships are very high value targets to potential enemies and so carry a heavy gun armament of eight 4.5-inch guns disposed in four twin turrets (one forward, one aft and one on each beam) in addition to smaller close range armament.

HMS Montclare

MONTCLARE CLASS

Ship	Completed	Builder
MONTCLARE	18.12.21 (L)	J. Brown & Co (Clydebank)

Displacement 19,600 tons (21,100 tons) **Dimensions** 563ft x 70ft 3in x 27ft 9in
Machinery Parsons SR geared turbines, 2 shafts, 13,500 shp **Speed** 17 knots
Armament 4 x 4in, 19 x 20mm **Complement** 480 inc staff

Notes

A former Canadian Pacific liner she was requisitioned by the Admiralty on 28 August 1939 and converted to an Armed Merchant Cruiser. On 2 June 1942 she was sold to the Admiralty and converted to a Destroyer Depot Ship and subsequently converted again, in 1944, to a Submarine Depot Ship being based at Rothesay with the 3rd Submarine Flotilla.

HMS Tyne

DESTROYER DEPOT SHIPS
HECLA CLASS

Ship	Completed	Builder
TYNE	28.02.41	Scott's SB & Eng Co (Greenock)

Displacement 11,000 tons (14,000 tons FL) **Dimensions** 621ft 2in x 66ft x 20ft 7in
Machinery Parsons geared turbines, 4 Admiralty 3-drum boilers, 2 shafts, 7,500 ihp
Speed 17 knots **Armament** 8 x 4.5in, 8 x 2pdr, 13 x 20mm **Complement** 818

Notes

One of two purpose-designed Destroyer Depot Ships built during the war, they serve a
similar purpose to the Submarine Depot Ships, only in this instance supporting destroyer flotillas. They carry similar workshops and hotel services and can provide all of a
destroyer flotillas needs, except for refuelling. She is a part of the Mediterranean Fleet
and serves as the flagship of Flag Officer, Flotillas, as a Harbour Depot ship at Malta.

HMS Ranpura

HEAVY REPAIR SHIPS
RANPURA CLASS

Ship	Completed	Builder
RANPURA	13.09.24 (L)	Hawthorn Leslie (Hebburn)

Displacement 16,120 tons (18,250 tons FL) Dimensions 570ft x 71ft 3in x 28ft 6in
Machinery Quadruple expansion steam reciprocating, 2 shafts, 15,000 ihp Speed 17 knots Complement 600

Notes

A former P&O liner taken in hand at HM Dockyard Portsmouth in May 1944 to be converted to a Heavy Repair Ship, a job completed in January 1946. Unlike the Depot Ships, the Repair Ships were designed to repair and maintain the fleet and therefore in lieu of accommodation and administrative space carried a greater capacity in the way of workshops and craftsmen to effect all manner of ship repair. In fact such was the extent of the repair facilities, that the repair Ships were accompanied by Accommodation Ships to act as floating hostels for the specialist repair ratings.

126

HMS Woodbridge Haven

HAVEN CLASS

Ship	Completed	Builder
WOODBRIDGE HAVEN	19.10.45	Swan Hunter & Wigham Richardson

Displacement 1,652 tons (2,407 tons FL) Dimensions 307ft 6in x 38ft 6in x 12ft 9in
Armament 2 x 40mm, 3 x 20mm Machinery Reciprocating steam engine, 2 Admiralty
3-drum boilers, 5,500 shp Speed 19½ knots Complement 120

Notes

Originally intended to be completed as a frigate, but was completed as a Depot and
Repair ship for Light Coastal forces, with reduced armament and increased deckhouses and workshops, for service in the Far East, but the war finished prior to her
commissioning so she went straight into reserve at Harwich. In 1946 she was nomi-
nated as a Despatch Vessel for Flag Officer Submarines and for use as a Submarine
Target Ship for the Third Submarine Squadron based in the Clyde, duties which she
continues to this day.

HMS Perseus

FERRY CARRIER
COLOSSUS CLASS

Ship	Completed	Builder
PERSEUS (ex-EDGAR)	19.10.45	Vickers Armstrong (Walker)

Displacement 12,265 tons (16,500 tons FL) Dimensions 694ft 6in x 80ft 6in x 23ft Machinery Parsons SR geared turbines, 4 Admiralty 3-drum boilers, 2 shafts, 40,000 shp Speed 25 knots Armament 16 x 2pdr, 16 x 40mm Complement 1,076

Notes

Originally laid down as a carrier of the Colossus class named EDGAR she was completed as an Aircraft Maintenance Carrier. In 1949, she served as a trial vessel for the steam catapult and earlier this year spent time in the USA demonstrating the system. She was unable to operate aircraft due to deckhouses and cranes located on the flightdeck. On her return to the UK she entered refit at Portsmouth where much of the workshop equipment, deckhouses and steam catapult were removed and in June she was redesignated as a Ferry Carrier, in which role she can ferry up to 60 aircraft.

128

HMS Bulawayo

FLEET REPLENISHMENT SHIP
NORDMARK TYPE

Ship	Completed	Builder
BULAWAYO	06.01.39	Schichau (Elbing)

Displacement 10,848 tons (20,000 tons FL) **Dimensions** 584ft x 72ft 6in x 30ft 3in
Machinery Steam DR geared turbine, 2 Wagner boilers, 2 shafts, 21,950 shp **Speed**
21 knots **Complement** 292

Notes

The former German Navy fast fleet oiler NORDMARK she was allocated to the Royal
Navy by the Inter-Allied Repatriations Commission. She was to undergo refit for service
with the British Pacific Fleet but the war ended before she could deploy. In January 1946
she was renamed NORTHMARK and considered for service with the Royal Fleet
Auxiliary but this was cancelled on cost grounds. Eventually in 1947 she was refitted for
service with the Royal Navy, completing as HMS BULAWAYO in July of that year.

HMS Blackburn

AIRCRAFT TRANSPORTS
BLACKBURN CLASS

Ship	Completed	Builder
BLACKBURN	25.03.44 (L)	Blyth SB & Dry Dock Co
RIPON	15.03.45 (L)	J. Pollock (Faversham)
ROC	28.03.45 (L)	Blyth SB & Dry Dock Co
SKUA (ex-WALRUS)	28.03.45 (L)	Blyth SB & Dry Dock Co

Displacement 990 tons **Dimensions** 172ft 6in x 35ft x 13ft 6in **Machinery** Crossley 2-stroke diesels, 2 shaft, 960 bhp **Speed** 10½ knots

Notes

Rated as Aircraft Transports (Small), they are fitted with 6-ton and 12-ton derricks for handling aircraft. BLACKBURN is now a seagoing tender to the Clyde Division RNVR. SEAFOX was withdrawn from RN service in May 1951 and is now a victualling store issue ship in service with the RFA.

HMS Sea Valour

SALVAGE VESSELS
KING SALVOR CLASS

Ship	Completed	Builder
KING SALVOR (RFA)	17.07.42	W. Simons & Co (Renfrew)
OCEAN SALVOR (RFA)	23.09.43	W. Simons & Co (Renfrew)
PRINCE SALVOR (RFA)	08.09.43	Goole Shipbuilding & Repair
SALVAGE DUKE	24.11.43	W. Simons & Co (Renfrew)
SALVALOUR	04.09.45	Goole Shipbuilding & Repair
SALVESTOR (RFA)	30.09.42	W. Simons & Co (Renfrew)
SALVICTOR (RFA)	31.03.44	W. Simons & Co (Renfrew)
SALVIGIL	23.05.45	W. Simons & Co (Renfrew)
SALVIOLA (RFA)	25.07.45	W. Simons & Co (Renfrew)
SEA SALVOR (RFA)	00.02.44	Goole Shipbuilding & Repair

Displacement 1,440 tons (1,700 tons FL) **Dimensions** 216ft x 37ft 9in x 13ft 9in
Machinery Triple expansion, 2 shafts, 1,500 ihp **Speed** 12 knots **Complement** 52-72

Notes

A class of vessel designed for offshore or shallow water salvage operations, for rendering assistance to vessels in adverse weather conditions and for firefighting. The ships were designed for making 300 ton tidal lifts, distributed 150 tons at the bow and stern. Most of the ships were initially placed under commercial management but all have served either as RN manned or with the Royal Fleet Auxiliary during their careers. In 1948 SALVAGE DUKE was chartered by Turkey and renamed IMROZ. SALVALOUR is on charter to Mollers Towages Ltd. SALVIGIL has been on commercial charter since 1951. Also in 1951 SEA SALVOR sailed from Malta to Gibraltar to attend and salvage NAV BEDENHAM which had blown up in the harbour while discharging ammunition. This year SALVICTOR has deployed to Singapore to assist in the salvage of floating dock AFD 9 which had been sunk during the war. A further vessel SALVENTURE was transferred to Greece in 1950 and renamed RHN SOTIR.

HMS Salveda

SALVEDA CLASS

Ship	Completed	Builder
SALVEDA	15.05.43	Cammell Laird (Birkenhead)

Displacement 1,250 tons (1,360 tons FL) **Dimensions** 191ft x 34ft 6in x 17ft
Machinery Reciprocating steam engine, 2 SE cylindrical boilers, single shaft, 1,200 ihp
Speed 12 knots **Armament** 4 x 20mm **Complement** 62

Notes

Included in the 1942 Programme for ocean-going vessels, she was generally similar to
the King Salvor class and fitted with a comprehensive range of firefighting, lifting and towing equipment. In February 1947 she was chartered by Metal Industries (Salvage) Ltd,
Faslane and operated under the same name.

HMS Lifeline

KIN CLASS

Ship	Completed	Builder
DISPENSER (RFA)	10.43	Smith's Dock (Middlesborough)
HELP	01.43	Smith's Dock (Middlesborough)
KINBRACE (RFA)	05.45	Alexander Hall & Sons (Aberdeen)
KINGARTH (RFA)	12.44	Alexander Hall & Sons (Aberdeen)
KINLOSS	07.45	Alexander Hall & Sons (Aberdeen)
LIFELINE	10.43	Smith's Dock (Middlesborough)
SUCCOUR (RFA)	10.43	Smith's Dock (Middlesborough)
SWIN (RFA)	10.44	Alexander Hall & Sons (Aberdeen)
UPLIFTER	10.43	Smith's Dock (Middlesborough)

Displacement 950 tons (1,050 tons FL) Dimensions 179ft 2in x 39ft 3in x 11ft
Machinery Triple expansion steam, 1 return tube cylindrical boiler, 1 shaft, 600 ihp
Speed 9 knots Complement 34

Notes

Originally a class of 11 Coastal Salvage Vessels was planned but two were cancelled
and of the remaining nine, seven saw brief service as RFA's. All were equipped with lifting horns and heavy rollers forward which enabled them to lift 200 tons dead-weight over
the bows. KINGARTH had been on charter to the Greek government from1946-50 but
on return was placed in care and maintenance at Malta prior to entering reserve. DIS-
PENSER is undergoing refit on completion of which she too will enter reserve.

HMS Reclaim

DIVING VESSELS
KING SALVOR CLASS

Ship	Completed	Builder
RECLAIM	00.10.48	W. Simons & Co (Renfrew)

Displacement 1,440 tons (1,700 tons FL) **Dimensions** 216ft x 37ft 9in x 13ft 9in
Machinery Triple expansion, 2 shafts, 1,500 ihp **Speed** 12 knots **Complement** 52-72

Notes

A member of the King Salvor class Ocean Salvage Ships, she was completed as a deep diving and submarine rescue vessel. Originally named SALVERDANT she was fitted with specialised equipment including underwater television cameras and sonar and echosounding apparatus and attached to HMS Vernon, Portsmouth as a diving tender. She was also equipped for submarine rescue work. At the time of her commissioning in 1949, she was the RN's only vessel capable of carrying out deep diving operations. On 14 June 1951 she found the submerged wreck of the submarine AFFRAY, missing since 17 April, during which operation her new underwater television apparatus was used.

HMS Moormyrtle

BOOM WORKING & MOORING VESSELS
MOOR CLASS

Ship	Launched	Builder
First Series		
MOORDALE	15.08.19	Bow McLachlan & Co. (Paisley)
MOORFOWL	11.09.19	Bow McLachlan & Co. (Paisley)
MOORHILL	12.09.19	Bow McLachlan & Co. (Paisley)
Prototype Vessel		
MOORLAND	11.11.38	W. Simons & Co (Renfrew)
Second Series		
MOORSIDE	25.08.45	Goole Shipbuilding & Repair
Fourth Series		
MOORBURN	16.04.42	Goole Shipbuilding & Repair
MOORCOCK	27.06.42	Goole Shipbuilding & Repair

Ship	Launched	Builder
MOORESS	16.09.43	Goole Shipbuilding & Repair
MOORFIELD	28.04.41	W. Simons & Co (Renfrew)
MOORFIRE	24.05.41	HM Dockyard (Devonport)
MOORFLY	14.07.42	Goole Shipbuilding & Repair
MOORGRASS	25.07.42	Goole Shipbuilding & Repair
MOORGRIEVE	04.09.44	Goole Shipbuilding & Repair
MOORHEN	30.09.43	Goole Shipbuilding & Repair
MOORMYRTLE	15.03.45	Goole Shipbuilding & Repair
MOORPOUT	24.07.44	HM Dockyard (Chatham)

First Series

Displacement 767 tons Dimensions 138ft x 29 ft x 10ft 6in Machinery Triple expansion steam, single shaft, 500 ihp Speed 9 knots

Second Series

Displacement 1,000 tons Dimensions 149ft x 34 ft x 11ft Machinery Triple expansion steam, single shaft, 500 ihp Speed 10 knots

Prototype Series

Displacement 720 tons Dimensions 135ft x 31 ft x 10ft Machinery Triple expansion steam, single shaft, 500 ihp Speed 10 knots

Fourth Series

Displacement 1,000 tons Dimensions 149ft x 34 ft x 11ft Machinery Triple expansion steam, single shaft, 500 ihp Speed 10 knots

Notes

Traditionally static harbour defence was conducted by Gate Vessels and Mooring Vessels, the former tending to be dumb barges and the later self propelled, but capable of very limited range of operation. Post WWI the Admiralty combined the roles in the larger Boom Defence Vessels, capable of overseas deployment. During World War 2, the Moor class was developed, adopting the size and range of the Boom Defence Vessels and having a useful heavylift capability by way of the bow horns.

HMS Barova

BOOM DEFENCE VESSELS
BAR CLASS

Ship	Completed	Builder
BARBAIN	31.05.40	Blyth Dry Dock & SB Co. Ltd
BARBASTEL	02.11.45	Philip & Son (Dartmouth)
BARBECUE	10.05.45	Ardrossan Dockyard
BARBERRY	09.04.43	Ferguson (Port Glasgow)
BARBETTE	00.09.43	W. Simons & Co (Renfrew)
BARBICAN	00.00.38	Blyth Dry Dock & SB Co. Ltd
BARBOUR	09.08.41	Blyth Dry Dock & SB Co. Ltd
BARBORNE	20.05.42	W. Simons and Co (Renfrew)
BARBRIDGE	21.10.41	Lobnitz & Co Ltd (Renfrew)
BARBROOK	15.09.38	Blyth Dry Dock & SB Co. Ltd
BARCAROLE	18.1045	Ardrossan Dockyard
BARCASTLE	10.11.38	Blyth Dry Dock & SB Co. Ltd
BARCLIFF	05.07.40	Lobnitz & Co Ltd (Renfrew)
BARCLOSE	13.10.41	Blyth Dry Dock & SB Co. Ltd
BARCOCK	20.12.41	Blyth Dry Dock & SB Co. Ltd

Ship	Completed	Builder
BARCOMBE	08.02.39	Goole Shipbuilding & Repair
BARCOTE	27.06.40	Blyth Dry Dock & SB Co. Ltd
BARCROFT	19.04.39	Goole Shipbuilding & Repair
BARDELL	12.06.42	Blyth Dry Dock & SB Co. Ltd
BARDOLF	24.07.42	Blyth Dry Dock & SB Co. Ltd
BARFIELD	00.00.39	J. Lewis (Aberdeen)
BARFOAM	24.09.41	W. Simons & Co (Renfrew)
BARFOIL	23.12.42	Philip & Son (Dartmouth)
BARFOOT	04.03.43	J. Lewis (Aberdeen)
BARFORD	12.11.41	W. Simons & Co (Renfrew)
BARFOSS	11.03.42	W. Simons & Co (Renfrew)
BARFOUNT	11.02.42	W. Simons & Co (Renfrew)
BARGLOW	08.04.43	J. Lewis (Aberdeen)
BARHILL	16.02.43	Ferguson (Port Glasgow)
BARHOLM	10.08.43	Ardrossan Dockyard
BARILLA	20.05.43	J. Lewis (Aberdeen)
BARITONE	02.07.45	Philip & Son (Dartmouth)
BARKING	17.12.41	Lobnitz & Co Ltd (Renfrew)
BARKIS	21.06.45	Ferguson (Port Glasgow)
BARLAKE	20.12.40	Blyth Dry Dock & SB Co. Ltd
BARLANE	12.10.38	Lobnitz & Co Ltd (Renfrew)
BARLEYCORN	13.08.43	J. Lewis (Aberdeen)
BARLOW	19.10.38	W. Simons & Co (Renfrew)
BARMILL	15.03.41	Blyth SB & Dry Dock Co
BARMOND	02.03.43	W. Simons & Co (Renfrew)
BARMOUTH	00.00.39	W. Simons & Co (Renfrew)
BARNABY	07.05.43	W. Simons & Co (Renfrew)

139

Ship	Completed	Builder
BARNARD	1812.42	J. Lewis (Aberdeen)
BARNDALE	23.03.40	Lobnitz & Co Ltd (Renfrew)
BARNEATH	04.01.43	J. Lewis (Aberdeen)
BARNEHURST	21.02.40	Blyth SB & Dry Dock Co
BARNSTONE	09.04.40	Blyth SB & Dry Dock Co
BARNWELL	26.04.40	Lobnitz & Co Ltd (Renfrew)
BARON	29.06.44	Philip & Son (Dartmouth)
BARONIA	02.07.41	Charles Hill & Sons (Bristol)
BAROVA	29.09.41	Charles Hill & Sons (Bristol)
BARRAGE	00.00.38	Hall Russell (Aberdeen)
BARRANCA	00.00.38	Hall Russell (Aberdeen)
BARRHEAD	28.11.40	W Simons (Renfrew)
BARRICADE	24.06.38	Charles Hill & Sons (Bristol)
BARRIER	27.10.38	Charles Hill & Sons (Bristol)
BARRINGTON	24.12.40	W Simons & Co (Renfrew)
BARRYMORE	15.03.41	W Simons & Co (Renfrew)
BARSING	05.05.41	W Simons & Co (Renfrew)
BARSOUND	02.07.41	W Simons & Co (Renfrew)
BARSPEAR	08.06.43	Ferguson (Port Glasgow)
BARSTOKE	28.08.41	W Simons (Renfrew)
BARTHORPE	05.06.40	Lobnitz & Co Ltd (Renfrew)
BARTIZAN	29.10.43	Ardrossan Dockyard
BARWIND	17.12.42	Ferguson (Port Glasgow)

Displacement 730 tons (875 tons FL) Dimensions 173ft 9in x 32ft 3in x 9ft 6in Machinery Triple expansion steam engine, 2 SE boilers, 850 ihp Speed 11¾ knots Complement 32

140

Built under the 1935, 36, 37, 39 and World War II estimates these Admiralty designed vessels were capable of world wide deployment for boom defence duties, designed to carry out the duties of operating gates, laying booms, handling heavy moorings and for laying and transporting moorings and boom working gear. With the end of the war many were relegated to the reserve fleet. However, with a bow lift of 27 - 70 tons , in the post war era of wreck and harbour clearance, many of these vessels found useful further employment employed on salvage work. BARGLOW was recommissioned in 1951 and manned by a civilian crew to survey wrecks in the Dover Strait.

Two vessels, BARBRAKE and BARCROSS are on loan to the Republic of South Africa Navy and, in 1951, were renamed FLEUR and SOMERSET respectively. BARSTOKE is on charter to Burma and BARNEHURST is on loan to the Netherlands. Three vessels (BARBARIAN, BARBETTE and BARFAIR) have been transferred to Turkey. BARCOCK was on loan to Belgium but was returned in 1949.

HMS Sonnet

NET CLASS

Ship	Completed	Builder
BOWNET	07.06.39	Blyth Dry Dock & SB Co. Ltd
BURGONET	05.07.39	Blyth Dry Dock & SB Co. Ltd
DRAGONET	13.09.39	Blyth Dry Dock & SB Co. Ltd
FALCONET	03.05.39	Blyth Dry Dock & SB Co. Ltd
MAGNET	04.04.39	Smith's Dock (Middlesborough)
MARTINET	04.05.39	Smith's Dock (Middlesborough)
PLANET	09.03.39	Lobnitz & Co Ltd (Renfrew)
PLANTAGENET	00.00.39	Lobnitz & Co Ltd (Renfrew)
SIGNET	11.08.39	Blyth Dry Dock & SB Co. Ltd
SONNET	15.10.39	Blyth Dry Dock & SB Co. Ltd

Displacement 530 tons (750 tons FL) Dimensions 135ft x 30ft 6in x 9ft Machinery Triple expansion steam engine, Cylindrical boiler, 850 ihp Speed 11½ knots Complement 44

Notes

Similar to the Bar class in general layout but designed to operate in waters too shallow for the larger vessels. Could not operate as Gate Vessels as they only had one boiler and would have to withdraw from the gate for boiler cleaning.

142

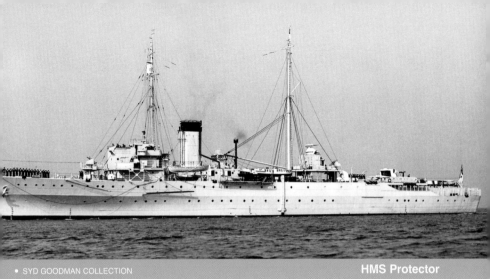

HMS Protector

NET LAYERS
GUARDIAN CLASS

Ship	Completed	Builder
PROTECTOR	31.12.36	Yarrow (Scotstoun)

Displacement 2,920 tons (3,610 tons FL) **Dimensions** 338ft x 50ft x 11ft 3in
Machinery Parsons geared turbines, 2 Admiralty 3-drum boilers, 2 shafts, 9,000 shp
Speed 20 knots **Armament** 2 x 4in, 6-10 x 20mm **Complement** 190

Notes

Designed to carry, lay and retrieve a net defence system in order to protect and render
safe, exposed anchorages or undefended harbours. She has a secondary role of target
towing.

HMS St Margarets

CABLE LAYERS
BULL CLASS

Ship	Completed	Builder
BULLFINCH	00.11.40	Swan Hunter & Wigham Richardson
ST MARGARETS	00.04.44	Swan Hunter & Wigham Richardson

Displacement 1,950 tons **Dimensions** 252ft x 36ft 3in x 16ft 3in **Machinery** Reciprocating steam engines, 2 Admiralty 3-drum boilers, two shafts, 1,300 ihp **Speed** 13 knots

Notes

The remaining pair of four vessels built for the Royal Navy during World War II. Fitted with tanks with a total capacity of 11,775 cubic feet. A cargo hold was fitted forward of the No 1 Cable tank for stowing cable buoys, grapnels etc. Fitted with 3 bow sheaves 3 ft 6 in. in diameter. Operated since 1947 by the Admiralty Cable Service, the ships operate under the Blue Ensign and carry the prefix ACS before their names.

The following year ST MARGARETS underwent a major refit at Sheerness, which included installing running water to the cabins, the fitting of range finders, gyro compass, new radio equipment, echo sounder and radar. Her hull was painted black with white upperworks and a buff funnel. She was based at Malta until 1951. She is now chartered out for operations in the Mediterranean and Red Sea.

144

HMS Lasso

LASSO TYPE

Ship	Completed	Builder
LASSO	17.03.38 (L)	J.I. Thornycroft & Co (Woolston)

Displacement 903 tons **Dimensions** 180ft x 35ft 1in x 9ft 8in **Machinery** Reciprocating Steam engine, 2 Admiralty 3-drum boilers, 2 shafts, 1,100 ihp **Speed** 13 knots

Notes

Originally laid down as a small cable layer capable of deploying cable over the bows from two internal cable tanks. Almost immediately she was employed as a tender to the Anti-Submarine School, Portland, leading some to suggest that her cable laying role may have more to do with A/S research than communications.

HMS Dwarf

TENDERS
DWARF CLASS

Ship	Completed	Builder
DWARF	20.08.36(L)	Philip & Son (Dartmouth)

Displacement 172 tons Dimensions 91ft x 19ft x 6ft 6in Machinery 2 sets triple expansion steam engines, 1 cylindrical boiler, 350 ihp Speed 9¼ knots Complement 12

Notes

Tender to Third Submarine Flotilla, Rothesay.

146

HMS Nightingale

MINING TENDERS

Ship	Completed	Builder
NIGHTINGALE	30.09.31	HM Dockyard (Portsmouth)
VESUVIUS	15.11.32	HM Dockyard (Portsmouth)

Displacement 298-302 tons Dimensions 106-110ft x 24ft 6in x 7ft 6in Machinery 2 sets triple expansion steam engines, 1 cylindrical boiler, 400 ihp Speed 10 knots Complement 15

Notes

Mining tenders to HMS Vernon at Portsmouth. The mainmast was removed from VESUVIUS in 1950 and NIGHTINGALE the following year.They now sport black hulls with grey upperworks.

HMS Diver

WAR PRIZE CLASS

Ship	Completed	Builder
DIPPER (ex-C30)	1943	Hamburg
DIVER (ex-C28)	1943	Hamburg

Displacement 102 tons Dimensions 88ft 10in x 16ft 6in x 9ft 8in Machinery Diesel
Speed 9 knots

Notes

Ex German Mine Locator vessels seized as war prizes. RN manned and attached to Experimental Minesweeping Flotilla, HMS LOCHINVAR, Port Edgar.

148

THE RESERVE FLEET
1952

At the end of World War II the Royal Navy had far more ships in service than it needed for peacetime operations and it was necessary to dispose of a large number of surplus vessels. However, wary of the poor decisions made at the end of World War I, many of the newer ships were placed into reserve so that, if necessary, the Royal Navy could be rapidly expanded.

However, in the intervening years, very little work has been carried out on these ships as they sat at their lay-up berths and little was done to preserve tham from the elements. As time passed many of these ships have reached a stage of obsolescence which would make their effectiveness in any future conflict somewhat limited. Indeed the baseline requirement for a vessel in Category A reserve, the highest state of readiness, was that the vessel should be at 3 months notice for operations (preferably 30 days).

In order to counter this deterioration and to place the vessels at a more practical state of readiness, the Government announced in 1950 a series of refits for these ships. Initially 89 vessels are to be refitted for operational duties, including seven destroyers, nine frigates and 16 fleet minesweepers. The rest are made up of Boom Defence Vessels, tank landing craft, minesweeping launches and MTBs. The work has been split between yards in the North-east, Clyde, Merseyside and Southampton.

Nearly 400 ships are in reserve and it is planned that most will enter the refit cycle to update their systems and bring them to higher states of readiness over the coming years. With most reserve ships concentrated in and around the Naval Base port areas it is also intended that the ships will be dispersed from their naval moorings, to various locations around the country and, as far as possible, berthing the vessels alongside jetties. It is also intended that certain of the ships, which are at a longer notice of readiness, should be removed to commercial ports where they are to be dehumidified and maintained by contractors.

The state of preparedness of the Reserve Fleet is certainly improving (indeed the new Category I standard requires a ship to be at 14 days notice and manned with a nucleus crew) and it is hoped that this policy will lead to substantial savings and that, in addition, a considerable number of naval personnel will become available to serve in the active Fleet.

SHIPS OF THE ROYAL NAVY (Reserve Fleet)
Pennant Numbers

Penn	Ship Name

Battleships

B17	DUKE OF YORK
B32	HOWE
B41	KING GEORGE V
B79	ANSON

Monitors

B98	ABERCROMBIE
B99	ROBERTS

Aircraft Carriers

R67	FORMIDABLE

Cruisers

C11	LIVERPOOL
C37	DIDO
C43	PHOEBE
C44	JAMAICA
C60	NIGERIA
C61	ARGONAUT
C80	MAURITIUS
C82	SIRIUS
C84	DIADEM
C89	ROYALIST

Submarines

S15	ALCIDE
S16	ALDERNEY
S17	ALLIANCE
S25	THULE
S32	TIPTOE
S34	TACITURN
S42	TABARD
S48	STURDY
S53	TRUNCHEON
S54	TURPIN
S61	SLEUTH
S62	SOLENT
S76	SIRDAR
S154	SELENE

Destroyers

D01	CAPRICE
D02	ZEST
D07	CAESAR
D09	DUNKIRK
D10	CASSANDRA
D15	CAVENDISH
D17	ALAMEIN
D23	TEAZER
D25	CARYSFORT
D26	COMET
D27	URANIA

Penn	Ship Name	Penn	Ship Name
D29	URSA	**Frigates**	
D30	CARRON		
D32	CAMPERDOWN	F05	ATHERSTONE
D33	TERPSICHORE	F12	BAMBOROUGH CASTLE
D38	NIZAM	F15	EGGESFORD
D39	ZEALOUS	F16	STEVENSTONE
D40	TROUBRIDGE	F21	DART
D43	MATAPAN	F22	WHEATLAND
D44	LAGOS	F24	BLENCATHRA
D52	CHAPLET	F25	SOUTHDOWN
D54	ZODIAC	F39	HIND
D56	PETARD	F49	PHEASANT
D58	MILNE	F55	SILVERTON
D62	JUTLAND	F56	TEST
D69	PALADIN	F57	BLACK SWAN
D72	WIZARD	F58	HART
D73	CAVALIER	F60	ALACRITY
D74	HOGUE	F70	FARNDALE
D77	TRAFALGAR	F75	HAYDON
D80	BARFLEUR	F79	BRISSENDEN
D81	ZEBRA	F81	STORK
D85	CAMBRIAN	F86	PELICAN
D91	CHILDERS	F87	EGLINTON
D95	ZENITH	F89	ALLINGTON CASTLE
D103	KEMPENFELT	F90	WOODCOCK
D121	TUMULT	F92	EXE
D125	NEPAL	F105	ALNWICK CASTLE
D135	MARNE	F111	FERNIE
D149	NORMAN	F112	ALBRIGHTON
D165	NOBLE	F116	AMETHYST
D169	ULYSSES	F118	TALYBONT
D186	MUSKETEER	F120	GARTH
D252	MATCHLESS	F128	WILTON
D273	METEOR	F130	BLANKNEY
D297	NAPIER	F132	BELVOIR
D298	WAGER	F134	BICESTER

Penn	Ship Name	Penn	Ship Name
F135	CATTISTOCK	F355	HADLEIGH CASTLE
F137	HAMBLEDON	F356	ODZANI
F145	WHADDON	F365	LOCHY
F146	CLEVELAND	F367	TAFF
F148	HOLDERNESS	F371	WYE
F150	BLEASDALE	F372	RUSHEN CASTLE
F152	COWDRAY	F387	BERKELEY CASTLE
F154	COTSWOLD	F388	DUMBARTON CASTLE
F155	BALLINDERRY	F391	LOCH KILLIN
F158	QUANTOCK	F413	FARNHAM CASTLE
F162	CROOME	F420	KENILWORTH CASTLE
F173	MELBREAK	F425	LOCH DUNVEGAN
F174	MIDDLETON	F431	LOCH TARBERT
F176	BRECON	F449	PEVENSEY CASTLE
F182	MEYNELL	F523	DOVEY
F190	LEDBURY	F525	RIBBLE
F192	PYTCHLEY	F530	OAKHAM CASTLE
F198	OAKLEY	F601	LOCH ARKAIG
F199	TETCOTT	F604	START BAY
F206	AVON VALE	F605	TREMADOC BAY
F217	SWALE	F608	PADSTOW BAY
F219	NESS	F616	WIGTOWN BAY
F221	CHELMER	F620	LOCH GORM
F222	TEVIOT	F636	CARNARVON BAY
F224	ROTHER	F644	CAWSAND BAY
F230	WEAR	F648	LOCH SCAVAIG
F232	TAY	F650	PORLOCK BAY
F235	JED	F691	LANCASTER CASTLE
F241	KALE	F692	OXFORD CASTLE
F248	WAVENEY	F693	MORPETH CASTLE
F252	HELFORD		
F254	ETTRICK		
F257	DERG	**Minelayer**	
F270	NENE		
F272	TAVY	M22	DABCHICK
F286	AMBERLEY CASTLE	M31	REDSHANK
F293	TEES	N11	MINER I
F294	TOWY	N16	MINER VI

Penn	Ship Name	Penn	Ship Name
N18	MINER VIII	M384	ROWENA
N25	STONECHAT	M389	HARE
N65	ARIADNE	M422	IMERSAY
N69	LINNET	M424	SANDRAY
		M426	SHILLAY
		M428	JASEUR
Minesweepers		M429	RONAY
		M431	TRODDAY
M01	ALBACORE	M423	VACEASAY
M17	SKIPJACK	M433	LAERTES
M49	COURIER	M434	VALLEY
M73	NIGER	M435	MAENAD
M81	TOCOGAY	M436	MAGICIENNE
M106	ACUTE	M438	MANDATE
M216	ESPIEGLE	M447	POLARIS
M221	ONYX	M448	PYRRHUS
M227	MUTINE	M450	ORSAY
M276	LENNOX	M454	MYRMIDON
M277	ORESTES	M455	MYSTIC
M293	PICKLE	M456	NERISSA
M298	RECRUIT	M462	ORCADIA
M302	THISBE	M463	OSSORY
M304	WATERWITCH		
M307	HOUND		
M325	PROVIDENCE	**Coastal Forces**	
M329	MOON		
M333	SEABEAR	P01	GREY GOOSE
M341	WIAY	P1505	PROUD FULSILIER
M354	SERENE	P1506	PROUD GRENADIER
M360	MARY ROSE	P1507	PROUD GUARDSMAN
M367	STORMCLOUD	P1508	PROUD HIGHLANDER
M376	GOLDEN FLEECE	P1509	PROUD KNIGHT
M377	LIONESS	P1519	PROUD LANCER
M381	MARMION	P1522	PROUD LEGIONARY
M382	SYLVIA	P1596	PROUD PATRIOT
M383	TANGANYIKA	P1598	PROUD PATROLLER

Penn	Ship Name	Penn	Ship Name
Auxiliaries		A189	PIONEER
		A191	BERRY HEAD
A117	ALAUNIA	A219	DODMAN POINT
A118	ARTIFEX	A225	MULL OF KINTYRE
A134	RAME HEAD	A226	MULL OF GALLOWAY
A145	GUARDIAN	A262	HARTLAND POINT
A153	AUSONIA	A309	SEAGULL
A158	DUNCANSBY HEAD	A315	BUCHAN NESS
A164	ADAMANT	A338	GRAEMSAY
A179	RESOURCE	A387	GIRDLE NESS
A180	WOOLWICH		

RESERVE SHIP READINESS STATES

Since January 1949

Category A: Operational Reserve - Ships fit for full operational service within three months of mobilisation and if possible to be maintained at 30 days notice.

Category B: Supplementary Reserve - Ships required for operational service but will only be required after Category A vessels.

Category C: Extended Reserve - Ships to be preserved for possible future employment. These vessels are not to be commissioned until after post-mobilisation expansion takes place.

Category Z: Disposal List - Ships no longer required for service.

Towards the end of 1952, this system is to be superceded by a new classification as follows:

Class I: Ships free from important defects, stored and manned by a nucleus crew and at 14 days notice to proceed to work-up base.

Class II: As above but dehumidified and at 30 days readiness.

Class III: Ships at extended readiness and requiring a refit before service.

Class IV: Ships no longer required for service.

154

HMS Anson

BATTLESHIPS
KING GEORGE CLASS

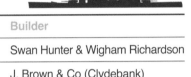

Ship	Completed	Builder
ANSON	22.06.42	Swan Hunter & Wigham Richardson
DUKE OF YORK	04.11.41	J. Brown & Co (Clydebank)
HOWE	29.08.42	Fairfield SB & Eng Co (Govan)
KING GEORGE V	11.12.40	Vickers Armstrong (Barrow)

Displacement 35,000 tons Dimensions 745ft x 103ft x 27ft 6in Machinery Parsons SR Geared Turbines, 8 Admiralty 3-drum boilers, 4 shafts, 110,000 shp Speed 28½ knots Armament 10 x 14in, 16 x 5.2.5in, 60-64 x 2pdr, 2-14 x 40mm, 8-14 x 20mm Complement 1,511 (war); 1,573 (Flag); 1,644 (Fleet Flag)

Notes

KING GEORGE V was Flagship of the Home Fleet until 1950 when placed in reserve. Since 1949 DUKE OF YORK was Flagship of the Reserve Fleet for two years but reduced to reserve in November 1951. ANSON paid off into reserve in 1949 following service with the Training Squadron. All three were 'cocooned' and laid up on the Gareloch, Scotland. HOWE remained in commission after the war and in 1946 became Flagship of the Training Squadron at Portland. She reduced to reserve r in 1950 and became headquarters of the Devonport Division, Reserve Fleet. It has been reported that in light of lessons learnt in Korea, the fire and damage control systems of the class are to be overhauled and brought up to date.

HMS Abercrombie

MONITORS
ABERCROMBIE CLASS

Ship	Completed	Builder
ABERCROMBIE	22.04.43	Vickers Armstrong (Walker)
ROBERTS	06.10.41	J. Brown & Co (Clydebank)

Displacement ROBERTS 7,973 tons (9,150 FL); ABERCROMBIE 8,536 (9,717 FL) Dimensions 354ft x 89ft 6in x 27ft (ROBERTS) 29ft (ABERCROMBIE) Machinery Parsons SR Geared Turbines, 2 Admiralty 3-drum boilers, 2 shafts, 4,800 shp Speed 12 knots Armament 2 x 15in, 8 x 4in, 16 x 2pdr, 0-8 x 40mm, 8-14 x 20mm Complement 442 (ROBERTS) 460 (ABERCROMBIE)

Notes

Post war ABERCROMBIE was placed into reserve at Sheerness. She wa used as an accommodation ship and in 1946 replaced EREBUS as the Turret Drill ship at Chatham and is now in use as a living ship for the Nore Reserve Fleet. ROBERTS is at Devonport where she has served as Turret Drill Ship and latterly as an accommodation ship for the reserve fleet.

HMS Formidable

AIRCRAFT CARRIERS
ILLUSTRIOUS CLASS

Ship	Completed	Builder
FORMIDABLE	24.11.40	Harland & Wolff (Belfast)

Displacement 23,207 tons (28,619 tons FL) Dimensions 753ft x 95ft x 29ft 6in
Machinery Parsons SR geared turbines, 6 Admiralty 3-drum boilers, 3 shafts, 110,000
shp Speed 31 knots Armament 16 x 4.5in, 21 x 40mm, 12 x 20mm, 40 x 2pdr, 54
aircraft Complement 1,600-1,785

Notes

In March 1947 the ship underwent a refit at Rosyth where her armament and equipment
was cocooned before she was reduced to reserve. She remained at Rosyth until 1949
when she was moved to Spithead and moored to a buoy off Ryde, Isle of Wight. In late
1952 she was moved from her mooring to Portsmouth Naval Base to prepare for an
extensive refit. She is scheduled to undergo a similar conversion to that of VICTORIOUS,
but with the delays and expenses being experienced it is unknown whether this will ever
go ahead.

HMS Jamaica

CRUISERS
FIJI CLASS

Ship	Completed	Builder
JAMAICA	29.06.42	Vickers Armstrong (Barrow)
MAURITIUS	01.01.41	Swan Hunter & Wigham Richardson
NIGERIA	23.09.40	Vickers Armstrong (Walker)

Displacement 8,000 tons (10,354 tons FL) Dimensions 555ft 6in x 62ft x 16ft 6in Machinery Parsons SR geared turbines, 4 Admiralty 3-drum boilers, 4 shafts, 72,500 shp Speed 31½ knots Armament 9 (NIGERIA 12) x 6in, 8 x 4in, 2-16 x 40mm, 4-12 x 20mm, 8-24 x 2-pdr, 6 x TT Complement 750

Notes

Following service in the Far East and off the coast of Korea JAMAICA returned to the UK in 1951 and was placed in reserve at Plymouth. After a period in reserve MAURITIUS re-commissioned in 1950 as Flagship in the East Indies and took part in operations in the Persian Gulf following unrest at Abadan. She returned to the UK in 1952 for a refit before being reduced to reserve. NIGERIA is in reserve at Plymouth.

HMS Diadem

MODIFIED DIDO CLASS

Ship	Completed	Builder
ROYALIST	10.09.43	Scott's SB & Eng Co (Greenock)
DIADEM	06.01.44	Hawthorn Leslie (Hebburn)

Displacement 5,900 tons (7,560 tons FL)   Dimensions 512ft x 50ft 6in x 15 ft
Machinery Parsons SR geared turbines, 4 Admiralty 3-drum boilers, 4 shafts, 62,000 shp   Speed 32 knots   Armament 8 x 5.25in, 12 x 2pdr, 12 x 40mm, 12 x 20mm, 6 x TT   Complement 588

Notes

Four turret versions of the original Dido class, omitting 'Q' turret. DIADEM served as Flagship of 2nd Cruiser Squadron, Home Fleet until 1950 when she was placed in Reserve. ROYALIST paid off into reserve in 1946. Two further ships of this class, BEL-LONA and BLACK PRINCE are serving with the Royal New Zealand Navy.

HMS Phoebe

DIDO CLASS

Ship	Completed	Builder
ARGONAUT	08.08.42	Cammell Laird (Birkenhead)
DIDO	30.09.40	Cammell Laird (Birkenhead)
PHOEBE	30.09.40	Fairfield SB & Eng Co (Govan)
SIRIUS	06.05.42	HM Dockyard (Portsmouth)

Displacement 5,770 tons (7,120-7,515 tons FL) Dimensions 512ft x 50ft 6in x 14ft Machinery Parsons SR geared turbines, 4 Admiralty 3-drum boilers, 4 shafts, 64,000 shp Speed 32¼ knots Armament 8 (DIDO/SIRIUS 10) x 5.25in, 12 x 2pdr, 2 x 40 mm, 4-13 x 20mm, 6 x TT Complement 550-620

Notes

ARGONAUT returned from service with the British Pacific Fleet at the end of World War II and reduced to reserve at Portsmouth. SIRIUS reduced to reserve at Portsmouth in 1949 and PHOEBE paid off into reserve in 1951 following service with the Mediterranean Fleet. DIDO was refitted at Chatham in 1945, but on completion in 1947, due to economic constraints and a manning shortage she was reduced to reserve at Portsmouth. This year she assumed the role of Flagship, Reserve Fleet.

HMS Liverpool

TOWN CLASS

Ship	Completed	Builder
LIVERPOOL	02.11.38	Fairfield SB & Eng Co (Govan)

Displacement 9,400 tons (12,860 tons FL) **Dimensions** 592ft x 62ft 6in x 17ft 6in
Machinery Parsons SR geared turbines, 4 Admiralty 3-drum boilers, 4 shafts, 82,500 shp **Speed** 32.3 knots **Armament** 9 x 6in, 8 x 4in, 26 x 2pdr, 8 x 40mm, 6 x TT
Complement 850

Notes

The sole survivor of the later Town, or Gloucester class of three ships. Her beam was slightly increased, installed power raised and gunnery control much improved. She served with the Mediterranean Fleet from 1945 before returning to Portsmouth this year to pay off into reserve.

161

HMS Alliance

SUBMARINES
'A' CLASS

Ship	Completed	Builder
ALCIDE	18.10.46	Vickers Armstrong (Barrow)
ALDERNEY	10.12.46	Vickers Armstrong (Barrow)
ALLIANCE	14.05.47	Vickers Armstrong (Barrow)

Displacement 1,120 tons (1,443 tons FL); 1,610 tons dived Dimensions 279ft 9in x 22ft 3in x 18ft 1in Machinery Supercharged diesel engines (4300 bhp); Electric motors (1250 bhp); 2 shafts Speed 19 knots (surfaced); 10 knots (dived) Armament 10 x 21-in TT (6 bow, 4 stern) up to 20 torpedoes or 26 mines; 1 x 4in deck gun in some Complement 60

Notes

Being relatively young submarines it is likely that they will undergo a modernisation pro-gramme, similar to the 'T' class, in the near future. In 1947, during early trials with the snort, ALLIANCE dived off Gibraltar at the start of a submerged tropical snort cruise which lasted 30 days and covered over 3,000 miles.

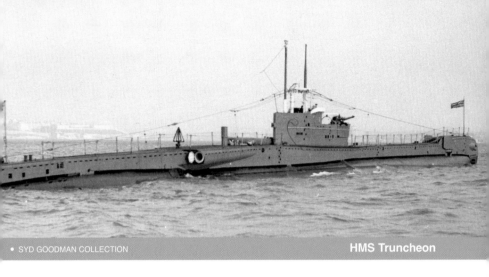

HMS Truncheon

'T' CLASS

Ship	Completed	Builder
TABARD	25.06.46	Scott's SB & Eng Co (Greenock)
TACITURN	08.10.44	Vickers Armstrong (Barrow)
THULE	13.05.44	HM Dockyard (Devonport)
TIPTOE	12.06.44	Vickers Armstrong (Barrow)
TRUNCHEON	25.05.45	HM Dockyard (Devonport)
TURPIN	18.12.44	HM Dockyard (Chatham)

Displacement 1,090 tons (1,442 FL); 1,571 tons dived Dimensions 273ft 3in x 26ft 7in x 15ft 10in Machinery Admiralty pattern diesel engines (2500 bhp); Electric motors (1450 bhp); 2 shafts Speed 15¼ knots (surfaced); 8¾ knots (dived) Armament 11 x 21-in TT (8 bow, 3 stern) up to 17 torpedoes or 12 mines; 1 x 4-in deck gun in some Complement 63-68

Notes

Five of these submarines (TABARD, TACITURN, TIPTOE, TRUNCHEON and TURPIN) have been assigned to the "Super T" modernisation programme begun in 1948. They will emerge with a streamlined hull, improved sensors and a longer hull to accommodate a greater number of batteries.

HMS Solent

'S' CLASS

Ship	Completed	Builder
SELENE	14.07.44	Cammell Laird (Birkenhead)
SIRDAR (ex-P76)	20.09.43	Scott's SB & Eng Co (Greenock)
SLEUTH	08.10.44	Cammell Laird (Birkenhead)
SOLENT	07.09.44	Cammell Laird (Birkenhead)
STURDY	29.12.43	Cammell Laird (Birkenhead)

Displacement 715 tons (854 FL); 990 tons dived Dimensions 217ft x 23ft 9in x 14ft 6in Machinery Admiralty diesel engines (1900 bhp); Electric motors (1300 bhp); 2 shafts Speed 14¾ knots (surfaced); 9 knots (dived) Armament 6-7 x 21in TT (6 bow, 1 stern) up to 12-13 torpedoes or 12 mines; 1 x 3in or 1 x 4in deck gun Complement 48

Notes

SELENE, SLEUTH and SOLENT underwent conversion to high speed submarine targets and cannot be considered as operational submarines.

XE 8

'XE' CRAFT

Ship	Completed	Builder
XE8	15.11.44	Broadbent (Huddersfield)

Displacement 30 tons (surfaced)/34 tons (dived) **Dimensions** 53ft x 5ft 9in
Machinery Diesel engine 42 bhp; Electric motor 30 bhp **Speed** 6½ knots (surfaced)
6 knots (dived) **Armament** 2 x side charges (4000lb each) **Complement** 5

Notes

With the announcement of a new class of midget submarine it is likely that this submarine will be deleted in the near future.

HMS Dunkirk

DESTROYERS
LATER BATTLE CLASS

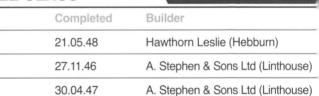

Ship	Completed	Builder
ALAMEIN	21.05.48	Hawthorn Leslie (Hebburn)
DUNKIRK	27.11.46	A. Stephen & Sons Ltd (Linthouse)
JUTLAND	30.04.47	A. Stephen & Sons Ltd (Linthouse)
MATAPAN	05.09.47	J. Brown & Co (Clydebank)

Displacement 2,380 tons (3,375 tons FL) Dimensions 379ft x 40ft 6in x 12ft 6in
Machinery Parsons geared turbines, 2 Admiralty 3-drum boilers, 2 shafts, 50,000 shp
Speed 31 knots Armament 5 x 4.5in, 8 x40mm, 10 x TT, 1 x Squid Complement
232-268 (337 in war)

Notes

JUTLAND paid off into reserve in May and her Ship's Company transferred to BAR
ROSA. The remaining three ships are in Category A reserve at Devonport.

HMS Barfleur

BATTLE CLASS

Ship	Completed	Builder
BARFLEUR	14.09.44	Swan Hunter & Wigham Richardson
CAMPERDOWN	18.06.45	Fairfield SB & Eng Co (Govan)
HOGUE	24.07.45	Cammell Laird (Birkenhead)
LAGOS	02.11.45	Cammell Laird (Birkenhead)
TRAFALGAR	23.07.45	Swan Hunter & Wigham Richardson

Displacement 2,315 tons (3,235-3,300 tons FL) Dimensions 379ft x 40ft 3in x 12ft 9in Machinery Parsons geared turbines, 2 Admiralty 3-drum boilers, 2 shafts, 50,000 shp Speed 32 knots Armament 4 x 4.5in, 10 x 40mm, 8-10 x TT Complement 247-308

Notes

BARFLEUR is undergoing a refit at Portsmouth to return her to active service. TRAFAL-GAR was recommissioned in February as a seagoing training ship for the reserve fleet. The remaining three vessels are in Category A reserve at Devonport.

167

HMS Comet

'CO' CLASS

Ship	Completed	Builder
COMET	06.06.45	Yarrow (Scotstoun)

Displacement 1,865 tons (2,515 tons FL) **Dimensions** 362ft 9in x 35ft 9in x 10ft **Machinery** Parsons SR geared turbines, 2 Admiralty 3-drum boilers, 2 shafts, 40,000 shp **Speed** 33 knots **Armament** 3-4 x 4.5in, 4 x 40mm, 2-6 x 20mm/2-pdr, 4 x TT **Complement** 186-222

Notes

The ship is in Category A reserve at Devonport.

HMS Childers

'CH' CLASS

Ship	Completed	Builder
CHAPLET	24.08.45	J.I. Thornycroft & Co (Woolston)
CHILDERS	19.12.45	Wm Denny & Bros (Dumbarton)

Displacement 1,885 tons (2,545 tons FL)   Dimensions 362ft 9in x 35ft 9in x 10ft
Machinery Parsons SR geared turbines, 2 Admiralty 3-drum boilers, 2 shafts, 40,000 shp   Speed 33 knots   Armament 3-4 x 4.5in, 4 x 40mm, 2-6 x 20mm/2pdr, 4 x TT
Complement 186-222

Notes

CHAPLET is in Category A reserve at Portsmouth, with CHILDERS in a similar state at Gibraltar.

HMS Cavalier

'CA' CLASS

Ship	Completed	Builder
CAESAR	05.10.44	J. Brown & Co (Clydebank)
CAMBRIAN	17.07.44	Scott's SB & Eng Co (Greenock)
CAPRICE	05.04.44	Yarrow (Scotstoun)
CARRON	06.11.44	Scott's SB & Eng Co (Greenock)
CARYSFORT	20.02.45	J.S. White & Co (Cowes)
CASSANDRA	28.07.44	Yarrow (Scotstoun)
CAVALIER	22.11.44	J.S. White & Co (Cowes)
CAVENDISH	13.12.44	J. Brown & Co (Clydebank)

Displacement 1,710 tons (2,530 tons FL)   **Dimensions** 362ft 9in x 35ft 9in x 10ft
Machinery Parsons SR geared turbines, 2 Admiralty 3-drum boilers, 2 shafts, 40,000

shp Speed 33 knots Armament 3-4 x 4.5in, 4 x 40mm, 2-6 x 20mm/2pdr, 8 x TT
Complement 186-222

Notes

CASSANDRA is at Sheerness; CAESAR and CAVENDISH at Devonport; CARRON and CAMBRIAN at Chatham. The remaining three ships are at Portsmouth. In November CARRON is scheduled to enter refit at Chatham for modernisation.

HMS Zest

'Z' CLASS

Ship	Completed	Builder
ZEALOUS	09.10.44	Cammell Laird (Birkenhead)
ZEBRA	13.10.44	Wm Denny & Bros (Dumbarton)
ZENITH	22.12.44	Wm Denny & Bros (Dumbarton)
ZEST	20.07.44	J.I. Thornycroft & Co (Woolston)
ZODIAC	23.10.44	J.I. Thornycroft & Co (Woolston)

Displacement 1,710 tons (2,530 tons FL) Dimensions 362ft 9in x 35ft 9in x 16ft
Machinery Parsons SR geared turbines, 2 Admiralty 3-drum boilers, 2 shafts, 40,000
shp Speed 33 knots Armament 3-4 x 4.5in, 6 x 40mm, 8 x TT Complement 186

Notes

ZEBRA and ZENITH remain in Category A reserve at Harwich. In September ZEALOUS
was moved from reserve at Penarth to Devonport to prepare for her Type 15 frigate conversion. ZEST joined the Nore Command in 1951 as an Air Training Ship until July 1952
when she was placed in reserve. She has been allocated to the Type 18 (A/S) frigate conversion programme, conceived as an advance over the Type 16. ZODIAC paid off at
Portsmouth in November following a period of operations with the 2nd Training Flotilla at
Portland. All except ZEST have been allocated to the Type 15 frigate conversion programme.

HMS Wizard

'W' CLASS

Ship	Completed	Builder
KEMPENFELT	25.10.43	J. Brown & Co (Clydebank)
WAGER	14.04.44	J. Brown & Co (Clydebank)
WIZARD	30.03.44	Vickers Armstrong (Barrow)

Displacement 1,710 tons (2,530 tons FL) Dimensions 362ft 9in x 35ft 9in x 16ft Machinery Parsons SR geared turbines, 2 Admiralty 3-drum boilers, 2 shafts, 40,000 shp Speed 33 knots Armament 4 x 4.7in, 5 x 40mm, 4 x 20mm, 8 x TT Complement 186

Notes

WIZARD remains in Category C reserve at Devonport despite being assigned to the Type 15 Frigate conversion programme in 1950. KEMPENFELT and WAGER are in Category A reserve at Simon's Town (South Africa) as part of the Commonwealth Strategic Reserve, and in February 1951 were assigned to the Type 62 AD frigate conversion programme. WESSEX and WHELP were similarly in reserve but were transferred to the South African Navy in 1950 and 1952 respectively and renamed JAN VAN RIEBEECK and SIMON VAN DER STEL (see page 328).

HMS Ulysses

'U' CLASS

Ship	Completed	Builder
ULYSSES	23.12.43	Cammell Laird (Birkenhead)
URANIA	18.01.44	Vickers Armstrong (Barrow)
URSA	01.03.44	J.I. Thornycroft & Co (Woolston)

Displacement 1,777 tons (2,508 tons FL) Dimensions 362ft 9in x 35ft 9in x 16ft
Machinery Parsons SR geared turbines, 2 Admiralty 3-drum boilers, 2 shafts, 40,000
shp Speed 34 knots Armament 4 x 4.7in, 4 x 40mm, 4 x 20mm, 8 x TT Complement
180

Notes

ULYSSES paid off in October 1952 to reduce to Category C reserve at Devonport. URA-
NIA is in reserve at Harwich and URSA at Portsmouth. URSA was allocated to the Type
62 AD frigate conversion programme, but being an intermediate destroyer design she
was unable to accommodate all of the radar equipment. All have been allocated to the
Type 15 frigate conversion programme.

174

HMS Tumult

'T' CLASS

Ship	Completed	Builder
TEAZER	13.09.43	Cammell Laird (Birkenhead)
TERPSICHORE	20.01.44	Wm Denny & Bros (Dumbarton)
TROUBRIDGE	08.03.43	J. Brown & Co (Clydebank)
TUMULT	02.04.43	J. Brown & (Clydebank)

Displacement 1,802 tons (2,530 tons FL) Dimensions 362ft 9in x 35ft 9in x 16ft
Machinery Parsons SR geared turbines, 2 Admiralty 3-drum boilers, 2 shafts, 40,000
shp Speed 34 knots Armament 4 x 4.7in, 4 x 40mm, 4 x 20mm, 8 x TT Complement
180

Notes

In 1951 it was agreed that TROUBRIDGE was to have been a part of the Type 62 AD
frigate conversion programme but is now expected to join the Type 16 limited conversion
programme like the remainder of the class. TUMULT is in Category B reserve at
Portsmouth, TEAZER and TERPSICHORE are in a similar state at Devonport.

175

HMS Petard

'P' CLASS

Ship	Completed	Builder
PALADIN	12.12.41	J. Brown & Co (Clydebank)
PETARD	15.06.42	Vickers Armstrong (Walker)

Displacement 1,640 tons (2,250 tons FL) **Dimensions** 345ft x 35ft x 20ft **Machinery** Parsons SR geared turbines, 2 Admiralty 3-drum boilers, 2 shafts, 40,000 shp **Speed** 34 knots **Armament** 4 x 4in, 4 x 40mm, 4 x 20mm, 4 x 2pdr, 8 x TT **Complement** 180

Notes

PALADIN was in Category B reserve at Harwich until 1951 when she commenced a refit at Chatham. In February 1951 PETARD was allocated to the Type 16 limited conversion programme but remains in reserve at Harwich.

HMS Noble

'N' CLASS

Ship	Completed	Builder
NAPIER	11.12.40	Fairfield SB & Eng Co (Govan)
NEPAL (ex-NORSEMAN)	29.05.42	J.I. Thornycroft & Co (Woolston)
NIZAM	19.12.40	J. Brown & Co (Clydebank)
NOBLE (ex-NERISSA)	04.11.40	J. Brown & Co (Clydebank)
NORMAN	29.09.41	J.I. Thornycroft & Co (Woolston)

Displacement 1,773 tons (2,384 tons FL)   Dimensions 356ft 6in x 35ft x 9ft
Machinery Parsons SR geared turbines, 2 Admiralty 3-drum boilers, 2 shafts, 40,000
shp Speed 36 knots Armament 6 x 4.7in, 4 x 40mm, 4 x 2pdr, 6 x 20mm, 10 x TT
Complement 220

Notes

The whole class is allocated to the Type 18 (A/S) frigate conversion programme, conceived in the summer of 1950 as an improvement over the current Type 16 programme.
It was announced in 1951 that NOBLE would be the first ship to be taken in hand with
the remainder to follow. To date there has been no movement with the programme and
NEPAL and NORMAN remain in Category C reserve at Devonport with the remainder in
reserve at Harwich.

177

HMS Meteor

'M' CLASS

Ship	Completed	Builder
MARNE	02.12.41	Vickers Armstrong (Walker)
MATCHLESS	26.02.42	A Stephen & Sons Ltd (Linthouse)
METEOR	12.08.42	A Stephen & Sons Ltd (Linthouse)
MILNE	06.08.42	Scott's SB & Eng Co (Greenock)
MUSKETEER	18.09.42	Fairfield SB & Eng Co (Govan)

Displacement 1,920 tons (2,735 tons FL) Dimensions 362ft 6in x 36ft 8in x 16ft 3in Machinery Parsons SR geared turbines, 2 Admiralty 3-drum boilers, 2 shafts, 48,000 shp Speed 36 knots Armament 6 x 4.7in, 1 x 4in, 4 x 2pdr, 10 x 20mm, 8 x TT Complement 220

Notes

MARNE and MUSKETEER in Category C reserve at Portsmouth and Harwich respectively have been assigned to the Type 62 AD frigate conversion programme. The need for an Aircraft Direction ship was first identified in 1947 under the Fleet Aircraft Direction Escort (FADE) project. The intention is to initially fit MARNE with Types 293Q, 960, 974, 982 and 983 radars. The remainder of the class will follow. However, MATCHLESS at Portsmouth, and METEOR and MILNE at Devonport are in Category C reserve.

HMS Brecon

HUNT CLASS (Type IV)

Ship	Completed	Builder
BRECON	18.12.42	J.I. Thornycroft & Co (Woolston)
BRISSENDEN	12.02.43	J.I. Thornycroft & Co (Woolston)

Displacement 1,175 tons Dimensions 296ft x 33ft 4in x 9ft Machinery ; Parsons SR geared turbines, 2 Admiralty 3-drum boilers, 2 shafts, 19,000 shp Speed 27 knots Armament 6 x 4in, 4 x 2pdr, 2 x 40mm, 2-8 x 20mm, 3 x TT Complement 170

Notes

This pair of Hunt class vessels were built to a private design that had been prepared pre-war by John I. Thornycroft & Company. They have a novel hull design, with a U-shaped forward section with a distinctive double knuckle, intended to increase low-speed efficiency and reduce rolling. Unlike the previous variants of the Hunt class these ships include a long forecastle extending for most of the length of the ship, increasing internal accommodation space and allowing the crew to fight the ship almost completely under cover. Both are in Category A reserve at Portsmouth.

HMS Bleasdale

HUNT CLASS (Type III)

Ship	Completed	Builder
ALBRIGHTON	22.02.42	J. Brown & Co (Clydebank)
BELVOIR	29.03.42	Cammell Laird (Birkenhead)
BLEASDALE	16.04.42	Vickers Armstrong (Walker)
EGGESFORD	21.01.43	J.S. White & Co (Cowes)
HAYDON	24.10.42	Vickers Armstrong (Walker)
MELBREAK	10.10.42	Swan Hunter & Wigham Richardson
STEVENSTONE	18.03.43	J.S. White & Co (Cowes)
TALYBONT	19.05.43	J.S. White & Co (Cowes)

Displacement 1,050 tons (1,435 tons FL) Dimensions 280ft x 31ft 6in x 7ft 9in Machinery Parsons SR geared turbines, 2 Admiralty 3-drum boilers, 2 shafts, 19,000 shp Speed 25 knots Armament 4 x 4in, 4 x 2pdr, 2 x 20/40mm, 2 x TT Complement 168

Notes

ALBRIGHTON is in reserve at Devonport; BELVOIR and BLEASDALE at Portsmouth. MELBREAK and STEVENSTONE are at Chatham with HAYDON at West Hartlepool. TALYBONT is to be laid up in a state of preservation at the Coal Dock, West Hartlepool from November. BLEASDALE is undergoing a short refit at Portsmouth.

Others of the class remain in service with overseas navies. GLAISDALE was transferred to Norway in 1946 and renamed NARVIK. During 1942 the Royal Hellenic Navy received BOLEBROKE, HATHERLEIGH and MODBURY were transferred being renamed PINDOS, KANARIS and MIAOULIS respectively. In 1946 a further two vessels, CATTERICK and TANATSIDE were transferred, being renamed ADMIRAL HASTINGS and ADRIAS, respectively, the latter to replace a previous vessel of the same name (the former BORDER) which had been damaged beyond repair.

HMS Farndale

HUNT CLASS (Type II)

Ship	Completed	Builder
AVON VALE	17.02.41	J. Brown & Co (Clydebank)
BICESTER	18.06.42	Hawthorn Leslie (Hebburn)
BLANKNEY	11.04.41	J. Brown & Co (Clydebank)
COWDRAY	29.07.42	Scott's SB & Eng Co (Greenock)
CROOME	29.06.41	A Stephen & Sons Ltd (Linthouse)
FARNDALE	27.04.41	Swan Hunter & Wigham Richardson
LEDBURY	11.02.42	J.I. Thornycroft & Co (Woolston)
MIDDLETON	10.01.42	Vickers Armstrong (Walker)
OAKLEY (II)	07.05.42	Yarrow (Scotstoun)
SILVERTON	28.05.41	J.S. White & Co (Cowes)
TETCOTT	11.12.41	J.S. White & Co (Cowes)
WHEATLAND	03.11.41	Yarrow (Scotstoun)
WILTON	18.02.42	Yarrow (Scotstoun)

Displacement 1,050 tons (1,430 tons FL) Dimensions 280ft x 31ft 6in x 7ft 9in Machinery Two Admiralty 3-drum boilers; Parsons SR geared turbines 19,000shp; 2 shafts Speed 25 knots Armament 6 x 4in, 4 x 2pdr, 2-4 x 20mm Complement 146

182

AVON VALE, BLANKNEY and SILVERTON are in reserve at Sheerness; BICESTER, COWDRAY and FARNDALE at Chatham; CROOME, WHEATLAND and WILTON at Devonport. The remainder are at Portsmouth.

It was announced on 27 October 1952 that BEDALE, LAMERTON and CHIDDING-FOLD are to be transferred to India where they will be renamed GODAVARI, GOMATI and GANGA respectively (see page 314). In October 1951 it was announced that BEAUFORT and ZETLAND were to be transferred on loan to Norway, free of charge, for a period of four years - their new names have yet to be announced. In July this year BLACKMORE, CALPE and EXMOOR were accepted on loan by Denmark - again, new names are not yet known. BRAMHAM and HURSLEY were transferred to Greece in 1943 where they operate as THEMISTOCLES and KRITI respectively. A third vessel, LAUDERDALE was transferred in 1946 and renamed AIAION.

HMS Cotswold

FRIGATES
HUNT CLASS (Type I)

Ship	Completed	Builder
ATHERSTONE	23.03.40	Cammell Laird (Birkenhead)
BLENCATHRA	14.12.40	Cammell Laird (Birkenhead)
CATTISTOCK	22.07.40	Yarrow (Scotstoun)
CLEVELAND	18.09.40	Yarrow (Scotstoun)
COTSWOLD	16.11.40	Yarrow (Scotstoun)
EGLINTON	28.08.40	Vickers Armstrong (Walker)
FERNIE	29.05.40	J. Brown & Co (Clydebank)
GARTH	01.07.40	J. Brown & Co (Clydebank)
HAMBLEDON	08.06.40	Swan Hunter & Wigham Richardson
HOLDERNESS	10.08.40	Swan Hunter & Wigham Richardson
MEYNELL	30.12.40	Swan Hunter & Wigham Richardson
PYTCHLEY	23.10.40	Scott's SB & Eng Co (Greenock)
QUANTOCK	06.02.41	Scott's SB & Eng Co (Greenock)
SOUTHDOWN	08.11.40	J.S. White & Co (Cowes)
WHADDON	28.02.41	A Stephen & Sons Ltd (Linthouse)

Displacement 1,000 tons (1,340 tons FL)   **Dimensions** 280ft x 29ft x 7ft 9in
Machinery Parsons SR geared turbines, 2 Admiralty 3-drum boilers, 2 shafts, 19,000
shp   **Speed** 25 knots   **Armament** 4 x 4in, 4 x 2pdr, 2 x 20mm   **Complement** 146

Notes

All reclassified as AA frigates in 1947. BLENCATHRA, FERNIE, MEYNELL, PYTCHLEY,
QUANTOCK and SOUTHDOWN all disarmed and reclassified as air targets.

EGLINTON is in reserve at Hartlepool; MEYNELL is at Sheerness and PYTCHLEY and
WHADDON are at Devonport. CATTISTOCK and CLEVELAND are at Cardiff and
ATHERSTONE and QUANTOCK are at Portsmouth. The remainder are at Harwich. All
are at Category C reserve with the exception of CATTISTOCK (Category B). EGLINTON
is undergoing a short refit at Hull.

COTTESMORE was transferred to Egypt in 1951 following a short refit by J.S. White &
Co (Cowes). She was initially renamed IBRAHIM EL AWAL, but within six months this
was changed to MOHAMED ALI.

HMS Amethyst

MODIFIED BLACK SWAN CLASS

Ship	Completed	Builder
ALACRITY	13.04.45	Wm Denny & Bros (Dumbarton)
AMETHYST	02.11.43	A Stephen & Sons Ltd (Linthouse)
HART	12.12.43	A Stephen & Sons Ltd (Linthouse)
HIND	11.04.44	Wm Denny & Bros (Dumbarton)
PHEASANT	12.05.43	Yarrow (Scotstoun)

Displacement 1,475 tons (1,925 tons FL) Dimensions 299ft 6in x 38ft 6in x 8ft 9in Machinery Parsons SR geared turbines, 2 Admiralty 3-drum boilers, 2 shafts, 4,300 shp Speed 19¾ knots Armament 6 x 4in, 6 x 40mm, Hedgehog Complement 192

Notes

AMETHYST returned to the UK at the end of 1952 following sevice in the Far East and reduced to reserve. HART is in reserve at Devonport with the remaining ships at Portsmouth.

HMS Woodcock

BLACK SWAN CLASS

Ship	Completed	Builder
BLACK SWAN	27.01.40	Yarrow (Scotstoun)
WOODCOCK	29.05.43	Fairfield SB & Eng Co (Govan)

Displacement 1,300 tons (1,750 tons FL) Dimensions 299ft 6in x 37ft 6in x 8ft 6in
Machinery Parsons SR geared turbines, 2 Admiralty 3-drum boilers, 2 shafts, 4,300
shp Speed 19¾ knots Armament 6 x 4in, 4 x 40mm, Hedgehog Complement 180

Notes

BLACK SWAN paid off into reserve at Portsmouth in May. She is scheduled to move
to Devonport. WOODCOCK is at Chatham.

187

HMS Stork

BITTERN CLASS

Ship	Completed	Builder
STORK	10.09.36	Wm Denny & Bros (Dumbarton)

Displacement 1,190 tons (1,600 tons FL)   **Dimensions** 282ft x 37ft x 8ft 3in
Machinery Parsons SR geared turbines, 2 Admiralty 3-drum boilers, 2 shafts, 3,300
shp **Speed** 18 knots **Armament** 4 x 4in 2 x 40mm **Complement** 125

Notes

Post war the ship operated as the Senior Officer's ship of the Fishery Protection
Squadron. She paid off into reserve at Portsmouth in 1948.

188

HMS Pelican

EGRET CLASS

Ship	Completed	Builder
PELICAN	02.03.39	J.I. Thornycroft & Co (Woolston)

Displacement 1,250 tons (1,680 tons FL) **Dimensions** 293ft x 37ft 6in x 8ft 6in **Machinery** Parsons SR geared turbines, 2 Admiralty 3-drum boilers, 2 shafts, 3,600 shp **Speed** 18 knots **Armament** 4 x 4in, 4 x 2pdr, 2 x 20mm **Complement** 188

Notes

She is fitted with a radar cabin abaft the bridge. She paid off into reserve at Chatham in 1951 following service with the Mediterranean Fleet.

189

HMS Tremadoc Bay

BAY CLASS

Ship	Completed	Builder
CARNARVON BAY	20.09.45	Henry Robb (Leith)
CAWSAND BAY	13.11.45	Blyth SB & Dry Dock Co
PADSTOW BAY	11.03.46	Henry Robb (Leith)
PORLOCK BAY	08.03.46	Charles Hill & Sons (Bristol)
START BAY	06.09.45	Harland & Wolff (Belfast)
TREMADOC BAY	11.10.45	Harland & Wolff (Belfast)
WIGTOWN BAY	19.01.46	Harland & Wolff (Belfast)

Displacement 1,580 tons (2,420 tons FL) **Dimensions** 307ft 6in x 38ft 6in x 12ft 9in **Machinery** Triple expansion, 2 Admiralty 3-drum boilers, 2 shafts, 5,500 ihp **Speed** 19½ knots **Armament** 4 x 4in, 6 x 40mm, 2 x 20mm, Hedgehog **Complement** 157

Notes

CAWSAND BAY went straight into reserve on completion and remains at Portsmouth as does START BAY. CARNARVON BAY is in reserve at Sheerness and PORLOCK BAY at Devonport. PADSTOW BAY is undergoing a refit at Dowsons, South Shields and WIGTOWN BAY similarly at Rutherford & Co Ltd at Liverpool. TREMADOC BAY paid off and was laid up in 1951 and is now docked at Silley Cox, Falmouth.

HMS Loch Scavaig

LOCH CLASS

Ship	Completed	Builder
LOCH ARKAIG	17.11.45	Caledon SB & Eng Co Ltd (Dundee)
LOCH DUNVEGAN	30.06.44	Charles Hill & Sons (Bristol)
LOCH GORM	18.12.44	Harland & Wolff (Belfast)
LOCH KILLIN	12.04.44	Burntisland Shipbuilding
LOCH SCAVAIG	22.12.44	Charles Hill & Sons (Bristol)
LOCH TARBERT	22.02.45	Ailsa SB Co (Troon)

Displacement 1,435 tons (2,260 tons FL) Dimensions 307ft x 38ft 6in x 12ft
Machinery Triple expansion (Double reduction geared turbines in LOCH ARKAIG and
LOCH TRALAIG), 2 Admiralty 3-drum boilers, 2 shafts, 5,500 ihp Speed 19½ knots
Armament 1 x 4in, 4 x 2pdr, 10 x 20mm, 2 x Squid Complement 103

Notes

LOCH DUNVEGAN, LOCH GORM, LOCH KILLIN are in reserve at Devonport. LOCH
TARBERT is in reserve at Portsmouth, while LOCH SCAVAIG entered reserve at
Sheerness in September.

HMS Tay

RIVER CLASS

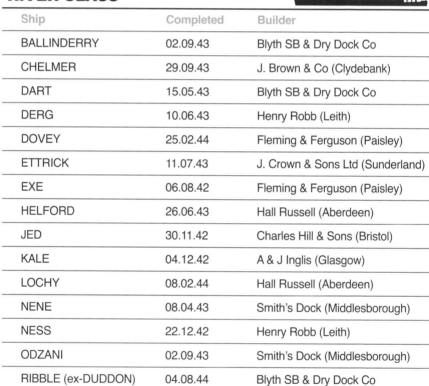

Ship	Completed	Builder
BALLINDERRY	02.09.43	Blyth SB & Dry Dock Co
CHELMER	29.09.43	J. Brown & Co (Clydebank)
DART	15.05.43	Blyth SB & Dry Dock Co
DERG	10.06.43	Henry Robb (Leith)
DOVEY	25.02.44	Fleming & Ferguson (Paisley)
ETTRICK	11.07.43	J. Crown & Sons Ltd (Sunderland)
EXE	06.08.42	Fleming & Ferguson (Paisley)
HELFORD	26.06.43	Hall Russell (Aberdeen)
JED	30.11.42	Charles Hill & Sons (Bristol)
KALE	04.12.42	A & J Inglis (Glasgow)
LOCHY	08.02.44	Hall Russell (Aberdeen)
NENE	08.04.43	Smith's Dock (Middlesborough)
NESS	22.12.42	Henry Robb (Leith)
ODZANI	02.09.43	Smith's Dock (Middlesborough)
RIBBLE (ex-DUDDON)	04.08.44	Blyth SB & Dry Dock Co
ROTHER	03.04.42	Smith's Dock (Middlesborough)

Ship	Completed	Builder
SWALE	24.06.42	Smith's Dock (Middlesborough)
TAFF	07.01.44	Charles Hill & Sons (Bristol)
TAVY	03.07.43	Charles Hill & Sons (Bristol)
TAY	05.08.42	Smith's Dock (Middlesborough)
TEES	28.08.43	Hall Russell (Aberdeen)
TEST	12.10.42	Hall Russell (Aberdeen)
TEVIOT	30.01.43	Hall Russell (Aberdeen)
TOWY	10.06.43	Smith's Dock (Middlesborough)
WAVENEY	16.09.42	Smith's Dock (Middlesborough)
WEAR	24.10.42	Smith's Dock (Middlesborough)
WYE	09.02.44	Henry Robb (Leith)

Displacement 1,370 tons (1,830 tons FL) Dimensions 301ft 6in x 36ft 9in x 14ft
Machinery Triple expansion, 2 Admiralty 3-drum boilers, 2 shafts, 5,500 ihp Speed 20
knots Armament 2 x 4in, 10 x 20mm, Hedgehog Complement 140

Notes

DART, NESS, ODZANI and TAFF are in reserve at Penarth. EXE, HELFORD, LOCHY
and TAVY are at Devonport. JED and KALE are at Cardiff. TEES is at Singapore, TOWY
at Portsmouth and WEAR at West Hartlepool. The remainder are in reserve at Harwich.
WAVENEY is refitting at Chatham, after which she will return to Harwich. DERG
(renamed WESSEX) was at Southampton from 1947 until this year as the Solent Division
RNR HQ ship. She has since been replaced by ERNE and has now entered reserve at
Portsmouth. A sistership, PLYM, was brought forward from reserve and prepared for special duties. On 10 June she sailed from Chatham for Australia, where, on 3 October, she
was expended when Britain's first atomic bomb was exploded at Monte Bello Island.

Several ships remain in service with overseas navies. FAL was transferred to Burma and
renamed MAYU. USK, NITH and SPEY were transferred to Egypt as ABIKIR, DOMIAT
and RASHEED rspectively. TRENT and BANN are operated by India as KUKRI and TIR.
AVON and AWE were transferred to Portugal as NUNO TRISTAO and DIOGO GOMES.
ANNAN and MONNOW are operated by Denmark as NIELS EBBESEN and HOLGER
DANSKE and Pakistan operate the former DEVERON and NADDER as ZULFIQUAR
and SHAMSHER.

HMS Dumbarton Castle

CASTLE CLASS

Ship	Completed	Builder
ALLINGTON CASTLE	19.06.44	Fleming & Ferguson (Paisley)
ALNWICK CASTLE	11.11.44	G. Brown & Co Ltd (Greenock)
AMBERLEY CASTLE	24.11.44	Austin & Son (Sunderland)
BAMBOROUGH CASTLE	30.05.44	J. Lewis & Sons Ltd (Aberdeen)
BERKELEY CASTLE	18.11.43	Barclay Curle & Co Ltd (Glasgow)
DUMBARTON CASTLE	25.02.44	Caledon SB & Eng Co Ltd (Dundee)
FARNHAM CASTLE	31.01.45	J. Crown & Sons Ltd (Sunderland)
HADLEIGH CASTLE	18.09.43	Smith's Dock (Middlesborough)
KENILWORTH CASTLE	22.11.43	Smith's Dock (Middlesborough)

Ship	Completed	Builder
LANCASTER CASTLE	15.09.44	Fleming & Ferguson (Paisley)
MORPETH CASTLE	13.07.44	W Pickersgill & Sons (Sunderland)
OAKHAM CASTLE	10.12.44	A & J Inglis (Glasgow)
OXFORD CASTLE	10.03.44	Harland & Wolff (Belfast)
PEVENSEY CASTLE	10.06.44	Harland & Wolff (Belfast)
RUSHEN CASTLE	24.02.44	Swan Hunter & Wigham Richardson

Displacement 1,060 tons (1,510 tons FL) Dimensions 252ft x 36ft 8in x 13ft 6in
Machinery Triple expansion, 2 Admiralty 3-drum boilers, 2,880 ihp Speed 16½ knots
Armament 1 x 4in, 6 x 20mm, 1 x Squid Complement 99

Notes

ALLINGTON CASTLE is in reserve at West Hartlepool. AMBERLEY CASTLE at Portsmouth and FARNHAM CASTLE at Sheerness. PEVENSEY CASTLE is at Chatham, and MORPETH CASTLE and OAKHAM CASTLE are at Devonport. OAKHAM CASTLE was at Devonport, but this year moved to Penarth where she joined BAMBOROUGH CASTLE, KENILWORTH CASTLE and RUSHEN CASTLE. The remaining ships are all in reserve at Harwich.

HMS Ariadne

FAST MINELAYERS
ARIADNE CLASS

Ship	Completed	Builder
ARIADNE	09.10.43	A Stephen & Sons Ltd (Linthouse)

Displacement 2,650 tons (3,475 tons FL)   Dimensions 418ft x 40ft x 11ft 3in
Machinery   Parsons SR geared turbines, 4 Admiralty 3-drum boilers, two shafts,
72,000shp Speed 35+ knots Armament 4-6 x 4in, 10 x 40mm, 2 x 20mm, 100 mines
Complement 246

Notes

Like her active sisters, ARIADNE spent her later war career, using her speed to transport
essential supplies, or her vast stores carrying capacity to help with repatriation duties in
the Pacific following VJ Day. She returned to the UK and was reduced to reserve at
Devonport. After the outbreak of war in Korea she was refitted at Immingham for possible further service but on completion of the refit she returned to reserve.

HMS Miner I

CONTROLLED MINELAYERS
MINER CLASS

Ship	Completed	Builder
MINER I	26.10.39	Philip & Son (Dartmouth)
MINER VI	30.05.42	Philip & Son (Dartmouth)
MINER VIII	15.05.43	Philip & Son (Dartmouth)

Displacement 300 tons (346-350 tons FL) **Dimensions** 110ft 3in x 26ft 5in x 8 ft
Machinery Ruston and Hornby diesels, 2 shafts, 360 bhp **Speed** 10 knots
Complement 32

Notes

Shortly before the outbreak of World War Two a programme of small Controlled
Minelayers was put in hand. Eight vessels were built, though MINER VII which was lost
during the fall of Singapore, was replaced. They have a capacity for laying up to 10
mines, but they are rarely used in that role.

197

HMS Linnet

LINNET CLASS

Ship	Completed	Builder
LINNET	00.06.38	Ardrossan Dockyard Co Ltd

Displacement 498 tons (560 tons FL) **Dimensions** 163ft 9in x 27ft 3in x 8ft **Machinery** Triple Expansion, one water tube boiler, 2 shafts, 400 ihp **Speed** 10½ knots **Armament** 1 x 20mm **Complement** 24

Notes

Built as a controlled minelayer, in which role she had a capacity to carry 12 mines, which she could lay and activate or deactivate as required. She has been placed in reserve at Rosyth where she is employed as a Static Pulsing Vessel.

HMS Stonechat

TRAWLER TYPE

Ship	Completed	Builder
DABCHICK	08.07.43	Cook, Welton & Gemmell
STONECHAT	12.11.44	Cook, Welton & Gemmell
REDSHANK	10.01.43	Cochrane Shipbuilders (Selby)

DABCHICK (ex THORNEY), STONECHAT

Displacement 545 tons (735 tons FL) Dimensions 164ft x 27ft 6in x 12ft 6in
Machinery Triple expansion, one cylindrical boiler, 1 shaft, 850 ihp Speed 12½ knots
Armament 1 x 20mm Complement 40

REDSHANK (ex TURBOT)

Displacement 590 tons (830 tons FL) Dimensions 162ft x 25ft 3in x 12ft 3in
Machinery Triple expansion steam, one cylindrical boiler, 1 shaft, 700 ihp Speed 11¼
knots Complement 35

Notes

The need for controlled minelayers in 1942 led to the conversion of several former A/S
and M/S trawlers. REDSHANK was the former Fish class trawler TURBOT and
DABCHICK the former Isles class trawler THORNEY. Another Isles class trawler,
STONECHAT was completed as a controlled minelayer, being the same as DABCHICK
except for being oil-fired. They coud carry up to 16 mines.

199

HMS Lennox

MINESWEEPERS
ALGERINE CLASS

Ship	Completed	Builder
Turbine Group		
ACUTE (ex-ALERT)	30.07.42	Harland & Wolff (Belfast)
ESPIEGLE	01.12.42	Harland & Wolff (Belfast)
HARE	10.11.44	Harland & Wolff (Belfast)
MUTINE	26.02.43	Harland & Wolff (Belfast)
ONYX	26.03.43	Harland & Wolff (Belfast)
PICKLE	15.10.43	Harland & Wolff (Belfast)
RECRUIT	14.01.44	Harland & Wolff (Belfast)
Reciprocating Group		
ALBACORE	16.06.42	Harland & Wolff (Belfast)
COURIER	31.08.44	Redfern (Toronto)
GOLDEN FLEECE	29.08.44	Redfern (Toronto)
HOUND	11.12.42	Lobnitz & Co Ltd (Renfrew)

Ship	Completed	Builder
JASEUR	27.10.44	Redfern (Toronto)
LAERTES	09.12.44	Redfern (Toronto)
LENNOX	18.01.44	Lobnitz & Co Ltd (Renfrew)
LIONESS	11.12.44	Redfern (Toronto)
MAENAD	16.11.44	Redfern (Toronto)
MAGICIENNE	11.05.45	Redfern (Toronto)
MANDATE	22.03.45	Redfern (Toronto)
MARMION (II)	29.05.45	Port Arthur Shipbuilding
MARY ROSE	24.04.44	Redfern (Toronto)
MOON (II)	06.07.44	Redfern (Toronto)
MYRMIDON (II)	09.07.45	Redfern (Toronto)
MYSTIC	02.08.45	Redfern (Toronto)
NERISSA	28.08.45	Redfern (Toronto)
NIGER	21.09.45	Lobnitz & Co Ltd (Renfrew))
ORCADIA	17.08.45	Port Arthur Shipbuilding
ORESTES	10.04.43	Lobnitz & Co Ltd (Renfrew)
OSSORY	29.09.45	Port Arthur Shipbuilding
POLARIS	29.10.45	Port Arthur Shipbuilding
PROVIDENCE	15.05.44	Redfern (Toronto)
PYRRHUS	02.11.45	Port Arthur Shipbuilding
ROWENA	06.09.44	Lobnitz & Co Ltd (Renfrew)
SEABEAR	22.06.44	Redfern (Toronto)
SERENE	14.09.44	Redfern (Toronto)
SKIPJACK (II)	29.04.44	Redfern (Toronto)
STORMCLOUD	28.03.44	Lobnitz & Co Ltd (Renfrew)
SYLVIA	17.05.44	Lobnitz & Co Ltd (Renfrew)

Ship	Completed	Builder
TANGANYIKA	07.07.44	Lobnitz & Co Ltd (Renfrew)
THISBE	08.06.44	Redfern (Toronto)
WATERWITCH	06.08.43	Lobnitz & Co Ltd (Renfrew)

Displacement Turbine Group: 850 tons (1,125 tons FL), Reciprocating Group: 1,010 tons (1,305 tons FL) Dimensions 235ft x 35ft 6in x 10ft 6in Machinery Turbine Group: Parsons SR geared turbines, 2 Admiralty 3-drum boilers, 2 shafts, 2,000 shp, Reciprocating Group: Reciprocating triple expansion steam, 2 Admiralty 3-drum boilers, 2 shafts, 2,400 shp Speed 16½ knots Armament 1 x 4in, 4-6 x 20mm Complement 85

Notes

Some of the ships have been in reserve since the end of World War II. ACUTE, COURIER, HARE, LAERTES, MOON, MUTINE, NERISSA, ORESTES, PICKLE, PROVIDENCE, SKIPJACK and THISBE are at Harwich. ALBACORE, MARY ROSE, SEABEAR and TANGANYIKA are at Chatham. HOUND, GOLDEN FLEECE, MANDATE, MYRMIDON, NIGER, ORCADIA, POLARIS,PYRRHUS and SERENE are at Devonport. LENNOX, MYSTIC, ONYX, OSSORY and WATERWITCH are at Portsmouth. ESPEIGLE is at West Hartlepool and MARMION at Sheerness. RECRUIT, ROWENA, STORMCLOUD and SYLVIA are at Malta. JASEUR, MAENAD and MAGICIENNE are at Singapore.

HMS Vaceasay

TRAWLERS
ISLES CLASS

Ship	Completed	Builder
Wreck Dispersal & Diving Vessels		
GRAEMSAY	18.06.43	Ardrossan Dockyard
Danlayers		
IMERSAY	08.12.44	Cochrane Shipbuilders (Selby)
ORSAY	11.05.45	Cochrane Shipbuilders (Selby)
RONAY	08.06.45	Cochrane Shipbuilders (Selby)
SANDRAY	27.12.44	Cook, Welton & Gemmell
SHILLAY	30.01.45	Cook, Welton & Gemmell
TOCOGAY	19.04.45	Cook, Welton & Gemmell
TRODDAY	13.05.45	Cook, Welton & Gemmell
VACEASAY	29.05.45	Cook, Welton & Gemmell

Ship	Completed	Builder
VALLEY	13.06.45	Cook, Welton & Gemmell
WIAY	17.07.45	Cook, Welton & Gemmell

Displacement 545 tons (735 tons FL) **Dimensions** 164ft x 27ft 6in x 14ft **Machinery** Triple expansion, one cylindrical boiler, 1 shaft, 850 ihp **Speed** 12 knots **Armament** 1 x 12pdr, 3 x 20mm **Complement** 40

Notes

The majority of the ships in reserve are Danlayers, converted from minesweepers in the run up to the D-Day landings. These ships would sail with the minesweeping flotillas and lay marker buoys to show the extent of the swept channels.

HMS Proud Legionary

COASTAL FORCES
PROUD CLASS

Ship	Completed	Builder
PROUD FUSILIER (ex-MTB 505)	11.05.45	British Powerboat Co (Hythe)
PROUD GRENADIER (ex-MTB 506)	31.05.45	British Powerboat Co (Hythe)
PROUD GUARDSMAN (ex-MTB 507)	30.11.45	British Powerboat Co (Hythe)
PROUD HIGHLANDER (ex-MTB 508)	22.11.45	British Powerboat Co (Hythe)
PROUD KNIGHT (ex-MTB 509)	29.01.46	British Powerboat Co (Hythe)
PROUD LANCER (ex-MTB 519)	14.02.46	British Powerboat Co (Hythe)
PROUD LEGIONARY (ex-MTB 522)	26.10.46	British Powerboat Co (Hythe)
PROUD PATRIOT (ex-MTB 496)	05.12.44	British Powerboat Co (Hythe)
PROUD PATROLLER (ex-MTB 498)	21.08.45	British Powerboat Co (Hythe)

Displacement 44 tons Dimensions 71ft 9in x 20ft 6in x 5ft 9in Machinery Three Packard petrol engines; 3 shafts; 4,050 bhp Speed 32 knots Armament 1 x 6pdr, 2 x 20mm (1 x twin), 4 x MG, 2 x 18in TT Complement 17

Notes

All refurbished British Powerboat Company craft. Originally cost £60,000 and were refitted between 1951-52 at a cost of £16,000 each. Received names in December 1952 and once refurbished all nine craft were laid up at Felixstowe.

HMS Grey Goose

GREY CLASS

Ship	Completed	Builder
GREY GOOSE	04.07.42	Wm Denny & Bros (Dumbarton)

Displacement 205 tons (260 tons) Dimensions 145ft 6in x 20ft x 5ft 6in Machinery 2 x Rolls-Royce RM 60 Gas Turbines, 12,000 shp Speed 35 knots Complement 27

Notes

Originally engined with Metro-Vick SR geared turbines. Taken in hand for Gas Turbine conversion in 1952.

RML 529

FAIRMILE 'B' RML CLASS

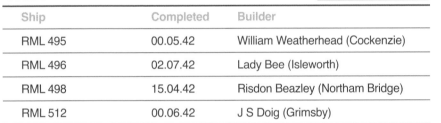

Ship	Completed	Builder
RML 495	00.05.42	William Weatherhead (Cockenzie)
RML 496	02.07.42	Lady Bee (Isleworth)
RML 498	15.04.42	Risdon Beazley (Northam Bridge)
RML 512	00.06.42	J S Doig (Grimsby)
RML 515	00.06.42.	Collins (Lowestoft)
RML 529	14.07.42	Jas Miller (St Monance)

Displacement 85 tons (130 FL) Dimensions 112ft x 18ft 4in x 5ft Machinery Hall Scott 12 cylinder petrol engines, 2 shafts, 1,200 bhp Speed 17¾ knots Armament 1 x 3pdr, 2 x .303 MG Complement 16

Notes

The Rescue Motor Launch (RML) is intended for search and rescue operations - in particular the recovery of downed pilots at sea. Fifty were built and these survivors differ from the standard 'B' design by the addition of a sick bay situated abaft the funnel and engine room hatchway. They carry a Sick Berth Attendant and basic medical supplies and operate as seagoing ambulances able to transfer recovered pilots to shore. They retain an armament and can conduct most roles of the basic Fairmile B.

207

HMS Seagull

SURVEY SHIPS
HALCYON CLASS

Ship	Completed	Builder
SEAGULL	30.05.38	HM Dockyard (Devonport)

Displacement 830 tons (1,330 tons FL) Dimensions 245ft x 33ft 6in x 7ft Machinery Parsons geared turbines, 2 Admiralty 3-drum boilers, 1,750 shp Speed 17 knots Complement 80

Notes

Originally a Halcyon class minesweeping sloop, at the end of the war was taken in hand, initially, at Rotterdam for conversion to a survey ship and later at HM Dockyard Chatham for installation of specialist hydrographic equipment. On completion in April 1946 the ship recommissioned and conducted surveys in Home Waters until March last year, when she paid off and reduced to reserve at Devonport.

HMS Adamant

SUBMARINE DEPOT SHIPS
ADAMANT CLASS

Ship	Completed	Builder
ADAMANT	28.02.42	Harland & Wolff (Belfast)

Displacement 12,700 tons (16,500 tons FL) **Dimensions** 658ft x 70ft 6in x 21ft 3in
Machinery Parsons geared turbines, 4 Admiralty 3-drum boilers, 2 shafts, 8,000 shp
Speed 17 knots **Armament** 8 x 4.5in, 16 x 2pdr, 4 x 40mm, 10 x 20mm **Complement**
1,273

Notes

Completed in 1942, she served in the Eastern Fleet with the 4th Submarine Flotilla and
in 1943 moved to Fremantle, Australia. She returned to the UK in 1950 since when she
has served as flagship of the Senior Officer, Reserve Fleet, Portsmouth. As a Submarine
Depot Ship she is equipped with all of the workshops necessary for supporting, repair-
ing and maintaining up to nine submarines and has the capacity to accommodate their
crews.

209

HMS Woolwich

DESTROYER DEPOT SHIPS
WOOLWICH CLASS

Ship	Completed	Builder
WOOLWICH	00.06.35	Fairfield SB & Eng Co (Govan)

Displacement 8,750 tons (10,200 tons FL)   Dimensions 608ft x 64ft x 16ft 6in
Machinery 2 sets Parsons triple reduction geared turbines, 4 Admiralty 3-drum boilers,
2 shafts, 6,500 shp Speed 15 knots Armament 4 x 4in, 2 x 20mm Complement 406

Notes

Carries a full range of machine tools for heavy repairs. Equipped with two 3-ton cranes,
a single 20-ton derrick and a similar 6-ton derrick. Unlike the latter clases of depot ship,
she is quite lightly armed carrying just 4 single 4-inch guns and various close range guns.
During the war she had magazines cabable of storing 200 depth charges and over 100
torpedoes for replenishing her destroyers.

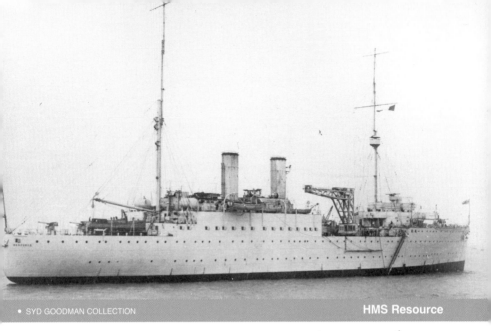

HMS Resource

RESOURCE CLASS

Ship	Completed	Builder
RESOURCE	27.11.28 (L)	Vickers-Armstrong (Barrow)

Displacement 12,300 tons (15,580 tons FL) Dimensions 534ft x 83ft 3in x 22ft 11in Machinery Parsons geared turbines, 4 Yarrow boilers, 2 shafts, 7,500 shp Speed 15½ knots Armament 4 x 4in (4 x single) Complement 581

Notes

Since returning to the UK at the end of World War II she has been the Senior Officer's ship of the Reserve Fleet at Portsmouth. She relinquished this role in 1951 and was paid off, her future uncertain.

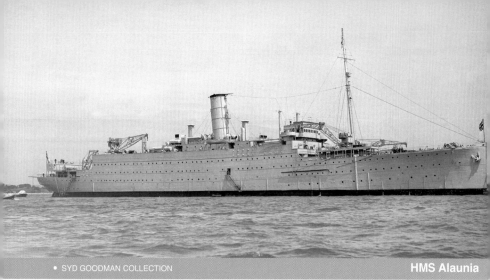

HMS Alaunia

HEAVY REPAIR SHIPS
ALAUNIA CLASS

Ship	Completed	Builder
ALAUNIA	07.02.28 (L)	J. Brown (Clydebank)
ARTIFEX (ex-AURANIA)	06.02.24 (L)	Swan Hunter & Wigham Richardson
AUSONIA	22.03.21 (L)	Armstrong Whitworth (Walker)

Displacement 19,000 tons (20,760 tons FL) Dimensions 519ft 9in x 65ft 3in x 31ft 6in Machinery Geared turbines, 2 shafts, 8,500 shp Speed 15 knots Complement 600

Notes

Former Cunard Liners taken over by the Admiralty during World War II. AURANIA was initially requisitioned in 1939 to operate as an Armed Merchant Cruiser, as was AUSONIA. Subsequently in 1942 both were sold to the Admiralty and converted as Heavy Repair Ships. AURANIA was renamed ARTIFEX on completion of the conversion. Since 1947 she has been based at Rosyth for Artificer Apprentice training. AUSONIA had remained in reserve in Scotland and Chatham since returning from the Far East at the end of the war. In 1951 she began a refit and, on completion, is reportedly scheduled to replace RANPURA. ALAUNIA was acquired in 1944 to operate as a Heavy Repair Ship and since 1949 has served as a Static Training Ship at Devonport.

HMS Pioneer

COLOSSUS CLASS

Ship	Completed	Builder
PIONEER (ex-MARS)	08.02.45	Vickers Armstrong (Barrow)

Displacement 12,265 tons (16,500 tons FL) **Dimensions** 694ft 6in x 80ft 6in x 23ft
Machinery Parsons SR geared turbines, 4 Admiralty 3-drum boilers, 2 shafts, 40,000
shp **Speed** 25 knots **Armament** 16 x 2pdr, 16 x 40mm **Complement** 1,076

Notes

Originally laid down as carrier a of the Colossus class named MARS she was completed as an Aircraft Maintenance Carrier. She returned to the UK at the end of WWII and paid off into reserve where she remains.

HMS Mull of Kintyre

MAINTENANCE SHIPS
HEAD CLASS

Ship	Completed	Builder
BERRY HEAD	20.03.45	Burrard Dry Dock (North Vancouver)
BUCHAN NESS	26.07.45	West Coast SB (Vancouver)
DODMAN POINT	03.10.45	Burrard Dry Dock (North Vancouver)
DUNCANSBY HEAD	08.08.45	Burrard Dry Dock (North Vancouver)
GIRDLE NESS	05.09.45	Burrard (South Yard Vancouver)
HARTLAND POINT	11.07.45	Burrard (South Yard Vancouver)
MULL OF GALLOWAY	15.05.45	North Van Ship Repair (Vancouver)
MULL OF KINTYRE	24.10.45	North Van Ship Repair (Vancouver)
RAME HEAD	18.08.45	North Van Ship Repair (Vancouver)

Displacement 8,580 tons (11,270 tons FL) Dimensions 441ft 6in x 57ft 3in x 20ft Machinery Steam reciprocating, 2 Foster Wheeler water-tube boilers, single shaft, 2,500 ihp Speed 11 knots Armament 16-32 x 20mm Complement 445

Notes

It was quickly realised during the war in the Pacific, that base facilities woud be few and far between and that it would therefore be essential that the Allies be able to support their fleet with mobile facilities. For the Royal Navy this involved the acquisition of a number of maintenance ships. Selection fell to the Victory ship design and construction in Canadian yards was undertaken to supply a basic maintenance ship design that could be adapted for vaious roles with little alteration from the original plan.

BERRY HEAD, DUNCANSBY HEAD and RAME HEAD were completed as Escort Maintenance Ships, each capable of supporting up to twenty-five escort ships. Basic structural modifications to the basic Victory ship design included plating over the large hatch covers and fitting decks in the holds. Superstructure was extended and additional deckhouses built. Workshops and foundries and heavy engineering spaces were installed. The original cargo handling derricks were retained and two ramped cargo lighters embarked.

BUCHAN NESS and GIRDLE NESS were completed as LCM Maintenance Ships, each required to maintain 54 major landing craft or up to 162 smaller vessels. Space provided in the original design for foundries and smithies was replaced by engine storage facilities.

DODMAN POINT and HARTLAND POINT were completed as LST Maintenance Ships, each required to maintain 36 LSTs.

MULL OF GALLOWAY and MULL OF KINTYRE were completed as Motor Craft Maintenance Ships each required to support HDMLs, BYMSs and MFVs. Again extra provision was made for spare engine stowage.

BEACHY HEAD had been on loan to the Royal Netherlands Navy as VULKAAN but was returned to the RN in 1950. It has been reported that the ship is to be transferred to Canada in the near future to join sistership FLAMBOROUGH HEAD which was transferred in 1951. BERRY HEAD is in reserve at Plymouth.

215

HMS Guardian

NET LAYERS
GUARDIAN CLASS

Ship	Completed	Builder
GUARDIAN	13.06.33	HM Dockyard (Chatham)

Displacement 2,860 tons (3,665 tons FL) Dimensions 338ft x 53ft x 11ft 3in
Machinery Parsons geared turbines, 2 Admiralty 3-drum boilers, 2 shafts, 6,500 shp
Speed 16 knots Armament 2 x 4in, 6-10 x 20mm Complement 181

Notes

Designed to carry, lay and retrieve a net defence system in order to protect and render
safe, exposed anchorages or undefended harbours. She has a secondary role of fleet
photography work. Nets, sinkers and buoys are stowed to port and starboard on the
upperdeck from just forward of the mainmast. The structure straddling the net handling
deck at the stern, and surmounted by a gun, is the photographic cabin. She is slightly
smaller and has less powerful machinery than her newer sister ship PROTECTOR.

216

SHIPS OF THE FUTURE FLEET

In addition to those vessels already listed which are under construction, there remain several programmes underway, but none of which have yet completed. Their details are listed below.

AIRCRAFT CARRIERS

Centaur Class

Ship	Laid Down	Builder
CENTAUR	30.05.44	Harland & Wolff (Belfast)
ALBION	23.03.44	Swan Hunter & Wigham Richardson
BULWARK	10.05.45	Harland & Wolff (Belfast)
HERMES (ex-ELEPHANT)	21.06.44	Vickers Armstrong (Barrow)

Displacement 23,300 tons (27,705 tons FL) Dimensions 737ft 9in x 123ft 6in x 28ft Machinery Parsons geared turbines, 4 x Admiralty three-drum boilers, 2 shafts, 78,000 shp Speed 28 knots Complement 1,035

Notes

All four ships were laid up incomplete following launch while their futures were decided - with the rapid pace of aircraft development and of carrier innovation, the opportunity was taken to redesign these vessels in order to incorporate many of the improvements. Work resumed and CENTAUR is scheduled to complete in 1953, pretty much to her original design. ALBION and BULWARK will follow but will complete with an angled flight deck and mirror landing sights although hydraulic catapults will be retained initially. HERMES construction was suspended in 1945 but resumed again in 1952 in order to clear the slipway. Her future is undecided at this time, but it is probable that she too will be completed to an improved design.

CRUISERS

Defence Class

Ship	Laid Down	Builder
DEFENCE	24.06.42	Scott's SB & Eng Co (Greenock)

217

Ship	Laid Down	Builder
TIGER	01.10.41	J. Brown & Co (Clydebank)
BLAKE	17.08.42	Fairfield SB & Eng Co (Govan)

Displacement 9,550 tons (11,700 tons FL) **Dimensions** 555ft 6in x 64ft x 23ft
Machinery Parsons geared turbines, 4 x Admiralty three-drum boilers, 2 shafts, 80,000 shp **Speed** 31½ knots **Complement** 800-850 estimated

Notes

These three vessels have been laid up incomplete since their launch, with all work suspended. The decision to complete these ships was made in 1951, but to date little sign of work has been noted. It is thought that problems with the design of a new type of rapid fire, water-cooled main armament is preventing a final configuration being determined and thereby further delaying the project.

SUBMARINES

Ex Class

Ship	Laid Down	Builder
EXCALIBUR	13.02.52	Vickers Armstrong (Barrow)
EXPLORER	20.07.51	Vickers Armstrong (Barrow)

Displacement 776 tons **Dimensions** 225ft 6in x 15ft 8in x 18ft 2in **Machinery** 2 x Vickers hydrogen peroxide turbines **Speed** Not known **Complement** 41-49

Notes

Experimental submarines ordered on 26 August 1947. Following on from the experience gained with the captured German U-Boat U-1407 (renamed HMS METEORITE) these two new vessels are to further test the application of High Test Peroxide (HTP) as a possible new fuel source for submarines.

X Class

Ship	Laid Down	Builder
X 51	Ordered	Vickers Armstrong (Barrow)

Ship	Laid Down	Builder
X 52	Ordered	Vickers Armstrong (Barrow)
X 53	Ordered	Vickers Armstrong (Barrow)
X 54	Ordered	Vickers Armstrong (Barrow)

Displacement 32 tons **Dimensions** 50ft 8in x 6ft x 7ft 6in **Machinery** 1 x Perkins P6 6-cylinder diesel, 1 x electric motor, 1 shaft **Speed** 6 knots approx **Complement** 5

Notes

Ordered in September 1951 to replace the worn out XE class of midget submarine.

Porpoise Class

Ship	Laid Down	Builder
CACHALOT	Ordered	Scott's SB & Eng. Co (Grenock)
FINWHALE	Ordered	Cammell Laird (Birkenhead)
GRAMPUS	Ordered	Cammell Laird (Birkenhead)
NARWHAL	Ordered	Vickers Armstrong (Barrow)
PORPOISE	Ordered	Vickers Armstrong (Barrow)
RORQUAL	Ordered	Vickers Armstrong (Barrow)

Displacement 1,605 tons standard (2,030 tons surfaced, 2,405 tons dived) **Dimensions** 295ft 3in x 26ft 6in x 18ft **Machinery** 2 ASR 1 turbocharged 16 cylinder diesel generator sets, 2 shafts, 3,680 bhp, 2 main batteries, electric drive 6,000 hp **Speed** 12 knots (surface) 17 knots (dived) **Armament** 8 x 21in TT **Complement** 71

Notes

The first class of patrol submarines to be constructed since the end of the war. It is intended that they will be able to undertake continuous submerged patrols using their snorting capabilities. They will have an all welded streamlined hull to allow greater underwater speed and deeper diving depths. All six submarines were ordered on 19 April 1951.

FRIGATES

Type 41 Anti-Aircraft Frigate

Ship	Laid Down	Builder
JAGUAR	Ordered	Wm Denny & Bros (Dumbarton)
LYNX	Ordered	J. Brown & Co (Clydebank)
PANTHER	Ordered	J. Brown & Co (Clydeside)
PUMA	Ordered	Scott's SB & Eng Co (Greenock)
LEOPARD	Ordered	HM Dockyard (Portsmouth)

Displacement 2,300 tons (2,520 tons FL) Dimensions 340ft x 40ft x 16ft Machinery Eight Admiralty Standard Range Diesels in three engine rooms, 2 shafts, 12,380 bhp Speed 24 knots Armament 4 x 4.5in (2 x twin), 1 x 40mm, Squid AS mortar Complement 205

Notes

These diesel engined vessels are designed for the protection of convoys against air attack. They are also expected to serve as medium destroyers in offensive operations. It remains to be seen whether they will make good fleet ships with their comparatively slow speed. Four ships were ordered on 28 June 1951 (JAGUAR, LYNX, PUMA and PANTHER). A fifth, LEOPARD, was ordered on 21 August 1951.

Type 61 Aircraft Direction Frigate

Ship	Laid Down	Builder
SALISBURY	23.01.52	HM Dockyard (Devonport)
CHICHESTER	Ordered	Fairfield SB & Eng Co (Govan)
LLANDAFF	Ordered	Hawthorn Leslie (Hebburn)
LINCOLN	Ordered	Fairfield SB & Eng Co (Govan)

Displacement 2,170 tons (2,350 tons FL) Dimensions 339ft 9in x 40ft x 15ft 6in Machinery Eight Admiralty Standard Range Diesels in three engine rooms, 2 shafts, 12,380 bhp Speed 24 knots Armament 2 x 4.5in (1 x twin), 2 x 40mm, Squid AS mortar Complement 210

220

This second group of diesel engined frigates is to be optimised for the direction of carrier-borne and shore based aircraft. Construction is to be all welded and comprising prefabricated blocks to enable rapid construction in an emergency. Four vessels were ordered on 28 June 1951 and bear the names of Cathedral Cities.

Type 14 Utility Anti-Submarine Frigate

Ship	Laid Down	Builder
BLACKWOOD	Ordered	J.I. Thornycroft (Southampton)
DUNCAN	Ordered	J.I. Thornycroft (Southampton)
DUNDAS	17.10.52	J.S. White & Co (Cowes)
EXMOUTH	Ordered	J.S. White & Co (Cowes)
GRAFTON	Ordered	J.S. White & Co (Cowes)
HARDY	Ordered	Yarrow (Scotstoun)
KEPPEL	Ordered	Yarrow (Scotstoun)
MALCOLM	Ordered	Yarrow (Scotstoun)
MURRAY	Ordered	A Stephen & Sons Ltd (Linthouse)
PALLISER	Ordered	A Stephen & Sons Ltd (Linthouse)
PELLEW	Ordered	Swan Hunter & Wigham Richardson
RUSSELL	Ordered	Swan Hunter & Wigham Richardson

Displacement 1,180 tons (1,535 FL) Dimensions 310ft x 33ft x 15ft 6in Machinery 1 geared steam turbine, 2 x Babcock & Wilcox boilers, 1 shaft Armament 3 x 40mm Bofors, 2 x Limbo AS mortar, 4 x 21in TT (2 x twin) Speed 27 knots Complement 140

Notes

A new class of small utility frigates designed primarily for A/S operations. They will have no main gun armament, but will carry a heavy anti-submarine weapon load including two triple A/S mortars and four 21-inch torpedo tubes. They will have a steam-powered machinery plant driving a single shaft. Twelve Type 14 frigates were ordered on 6 March 1951.

Type 12 Anti-Submarine Frigate

Ship	Laid Down	Builder
WHITBY	30.09.52	Cammell Laird (Birkenhead)
BLACKPOOL	Ordered	Harland & Wolff (Belfast)
EASTBOURNE	Ordered	Vickers Armstrong (Tyne)
SCARBOROUGH	Ordered	Vickers Armstrong (Tyne)
TENBY	Ordered	Cammell Laird (Birkenhead)
TORQUAY	Ordered	Harland & Wolff (Birkenhead)

Displacement 2,150 tons (2,560 tons FL) Dimensions 369ft 9in x 41ft x 17ft 6in Machinery 2 sets double reduction geared steam turbines, 2 shafts, 30,430 shp Speed 31 knots Armament 2 x 4.5in (1 x twin), 2 x 40mm (1 x twin), 12 x 21in TT (2 x twin, 8 x single), 2 x Limbo AS mortar Complement 221

Notes

Primarily designed for the location, detection and destruction of submarines, these first-rate frigates will be fitted with the latest underwater detection equipment and anti-submarine weapons. They will have good seakeeping qualities and sufficient power to enable them to maintain high speeds in rough seas. The first of class WHITBY was ordered on 2 February 1951. A further 5 frigates, BLACKPOOL, EASTBOURNE, SCARBOROUGH, TENBY and TORQUAY were all ordered on 6 March 1951.

MINE WARFARE VESSELS

Coastal Minesweepers

Ship	Laid Down	Builder
CONISTON (ex CMS 01)	09.07.52 (L)	J.I. Thornycroft & Co (Woolston)
ALCASTON (ex CMS 02)	03.07.51	J.I. Thornycroft & Co (Woolston)
ALFRISTON (ex CMS 03)	16.08.51	J.I. Thornycroft & Co (Woolston)
ALVERTON (ex CMS 04)	18.11.52 (L)	Camper & Nicholson Ltd (Gosport)
AMERTON (ex CMS 05)	09.07.51	Camper & Nicholson Ltd (Gosport)

Ship	Laid Down	Builder
APPLETON (ex CMS 06)	04.09.52 (L)	Goole Shipbuilding Ltd
BEACHAMPTON (ex CMS 07)	09.04.51	Goole Shipbuilding Ltd
BEVINGTON (ex CMS 08)	13.09.51	White's Shipyard (Southampton)
BICKINGTON (ex CMS 09)	21.09.51	White's Shipyard (Southampton)
BILDESTON (ex CMS 10)	09.06.52 (L)	J. S. Doig (Grimsby)
EDDERTON (ex CMS 11)	01.11.52 (L)	J. S. Doig (Grimsby)
BOULSTON (ex CMS 12)	05.10.52 (L)	Richards Ironworks (Lowestoft)
BRERETON (ex CMS 13)	25.09.51	Richards Ironworks (Lowestoft)
BRINTON (ex CMS 14)	08.08.52 (L)	Cook, Welton & Gemmell
BRONINGTON (ex CMS 15)	30.05.51	Cook, Welton & Gemmell
BURNASTON (ex CMS 16)	03.05.51	Fleetlands Shipyard (Gosport)
BUTTINGTON (ex CMS 17)	26.11.51	Fleetlands Shipyard (Gosport)
CALTON (ex CMS 18)	18.02.52	Wivenhoe Shipyard Ltd
CARHAMPTON (ex CMS 19)	Ordered	Wivenhoe Shipyard Ltd
CAUNTON (ex CMS 20)	28.01.52	Montrose Shipyard Ltd
CHEDISTON (ex CMS 21)	30.04.52	Montrose Shipyard Ltd
CHILCOMPTON (ex CMS 22)	27.12.51	Herd & McKenzie
CLARBESTON (ex CMS 23)	12.03.52	Richards Ironworks (Lowestoft)
CRICHTON (ex CMS 24)	21.04.52	J. S. Doig (Grimsby)
CUXTON (ex CMS 25)	02.07.52	Camper & Nicholson Ltd (Gosport)
DALSWINTON (ex CMS 26)	26.03.52	White's Shipyard (Southampton)
DARLASTON (ex CMS 27)	30.09.52	Cook, Welton & Gemmell
DERRITON (ex CMS 28)	17.12.52	J.I. Thornycroft & Co (Woolston)
OULSTON (ex-CMS 29)	Ordered	J. S. Doig (Grimsby)
HIGHBURTON (ex-CMS 30)	Ordered	J.I. Thornycroft & Co (Woolston)
HICKLETON (ex-CMS 31)	Ordered	J.I. Thornycroft & Co (Woolston)

Ship	Laid Down	Builder
BLAXTON (ex CMS 32)	Ordered	J.I. Thornycroft & Co (Woolston)
BOSSINGTON (ex-CMS 33)	Ordered	J.I. Thornycroft & Co (Woolston)
ESSINGTON (ex-CMS 34)	Ordered	Camper & Nicholson Ltd (Soton)
FENTON (ex-CMS 35)	Ordered	Camper & Nicholson Ltd (Soton)
FITTLETON (ex-CMS 36)	15.09.52	White's Shipyard (Itchen)
FLOCKTON (ex-CMS 37)	Ordered	White's Shipyard (Itchen)
FLORISTON (ex-CMS 38)	08.12.52	Richards Ironworks (Lowestoft)
SOMERLEYTON (ex-CMS 39)	Ordered	Richards Ironworks (Lowestoft)
GAVINTON (ex-CMS 40)	29.09.52	J. S. Doig (Grimsby)
GLASSERTON (ex-CMS 41)	Ordered	J. S. Doig (Grimsby)
HAZELTON (ex-CMS 42)	Ordered	Cook, Welton & Gemmell
HEXTON (ex-CMS 43)	Ordered	Cook, Welton & Gemmell
DUNKERTON (ex CMS 44)	25.09.52	Goole Shipbuilding Ltd
DUFTON	Ordered	Goole Shipbuilding Ltd
HODGESTON	22.09.52	Fleetlands Shipyard (Gosport)
HUBBERSTON	Ordered	Fleetlands Shipyard (Gosport)
ILMINGTON	24.12.52	Camper & Nicholson Ltd (Gosport)
BADMINTON	Ordered	Camper & Nicholson Ltd (Gosport)
INVERMORISTON	03.11.52	Dorset Yacht Company (Poole)
IVESTON	22.10.52	Philip & Son (Dartmouth)
JACKTON	Ordered	Philip & Son (Dartmouth)
KEDLESTON	26.11.52	Wm Pickersgill & Sons (Sunderland)
KELLINGTON	Ordered	Wm Pickersgill & Sons (Sunderland)
DILSTON	Ordered	Cook, Welton & Gemmell
PENSTON	Ordered	Cook, Welton & Gemmell
PICTON	Ordered	Cook, Welton & Gemmell
ALDINGTON	Ordered	Camper & Nicholson Ltd (Soton)

Ship	Laid Down	Builder
THANKERTON	Ordered	Camper & Nicholson Ltd (Soton)
POLLINGTON	Ordered	Camper & Nicholson Ltd (Soton)
PUNCHESTON	Ordered	Richards Ironworks (Lowestoft)
QUAINTON	Ordered	Richards Ironworks (Lowestoft)
RENNINGTON	Ordered	Richards Ironworks (Lowestoft)
RODINGTON	Ordered	Fleetlands Shipyard (Gosport)
SANTON	Ordered	Fleetlands Shipyard (Gosport)
SEFTON	Ordered	White's Shipyard (Itchen)
SHAVINGTON	Ordered	White's Shipyard (Itchen)
SHERATON	Ordered	White's Shipyard (Itchen)
SHOULTON	Ordered	Montrose Shipyard Ltd
SINGLETON	Ordered	Montrose Shipyard Ltd
SULLINGTON	Ordered	J. S. Doig (Grimsby)
SWANSTON	Ordered	J. S. Doig (Grimsby)
TARLTON	Ordered	J. S. Doig (Grimsby)

Displacement 360 tons (425 FL) Dimensions 153ft x 28ft 9in x 8ft Machinery Mirrlees diesels driving two shafts, 2,500 bhp Armament 1 x 40mm, 2 x 20mm Speed 15 knots Complement 30 average

Notes

These are the first of a new type of coastal minesweeper designed to counter the latest generation of sea mine. They have a double mahogany hull over an aluminium alloy frame, designed for the lowest possible magnetic signature. J.I Thornycroft & Co Ltd of Woolston have been selected as the parent firm for the group of shipbuilders who will produce these ships. The first batch of ships were ordered on 9 September 1950 (CMS 01-15) followed by CMS 16-17 on 20 October 1950. A further batch of ten were ordered on 4 April 1951 (CMS 18-27) with another order for 17 ships being placed in on 28 September 1951 (CMS 28-44). A further four orders were placed in 1952 as follows: M1145-49 (14 February); M1150-51 (19 March); M1152-54 (21 April); M1155-97 (22 March) and M1168-1186 (17 June).

Originally these vessels were to be un-named carrying a CMS designation followed by a number. It was further determined that they be named after insects, with a colour prefix denoting their specific roles. By March 1952 village names (with the suffix -ton) were being assigned to the ships and the CMS numbers being replaced by four figure pennants in the 1100 series preceded by the letter 'M'. Therefore CMS 01 became M1101 etc. Although no ship was launched bearing the proposed Insect class names, they have been included here for completeness.

CONISTON (ex-RED ANT); ALCASTON (ex-BLUE ANT); ALFRISTON (ex-GREEN ANT); ALVERTON (ex-GOLDEN ANT); AMERTON (ex-RED APHIS); APPLETON (ex-BLUE APHIS); BEACHAMPTON (ex-GREEN APHIS); BEVINGTON (ex-GOLDEN APHIS); BICKINGTON (ex-RED BEE); BILDESTON (ex-BLUE BEE); EDDERTON (ex-GREEN BEE); BOULSTON (ex-GOLDEN BEE); BRERETON (ex-RED BEETLE); BRINTON (ex-BLUE BEETLE); BRONINGTON (ex-GREEN BEETLE); BURNASTON (ex-GOLDEN BEETLE); BUTTINGTON (ex-RED BUTTERFLY); CALTON (ex-BLUE BUTTERFLY); CARHAMPTON (ex-GREEN BUTTERFLY); CAUNTON (ex-GOLDEN BUTTERFLY); CHEDISTON (ex-RED CENTIPEDE); CHILCOMPTON (ex-BLUE CENTIPEDE); CLARBESTON (ex-GREEN CENTIPEDE); CRICHTON (ex-GOLDEN CENTIPEDE); CUXTON (ex-RED CICALA); DALSWINTON (ex-BLUE CICALA); DARLASTON (ex-GREEN CICALA); DERRITON (ex-GOLDEN CICALA); OULSTON (ex-RED COCKCHAFER); HIGHBURTON (ex-BLUE COCKCHAFER); HICKLETON (ex-GREEN COCKCHAFER); BLAXTON (ex-GOLDEN COCKCHAFER); BOSSINGTON (ex-EMBLE-TON; ex-RED CRICKET); ESSINGTON (ex-BLUE CRICKET); FENTON (ex-GREEN CRICKET); FITTLETON (ex-GOLDEN CRICKET); FLOCKTON (ex-RED DRAGONFLY); FLORISTON (ex-BLUE DRAGONFLY); SOMERLEYTON (ex-GAMSTON, ex-GREEN DRAGONFLY); GAVINTON (ex-GOLDEN DRAGONFLY); GLASSERTON (ex-RED FIREFLY); HAZELTON (ex-BLUE FIREFLY); HEXTON (ex-GREEN FIREFLY); DUNKER-TON (ex-GOLDEN FIREFLY); BADMINTON (ex-ILSTON); MONKTON (ex-KELTON); KIL-DARTON (ex-LISTON); DILSTON (ex-PILSTON); ALDINGTON (ex-PITTINGTON).

Thorpe Class

Ship	Laid Down	Builder
CUTTHORPE (ex-AMS 01)	Ordered	J.S. White & Co (Cowes)
AINTHORPE (ex-AMS 02)	Ordered	Camper & Nicholson Ltd (Gosport)
BILSTHORPE (ex-AMS 03)	Ordered	Camper & Nicholson Ltd (Gosport)

Ordered on 9 September 1950 these vessels are similar to the CMS but are to be built of composite materials. The vessels were previously named BLACK ANT (CUTTHOR-PE); GREY ANT (AINTHORPE) and SILVER ANT (BILSTHORPE).

226

Inshore Minesweepers

Ship	Laid Down	Builder
INGLESHAM (ex-IMS 01)	23.04.52 (L)	J.S. White & Co (Cowes)
ALTHAM (ex-IMS 02)	02.12.52 (L)	Camper & Nicholson Ltd (Gosport)
ARLINGHAM (ex-IMS 03)	30.07.51	Camper & Nicholson Ltd (Gosport)
ASHELDHAM (ex-IMS 04)	30.09.52 (L)	Philip & Son (Dartmouth)
BASSINGHAM (ex-IMS 05)	24.06.52 (L)	Vosper
BEDHAM (ex-IMS 06)	29.06.51	J. L. Bolson (Poole)
BISHAM (ex-IMS 07)	26.11.51	J. L. Bolson (Poole)
BLUNHAM (ex-IMS 08)	12.06.52 (L)	Brooke Marine (Lowestoft)
BODENHAM (ex-IMS 09)	21.08.52 (L)	Brooke Marine (Lowestoft)
BOREHAM (ex-IMS 10)	21.10.52 (L)	Brooke Marine (Lowestoft)
BOTTISHAM (ex-IMS 11)	29.06.51	Ailsa SB Co Ltd (Troon)
BRANTINGHAM (ex-IMS 12)	30.08.51	Ailsa SB Co Ltd (Troon)
BRIGHAM (ex-IMS 13)	12.03.51	Berthon Boat
BUCKLESHAM (ex-IMS 14)	14.09.51	Ardrossan
CARDINGHAM (ex-IMS 15)	24.06.52 (L)	Herd & Mackenzie (Buckie)
CHELSHAM (ex-IMS 16)	09.07.52 (L)	Jones (Buckie)
CHILLINGHAM (ex-IMS 17)	19.12.52 (L)	McLean & Sons
COBHAM (ex-IMS 18)	14.03.51	Fairlie Yacht
CRANHAM (ex-IMS 19)	27.10.52	J.S. White & Co (Cowes)
FRETTENHAM (ex-IMS 20)	Ordered	J.S. White & Co (Cowes)
DARSHAM (ex-IMS 21)	19.11.52 (L)	Jones (Buckie)
DAVENHAM (ex-IMS 22)	18.09.51	Weatherhead
DITTISHAM (ex-IMS 23)	06.11.52	Fairlie Yacht Slip (Glasgow)
DOWNHAM (ex-IMS 24)	30.06.52	J.S. White & Co (Cowes)
EDLINGHAM (ex-IMS 25)	Ordered	Weatherhead (Cockenzie)

Ship	Laid Down	Builder
ELSENHAM (ex-IMS 26)	Ordered	Ailsa SB Co Ltd (Troon)
ETCHINGHAM (ex-IMS 27))	Ordered	Ailsa SB Co Ltd (Troon)
EVERINGHAM (ex-IMS 28)	Ordered	Philip (Dartmouth)
FELMERSHAM (ex-IMS 29)	24.09.52	Camper & Nicholson Ltd (Gosport)
FLINTHAM (ex-IMS 30)	30.10.52	J. L. Bolson (Poole)
DAMERHAM (ex-IMS 31)	12.08.52	Brooke Marine (Lowestoft)
FRITHAM (ex-IMS 32)	19.09.52	Brooke Marine (Lowestoft)
GLENTHAM (ex-IMS 33)	Ordered	Ardrossan Dockyard
GREETHAM (ex-IMS 34)	09.09.52	Herd & Mackenzie (Buckie)
HALSHAM (ex-IMS 35)	13.11.52	Jones (Buckie)
HARPHAM (ex-IMS 36)	08.09.52	Jones (Buckie)
HAVERSHAM (ex-IMS 37)	26.12.52	McLean & Sons
LASHAM (ex-IMS 38)	05.08.52	Weatherhead
HOVINGHAM (ex-IMS 39)	Ordered	Fairlie Yacht Slip (Glasgow)
ISHAM (ex-IMS 40)	Ordered	Weatherhead (Cockenzie)
KINGHAM (ex-IMS 41)	Ordered	Weatherhead (Cockenzie)
HILDERSHAM (ex-IMS 42)	Ordered	Vosper (Portsmouth)
LEDSHAM (ex-IMS 43)	Ordered	Bolson (Poole)
LITTLEHAM (ex-IMS 44)	Ordered	Brooke Marine (Lowestoft)
LUDHAM (ex-IMS 45)	Ordered	Fairlie Yacht Slip
MERSHAM (ex-IMS 46)	Ordered	Harris (Appledore)
MICKLEHAM (ex-IMS 47)	Ordered	Bethon Boat Co (Lymington)
MILEHAM (ex-IMS 48)	Ordered	Blackmore (Bideford)

Displacement 120 tons (159 FL)   Dimensions 106ft 6in x 21ft 3in x 5ft 6 in
Machinery Davey Paxman diesels driving two shafts, 1,100 bhp   Speed 14 knots
Armament 1 x 40mm or 1 x 20mm   Complement 15

Another new type of minesweeper, these smaller vessels are designed to operate in shallow waters such as rivers and estuaries. The early boats are of composite construction but it is intended that most of the later boats will feature wooden hulls. IMS 01-13 ordered 09 September 1950 and IMS 14-18 on 29 September. IMS 19-24 ordered on 23 April 1951 while the next batch IMS 25-47 were ordered on 17 October with the final order for the year being placed on 20 November 1951 for IMS 48.

Similar to the coastal minesweepers these boats were initially to have been un-named, carrying just the IMS designator and a number. Again they were renamed and assigned Bird names with a colour prefix. Just as in the earlier class these names have now given way to village names (with the suffix -ham). The earlier names are included here for completeness.

INGLESHAM (RED BANTAM); ALTHAM (ex-BLUE BANTAM); ARLINGHAM (ex-GREEN BANTAM); ASHELDHAM (ex-GOLDEN BANTAM); BASSINGHAM (ex-RED BULLFINCH); BEDHAM (ex-BLUE BULLFINCH); BISHAM (ex-GREEN BULLFINCH); BLUNHAM (ex-GOLDEN BULLFINCH); BODENHAM (ex-RED CHAFFINCH); BOREHAM (ex-BLUE CHAFFINCH); BOTTISHAM (ex-GREEN CHAFFINCH); BRANTINGHAM (ex-GOLDEN CHAFFINCH); BRIGHAM (ex-RED CROW); BUCKLESHAM (ex-BLUE CROW); CARDINGHAM (ex-GREEN CROW); CHELSHAM (ex-GOLDEN CROW); CHILLINGHAM (ex-RED CUCKOO); COBHAM (ex-BLUE CUCKOO); CRANHAM (ex-GREEN CUCKOO); FRETTENHAM (ex-GOLDEN CUCKOO); DARSHAM (ex-RED DOVE); DAVENHAM (ex-BLUE DOVE); DITTISHAM (ex-GREEN DOVE) and DOWNHAM (ex-GOLDEN DOVE).

Inshore Minehunters

Ship	Laid Down	Builder
DINGLEY (ex-BMS 01)	03.09.52 (L)	J.S. White & Co (Cowes)
AVELEY (ex-BMS 02)	09.10.51	J.S. White & Co (Cowes)
BREARLEY (ex-BMS 03)	19.09.51	J.S. White & Co (Cowes)
BRENCHLEY (ex-BMS 04)	16.09.51	Saunders Roe (Anglesey)
BRINKLEY (ex-BMS 05)	16.09.51	Saunders Roe (Anglesey)
BROADLEY (ex-BMS 06)	19.12.51	Blackmore
BROOMLEY (ex-BMS 07)	19.11.51	P. K. Harris

Ship	Laid Down	Builder
BURLEY (ex-BMS 08)	01.10.51	Dorset Yacht Company
CHAILEY (ex-BMS 09)	18.11.52	Saunders Roe (Anglesey)
CRADLEY (ex-BMS 10)	14.11.52	Saunders Roe (Anglesey)
CUFFLEY (ex-BMS 11)	Ordered	J.S. White & Co (Cowes))
DOWNLEY (ex-BMS 12)	Ordered	J.S. White & Co (Cowes)
EDGELEY (ex-BMS 13)	Ordered	Dorset Yacht Co (Hamworthy)

Displacement 123 tons (164 tons FL) Dimensions 106ft 9in x 21ft 9in x 5ft 6in Machinery 2 x 8-cyl Davey Paxman diesels, 2 shafts, 7,000 bhp Armament 1 x 40mm or 1 x 20mm Speed 13 knots Complement 15

Notes

Similar to the Inshore Minesweepers, these vessels are designed for the detection of mines in shallow waters. Their hull design is similar but are all of composite construction. Their superstructure is longer to accommodate the detection gear and operation room. As a consequence of not needing to tow sweep wires they have a less powerful engines than the inshore minesweepers. BMS 01-03 were ordered on 9 September 1950. BMS 04-08 were ordered 23 April 1951 and BMS 09-13, 17 October 1951.

Name Changes

These ships also underwent several name changes before village names with the suffix -ley were finally adopted. Once again, their original Bird names have been listed here for completeness.

AVELEY (ex-GREY BANTAM); BREARLEY (ex-SILVER BANTAM); BRENCHLEY (ex-WHITE BANTAM); BRINKLEY (ex-BLACK BULLFINCH); BROADLEY (ex-GREY BULLFINCH); BROOMLEY (ex-SILVER BULLFINCH); BURLEY (ex-WHITE BULLFINCH); DINGLEY (ex-BLACK BANTAM)

COASTAL FORCES

Bold Class

Ship	Laid Down	Builder
BOLD PIONEER	18.08.51(L)	J.S. White & Co (Cowes)

230

Displacement 138 tons **Dimensions** 122ft 9in x 25ft x 6ft 9in **Machinery** 2 Metro-Vick G2 turbines supplemented by 2 Mercedes diesel engines, 4 shafts **Armament** 1 x 4.5in, 4 x TT **Speed** 43 knots **Complement** 20

Notes

Two large fast attack craft intended to be powered by both diesel and gas turbine machinery. The diesels will be used for cruising at around 16 knots, whereas the gas turbines will be able to drive the craft in excess of 40 knots. It is reported that both vessels will sport a different hull design, one with a rounded keel and the other with a hard chine.

Dark Class

Ship	Laid Down	Builder
DARK ADVENTURER	Ordered	Saunders Roe (Beaumaris)
DARK AGGRESSOR	Ordered	Saunders Roe (Beaumaris)
DARK ANTAGONIST	Ordered	Saunders Roe (Beaumaris)
DARK AVENGER	Ordered	Saunders Roe (Beaumaris)
DARK BATTLER	Ordered	Saunders Roe (Beaumaris)
DARK BITER	Ordered	Saunders Roe (Beaumaris)
DARK BUCCANEER	Ordered	Vosper (Portchester)
DARK CLIPPER	Ordered	Vosper (Portchester)
DARK FIGHTER	Ordered	Taylor (Chertsey)
DARK GLADIATOR	Ordered	Taylor (Chertsey)
DARK HERO	Ordered	McGruer (Clynder)
DARK HIGHWAYMAN	Ordered	Vosper (Portchester)
DARK HORSEMAN	Ordered	McGruer (Clynder)
DARK HUNTER	Ordered	Miller (St. Monance)
DARK HUSSAR	Ordered	Thornycroft (Hampton)

Ship	Laid Down	Builder
DARK INTRUDER	Ordered	Morgan Giles (Teignmouth)
DARK INVADER	Ordered	Morgan Giles (Teignmouth)
DARK KILLER	Ordered	Thornycroft (Hampton)
DARK ROVER	Ordered	Vosper (Portchester)

Displacement 50 tons (64 tons FL) Dimensions 71ft 4in x 19ft 5in x 6ft 1in
Machinery 2 x Napier Deltic Diesels; 5,000 shp Speed 40+ knots Complement 15

Notes

The first six vessels (ADVENTURER, AGGRESSOR, ANTAGONIST, BITER, AVENGER and BATTLER) were ordered on 27 February 1951. A further order for 10 vessels (ROVER, BUCCANEER, CLIPPER, HIGHWAYMAN, KILLER, HUSSAR, FIGHTER, GLADIATOR HERO and HUNTER) was placed 18 December 1951. INTRUDER and INVADER were ordered on 22 January 1952 while the final order this year for HORSEMAN was placed on 28 May 1952 bringing the total number ordered to date to 19 vessels. They are designed as Interchangeable MTB/MGBs: as torpedo boats they will be armed with a single 40mm gun and up to 21-inch torpedoes whilst as gun boats they will mount a single 4.5-inch gun and one 40mm gun. To be fitted with Napier Deltic 16 cylinder diesel engines driving two shafts for a top speed of around 40 knots. Wooden hull over alloy frames.

Gay Class

Ship	Laid Down	Builder
GAY ARCHER	20.08.52(L)	Vosper (Portchester)
GAY BOMBADIER	20.08.52(L)	Vosper (Portchester)
GAY BOWMAN	19.12.52(L)	Vosper (Portchester)
GAY BRUISER	19.12.52(L)	Vosper (Portchester)
GAY CARABINEER	22.01.53(L)	Thornycroft (Hampton)
GAY CAVALIER	23.01.53(L)	Taylor (Chertsey)
GAY CENTURION	03.09.52(L)	Thornycroft (Hampton)
GAY CHARGER	12.01.53(L)	Morgan Giles (Teignmouth)
GAY CHARIOTEER	12.06.53(L)	Morgan Giles (Teignmouth)

Ship	Laid Down	Builder
GAY DRAGOON	28.01.53(L)	Taylor (Chertsey)
GAY FENCER	18.02.53(L)	McGruer & Co Ltd (Clynder)
GAY FORESTER	Building	McGruer & Co Ltd (Clynder)

Displacement 50 tons (65 tons FL)   **Dimensions** 75ft 2in x 20ft 1in x 4ft 2in
Machinery Three Packard 4M-2500 Marine Petrol Engines   **Armament** As MTB: 2 x 20mm Oerlikon (1 x twin) or 1 x 40mm Bofors (Single), 2 x 21in TT. As MGB: 1 x 4.5in, 2 x 20mm Oerlikon (1 x twin)   **Speed** 40 knots   **Complement** 13

Notes

In 1951 the Admiralty ordered 12 Type "B" "Short" Interchangable Fast Attack Craft under contract No BR 8E/52143/51 from Vosper Ltd (Portchester) as an interim measure until the Type "A" (Dark) became operationally available. The first four vessels (ARCHER, BOMBADIER, BOWMAN and BRUISER) were ordered 27 February 1951. This was followed on 4 May 1951 by the remaining eight vessels.

Ford Class Seaward Defence Boats

Ship	Laid Down	Builder
SHALFORD	29.10.51	Yarrow
ABERFORD	29.10.51	Yarrow
AXFORD	25.12.51	Simons
BECKFORD	25.12.51	Simons
BRAYFORD	14.12.51	A & J Inglis (Glasgow)
BRYANSFORD	14.12.51	A & J Inglis (Glasgow)
CAMBERFORD	Ordered	Vosper (Portchester)
DESFORD	Ordered	Vosper (Portchester)
DROXFORD	Ordered	Pimblott
DUBFORD	12.12.51	White
GIFFORD	Ordered	Dunston
GLASSFORD	Ordered	Dunston

Ship	Laid Down	Builder
GREATFORD	25.10.51	White
HINKSFORD	Ordered	Richards Ironworks (Lowestoft)
ICKFORD	Ordered	Rowhedge Ironworks
KINGSFORD	Ordered	Rowhedge Ironworks
MARLINGFORD	Ordered	Yarwood
MAYFORD	Ordered	Richards Ironworks

Displacement 120 tons (160 tons FL) Dimensions 117ft 3in x 20ft x 5ft Machinery 2 x Davey Paxman Diesels; Foden on centre shaft; 3 shafts Speed 18 knots Armament 1 x 40mm Bofors; 1 x Squid; DC rails Complement 18 estimated

Notes

An entirely new design of naval vessel designed to detect, locate and destroy submarines in the approaches to defended ports. They are to be equipped with both advances anti-submarine detection equipment and a heavy anti-submarine armament fit. the first two vessels, SHALFORD and ABERFORD, were ordered on 6 April 1951; AXFORD, BECKFORD, BRAYFORD BRYANSFORD, CAMBERFORD and DUFFORD on 3 May 1951; GREATFORD, DUBFORD, GIFFORD, GLASSFORD and DROXFORD on 11 May; MAYFORD, HINKSFORD, ICKFORD, KINGSFORD and MARLINGFORD ordered on 31 May 1952.

SURVEY VESSELS

Ship	Laid Down	Builder
VIDAL	05.07.50	HM Dockyard (Chatham)

Displacement 1,940 tons (2,200 tons FL) Dimensions 315ft x 40ft x 11ft Machinery 4 x diesel engines driving two shafts through reverse and reduction gear boxes; 8,300 bhp Speed 15 knots Complement 161

Notes

Designed by the Admiralty from the start for surveying and hydrographic operations. Ordered on 20 June 1949, she was launched on 31 July 1951. The design incorporates a flight deck and hangar for the operation of a helicopter. Another survey vessel, WHAR-

TON, ordered on 4 May 1949, was cancelled on 19 September 1951, before construction had begun.

ROYAL YACHT

Ship	Laid Down	Builder
Unnamed	16.06.52	J. Brown & Co (Clydebank)

Displacement 4,000 tons approx Dimensions 413ft x 55ft x 16ft Machinery Single reduction geared steam turbines; 2 shafts Speed 21 knots

Notes

A new Royal Yacht was ordered 5 February 1952 to replace the VICTORIA & ALBERT which is no longer seaworthy. The new ship, when not in use by the Queen, or in time of war, will be able to be quickly converted into a small hospital ship. The ship will feature a modified cruiser stern and a raked bow and will be fitted with stabilisers to reduce roll in bad weather.

FLEET OILERS

Tide Class

Ship	Laid Down	Builder
TIDEREACH	Ordered	Swan Hunter & Wigham Richardson
TIDERACE	Ordered	J.L. Thompsons (Sunderland)
TIDERANGE	Ordered	J. Laing & Sons (Sunderland)

Displacement 26,417 tons FL Dimensions 583ft 4in x 71ft 4in x 32ft Machinery 2 x Double reduction geared turbines; 3 x Boilers; 1 shaft Speed 17 knots approx Complement 90

Notes

Building on the experience of the Wave class and RFA OLNA this new class of tanker is intended to offer true replenishment at sea capabilities with positions for refuelling on both sides and astern. Three were ordered on 22 January 1952 for the Royal Fleet Auxiliary, with a fourth vessel, TIDE AUSTRAL, being ordered by the Royal Australian Navy.

STORE SHIPS

Retainer Class

Ship	Completed	Builder
RESURGENT	15.02.51	Scott's SB & Eng Co (Greenock)
CHUNGKING	31.07.50	Scott's SB & Eng Co (Greenock)

Displacement 8,669 tons (14,400 tons FL) Dimensions 477ft 2in x 62ft 2in x 25ft 1in
Machinery Single 6-cylinder Doxford diesel engine, 1 shaft, 6500 bhp Speed 15 knots
Complement 132

Notes

Originally built as cargo/passenger liners for their owners' China - Hong Kong - Amoy - Indonesia trade these vessels were chartered as stores carriers. CHANGCHOW was purchased by the Admiralty in February 1952 and renamed RESURGENT. They are expected to undergo a conversion in the long term into full cargo configuration.

THE ROYAL FLEET AUXILIARY 1952

In1905, the Lords Commissioners of the Navy determined that "*the title HMS shall in future be strictly confined to commissioned ships flying the white ensign*" and further "*that auxiliaries which belong to the Admiralty shall in future be styled Royal Fleet Auxiliaries*" and bear the prefix RFA. Thus was born the modern day RFA, manned by merchant navy personnel and comprising a varied fleet of specialist vessels to support the Royal Navy in its activities and operations around the world.

During World War II the RN fleet could rely upon a myriad of naval bases and supporting bases around the world for its everyday needs, be that fuel, solid stores, ammunition, or even basics such as water. As the war moved into the Pacific and the availability of shoreside support became ever more remote, the RN had to rely more and more on the 'fleet train', a fleet of specialist ships able to provide such support as was needed, while still at sea. Methods and techniques for transferring fuel and stores, were developed and rapidly advanced. Refuelling of ships at sea was in its infancy, with fuel oil not long having taken over from coal. Early operations, using the astern refuelling method, were laborious and inefficient, but this soon gave way to the beam methods using derricks and jackstays, allowing more than one vessel to be refuelled at a time. Advances are still being made today and the next generation of tanker will enable several types of fuel to be transferred to a ship at the same time using more than one refuelling point. Advances in aviation, particularly the advent of the helicopter, has given planners another option in so far as solid loads can be moved between ships by underslung loads carried by helicopter.

Today the Royal Fleet Auxiliary will be found wherever the RN is operating, enabling it to range far and wide without the need to return to port.

Tugs

While not necessarily RFA vessels, there is no single authority or organisation for the operation of Fleet and Harbour tugs, therefore I have included these vessels in this section for ease of reference.

The Admiralty own and operate a large fleet of tugs necessary to support the Royal Navy in all its activities. Some are purely ocean-going in nature, such as the large salvage tugs, while others have a minimal sea-going capability. These Fleet tugs provide for coastal towing, search and rescue and target towing duties. The majority though are harbour tugs, responsible for moving vessels in and around the various ports and naval bases and these vessels generally come under the all-encompassing title of 'Yardcraft'.

Some are RN manned, some RFA, but many are managed and operated by the various departments in the dockyards and naval bases. Captains of Dockyards and King's (Queen's) Harbour Masters and their equivalents in smaller ports, who are responsible for ship's movements within the port area, operate the majority of the tugs. Some of the specialised smaller tugs are operated by the RN's various supply departments. A system of coloured bands around the funnels give an indication as to the operating department (Blue for Captain of Dockyard; Red for the Royal Naval Armament Depot, Green for the Victualling Department and White for the Naval Stores Department).

SHIPS OF THE ROYAL FLEET AUXILIARY
Pennant Numbers

Penn	Ship Name	Penn	Ship Name
A100	WAVE EMPEROR	A168	BROOMDALE
A103	BACCHUS	A169	BROWN RANGER
A104	EAGLESDALE	A170	ECHODALE
A105	EASEDALE	A173	ENNERDALE
A106	BELGOL	A182	WAVE KING
A107	EDDYBAY	A184	MAINE
A108	WAVE MONARCH	A186	FORT ROSALIE
A109	ABBEYDALE	A190	EDDYCLIFF
A110	BOXOL	A192	SPA
A114	DERWENTDALE	A193	WAVE MASTER
A115	AIRSPRITE	A198	EDDYROCK
A116	CELEROL	A202	EDDYREEF
A119	WAVE LAIRD	A204	ROBERT DUNDAS
A120	LIMOL	A207	WAVE PRINCE
A123	ELMOL	A210	WAVE REGENT
A126	FORTOL	A211	WAVE SOVEREIGN
A127	BIRCHOL	A212	WAVE RULER
A128	BISHOPDALE	A213	FRESHBROOK
A129	WAVE PREMIER	A214	SEA FOX
A130	GOLD RANGER	A215	WAVE PROTECTOR
A132	EDDYBEACH	A216	OLNA
A133	ARNDALE	A220	WAVE VICTOR
A135	NORDENFELT	A222	SPAPOOL
A137	LARCHOL	A224	SPABROOK
A144	DINGLEDALE	A227	SPABECK
A151	DEWDALE	A229	FORT DUQUESNE
A152	GREEN RANGER	A230	FORT LANGLEY
A154	ELDEROL	A236	FORT CHARLOTTE
A155	PRESTOL	A237	FORT CONSTANTINE
A157	BLUE RANGER	A238	AMHERST
A160	FORT DUNVEGAN	A241	ROBERT MIDDLETON
A162	SERBOL	A242	WAVE BARON
A163	BLACK RANGER	A244	WAVE COMMANDER
A167	TEAKOL	A245	WAVE CONQUEROR

Penn	Ship Name	Penn	Ship Name
A246	WAVE DUKE	A376	GATLING
A247	WAVE GOVERNOR	A377	MAXIM
A248	WAVE LIBERATOR	A378	KINTERBURY
A249	WAVE KNIGHT	A379	THROSK
A250	PETROBUS	A380	CEDARDALE
A252	NASPRITE	A395	ENFIELD
A253	PHILOL		
A257	SPABURN	X05	DENBYDALE
A258	EDDYCREEK	X47	FRESHTARN
A260	SPALAKE	X60	FRESHBURN
A261	EDDYFIRTH	X63	FRESHFORD
A265	WAVE CHIEF	X76	FRESHPOND
A284	ROWANOL	X99	FRESHPOOL
A285	FORT BEAUHARNOIS	X102	FRESHET
A287	WAR HINDOO	X109	FRESHENER
A295	EDDYNESS	X113	FRESHSPRAY
A300	OAKOL	X117	FRESHMERE
A316	FORT SANDUSKY	X118	FRESHSPRING
A349	FRESHWATER	X120	FRESHLAKE
A357	SURF PATROL	X121	FRESHWELL
A365	SURF PIONEER		
A375	SNIDER	Y39	CHATTENDEN

RFA Olna

FAST REPLENISHMENT TANKER
OLNA CLASS

Ship	Completed	Builder
OLNA	27.04.45	Swan Hunter & Wigham Richardson

Displacement 17,000 tons (25,096 tons FL)   Dimensions 583ft 6in x 70ft 3in x 31ft 9in   Machinery Turbo-electric, 3 x Babcock & Wilcox boilers, 13,000 shp   Speed 17 knots   Complement 77

Notes

Acquired from the Shell Oil Company during the war to meet the need for a fast tanker able to oil at sea she commissioned as HMS OLNA in 1945 with an oiling at sea rig built on a platform on the starboard side upperdeck. She was retained after the war as her RAS equipment was so advanced and today she continues to develop and trial new RAS techniques and equipment. After several years operating between the Indian Ocean and Australia she returned to the UK in 1952 and participated in Exercise Mainbrace, a major NATO exercise in the North Sea and Arctic Ocean.

RFA Wave Protector

REPLENISHMENT TANKERS
WAVE CLASS

Ship	Completed	Builder
WAVE BARON	01.04.46	Furness SB Co Ltd (Haverton)
WAVE CHIEF	27.07.46	Harland & Wolff (Govan)
WAVE COMMANDER	23.08.44	Furness SB Co Ltd (Haverton)
WAVE CONQUEROR	00.03.44	Furness SB Co Ltd (Haverton)
WAVE DUKE	17.01.45	J. Laing & Son (Sunderland)
WAVE EMPEROR	20.12.44	Furness SB Co Ltd (Haverton)
WAVE GOVERNOR	08.03.45	Furness SB Co Ltd (Haverton)
WAVE KING	21.07.44	Harland & Wolff (Govan)
WAVE KNIGHT	31.05.46	J. Laing & Son (Sunderland)
WAVE LAIRD	30.09.46	J. Laing & Son (Sunderland)
WAVE LIBERATOR	00.06.44	Furness SB Co Ltd (Haverton)
WAVE MASTER	00.12.44	J. Laing & Son (Sunderland)
WAVE MONARCH	03.11.44	Harland & Wolff (Govan)
WAVE PREMIER	06.12.46	Furness SB Co Ltd (Haverton)
WAVE PRINCE	00.03.46	J. Laing & Son (Sunderland)

Ship	Completed	Builder
WAVE PROTECTOR	18.10.44	Furness SB Co Ltd (Haverton)
WAVE REGENT	31.05.45	Furness SB Co Ltd (Haverton)
WAVE RULER	00.04.46	Furness SB Co Ltd (Haverton)
WAVE SOVEREIGN	28.02.46	Furness SB Co Ltd (Haverton)
WAVE VICTOR	00.02.44	Furness SB Co Ltd (Haverton)

Displacement 11,600 - 11,955 tons (16,650 tons FL) Dimensions 492ft 6in x 64ft 4in x 28ft 6in Machinery Metro-Vick double reduction geared turbines (in WAVEs, BARON, CHIEF, COMMANDER, CONQUEROR, DUKE and LAIRD) Parsons double reduction geared turbines in remainder, water tube boilers, single shaft, 6,800 shp Speed 15 knots Complement 60

Notes

Originally purchased during the war for freighting duties these ships had an arrangement for refuelling over the stern. With post war developments in refuelling techniques eight of the ships (WAVEs BARON, CHIEF, KNIGHT, MASTER, PRINCE, RULER, SOVEREIGN and VICTOR) were modernised for abeam refuelling and received interim rigs forward and aft of the bridge comprising a goalpost and derrick arrangement. Even so these ships are deemed too slow for fleet work and their pumping capacity is woefully short. Add this to their somewhat thirsty machinery plant, these vessels are far from ideal for the modern day refuelling role. WAVE LIBERATOR is undergoing a refit at Harland and Wolff. In October WAVE KING and WAVE PRINCE were deployed in support of Operation Hurricane 1, Britain's first atomic tests at Monte Bello off the west coast of Australia. WAVE BARON, WAVE CHIEF, WAVE KNIGHT, WAVE PREMIER and WAVE SOVEREIGN have been engaged in operations off Korea. During these operations WAVE CHIEF, which has now returned to the UK, conducted 66 replenishments at sea, pumping over 37,000 tons of fuel to Allied warships. As is the nature of such things, a competitive element has crept in to these evolutions and ship's companies are still trying to beat the record set by WAVE KNIGHT and the Canadian destroyer ATHABASKAN of 105 seconds from the shooting of the gun line to the pumping of fuel. On 23 May WAVE CONQUEROR was badly damaged aft off Immingham when she was hit by a Norwegian vessel. She is at Smith's Dock (Middlesborough) for repairs.

RFA Black Ranger

RANGER CLASS

Ship	Completed	Builder
BLACK RANGER	28.01.41	Harland & Wolff (Govan)
BLUE RANGER	05.06.41	Harland & Wolff (Govan)
BROWN RANGER	10.04.41	Harland & Wolff (Govan)
GOLD RANGER	25.09.41	Caledon SB & Eng Co Ltd (Dundee)
GREEN RANGER	04.12.41	Caledon SB & Eng Co Ltd (Dundee)

Displacement 3,313 - 3,417 tons Dimensions 365ft 3in x 47ft x 20ft (355ft 3in x 48ft 3in x 22ft 6in GOLD & GREEN) Machinery 1 6-cylinder Burmeister & Wain diesel; 1 shaft, 3,500 bhp (1 4-cylinder Doxford diesel, 2800 bhp (GOLD & GREEN)) Speed 14 knots Complement 40

Notes

The funnel on these ships is offset to port. GOLD RANGER and GREEN RANGER are 10 feet longer than the first three ships. In October GOLD RANGER deployed in support of Operation Hurricane 1, Britain's first atomic tests at Monte Bello off the west coast of Australia.

RFA Arndale

FREIGHTING TANKERS
EARLY DALE CLASS

Ship	Completed	Builder
ABBEYDALE	04.03.37	Swan Hunter & Wigham Richardson
ARNDALE	28.09.37	Swan Hunter & Wigham Richardson
BISHOPDALE	06.06.37	J. Lithgow (Port Glasgow)
BROOMDALE	03.11.37	Harland & Wolff (Govan)

Displacement 8,129 - 8,402 tons (17,210 -17,357 tons FL) Dimensions 481ft 6in x 62ft x 27ft 6in Machinery Doxford diesels (in first two) Burmeister & Wain diesels in others, single shaft, 2,850 bhp Speed 11½ knots Complement 40

Notes

These vessels were originally taken over from the British Tanker Co Ltd while they were under construction. All are employed as freighting tankers.

RFA Dingledale

LATER DALE CLASS

Ship	Completed	Builder
CEDARDALE	25.05.39	Blythswood SB Co Ltd (Scotstoun)
DENBYDALE	30.01.41	Blythswood SB Co Ltd (Scotstoun)
DERWENTDALE	30.08.41	Harland & Wolff (Govan)
DEWDALE	14.06.41	Cammell Laird (Birkenhead)
DINGLEDALE	10.09.41	Harland & Wolff (Govan)
EAGLESDALE	10.01.42	Furness SB Co Ltd (Haverton)
EASEDALE	12.02.42	Furness SB Co Ltd (Haverton)
ECHODALE	04.03.41	Hawthorn Leslie (Hebburn)
ENNERDALE	11.07.41	Swan Hunter & Wigham Richardson

Displacement 8,129 - 8,402 tons (17,210 -17,357 tons FL) Dimensions 483ft x 59ft 6in x 27ft 6in Machinery Burmeister & Wain 4-cycle diesels, single shaft, 3,600 bhp Speed 13 knots Complement 40

Notes

There are differences in machinery and dimensions, but all are pretty much built to the same design. DENBYDALE was damaged by Italian frogmen at Gibraltar on 19 September 1942. Her machinery was removed to re-engine DERWENTDALE. Is now used as a fuelling and accommodation hulk at Gibraltar. CEDARDALE stranded near Mina-al-Ahmadi but was refloated with little damage. DERWENTDALE is refitting on the Clyde and ECHODALE it undertaking freighting duties in support of Korean operations.

246

RFA Surf Patrol

SURF CLASS

Ship	Completed	Builder
SURF PATROL	17.07.51	Bartram & Sons Ltd (Sunderland)
SURF PIONEER	28.11.51	Bartram & Sons Ltd (Sunderland)

Displacement 11,500 tons (15,800 tons FL) Dimensions 469ft 6in x 60ft 6in x 27ft 6in Machinery Westgarth 4-cylinder diesel, 4,400 bhp (SURF PATROL); NEME Diesel, 4,250 bhp (SURF PIONEER), 1 shaft Speed 13¾ knots

Notes

The two ships in this Class were originally ordered by Polish owners and both were jointly commandeered by the Admiralty and the Foreign Office under the Defence Regulations and Enactments during the Korean War. They were originally named TATRY (SURF PATROL) and BESKIDY (SURF PIONEER).

RFA War Hindoo

WAR CLASS

Ship	Completed	Builder
WAR HINDOO	30.10.19	Wm Hamilton & Co (Port Glasgow)

Displacement 11,680 tons Dimensions 412ft x 52ft 3in x 25ft 8in Machinery Triple Expansion Steam Engine, 3,000 ihp Speed 10 knots Complement 40-45

Notes

Hired by Shell Oil in April 1950 for use as a storage tanker at Gibraltar. On return went back to freighting. In 1952 following repairs at Immingham (Aug-Dec) she sailed for Malta where she is to be laid up as a fuelling hulk.

RFA Eddybay

COASTAL TANKERS
EDDY CLASS

Ship	Completed	Builder
EDDYBAY	29.11.52	Caledon SB & Eng Co Ltd (Dundee)
EDDYBEACH	25.04.52	Caledon SB & Eng Co Ltd (Dundee)
EDDYCLIFF	25.08.52(L)	Blythswood SB Co Ltd (Scotstoun)
EDDYCREEK	Ordered	Lobnitz & Co Ltd (Renfrew)
EDDYFIRTH	25.04.52(LD)	Lobnitz & Co Ltd (Renfrew)
EDDYNESS	Ordered	Blyth SB & Dry Dock Co
EDDYREEF	Ordered	Caledon SB & Eng Co Ltd (Dundee)
EDDYROCK	15.12.52(L)	Blyth SB & Dry Dock Co

Displacement 2,157-2,300 tons (4,165 tons FL) Dimensions 286ft 5in x 44ft 1in x 17ft 3in Machinery Lobnitz Triple Expansion Steam Engine, 2 Scotch boilers, single shaft, 1,750 ihp Speed 12 knots Complement 38

Notes

Designed as Fleet Attendant Tankers this role has rapidly been overtaken by advances in replenishment at sea capabilities and they are now employed as coastal tankers with a cargo capacity of 1,650 tons carried in 4 tanks. The first two vessels were ordered on 1 March 1949, with a second batch of six ordered on 23 January 1951. Two further vessels, EDDYCOVE and EDDYMULL, were ordered on 27 March 1951 but cancelled in 1952.

RFA Oakol

1500 TON CLASS

Ship	Completed	Builder
BIRCHOL	12.06.46	Lobnitz & Co Ltd (Renfrew)
OAKOL	01.11.46	Lobnitz & Co Ltd (Renfrew)
ROWANOL	21.08.46	Lobnitz & Co Ltd (Renfrew)
TEAKOL	14.01.47	Lobnitz & Co Ltd (Renfrew)

Displacement 2,670 tons (3,200 tons FL)　Dimensions 263ft x 38ft 6in x 17ft 6in
Machinery　Triple Expansion Steam Engine; 1 shaft, 1,140 ihp　Speed 11 knots
Complement 26

Notes

ROWANOL is based at Malta and regularly supports the Mediterranean Fleet during
Fleet Cruises. BIRCHOL and OAKOL are based in the Far East (at Hong Kong and
Singapore respectively) where they service and supply those vessels operating off Korea.

250

RFA Fortol

2nd 2000 TON CLASS

Ship	Completed	Builder
BELGOL	19.10.17	Irvine (West Hartlepool)
CELEROL	10.09.17	Short (Sunderland)
FORTOL	31.08.17	A McMillan (Dumbarton)
PRESTOL	14.12.17	Napier & Miller (Glasgow)
SERBOL	00.03.18	Caledon SB & Eng Co Ltd (Dundee)

Displacement 5,049-5,660 tons FL   Dimensions 342ft 6in x 41ft 6in x 22ft 6in
Machinery Triple expansion engine, 1 shaft, 3,375 ihp   Speed 14 knots   Complement 42

Notes

Looking more akin to a cargo vessel than a conventional tanker, in addition to their oil cargo, these vessels could also carry up to 5000 gallons of lubricating oil. SERBOL has an upright funnel and mast arrangement.

RFA Elderol

2nd 1000 TON CLASS

Ship	Completed	Builder
BOXOL	27.09.17	Barclay Curle & Co Ltd (Glasgow)
ELDEROL	23.06.17	Swan Hunter & Wigham Richardson
ELMOL	27.08.17	Swan Hunter & Wigham Richardson
LARCHOL	09.08.17	Lobnitz & Co Ltd (Renfrew)
LIMOL	18.12.17	Lobnitz & Co Ltd (Renfrew)
PHILOL	00.08.16	Tyne Iron Shipbuilding

Displacement 2,365 - 2,400 tons Dimensions 220ft x 34ft 9in x 16ft 2in Machinery Triple Expansion Steam Engine, single shaft, 700 ihp Speed 11½ knots Complement 19

Notes

BOXOL was sold in 1948 and renamed PORTNALL. She was re-purchased by the Admiralty in 1951 for further service during the Korean War. She was renamed BOXOL in 1952 and was based at Gibraltar.

RFA Airsprite

SPIRIT CARRIERS
SPRITE CLASS

Ship	Completed	Builder
AIRSPRITE	16.02.43	Blythswood SB Co Ltd (Scotstoun)
NASPRITE	11.02.41	Blythswood SB Co Ltd (Scotstoun)

Displacement 965 tons **Dimensions** 204ft 6in x 33ft 3in x 12ft 9in **Machinery** Triple expansion steam engine, two SE cylindrical boilers, single shaft, 900 ihp **Speed** 11 knots **Complement** 30

Notes

Designed by the Admiralty to transport petrol in bulk, although they also have capacity to accommodate lubricating oil. 533 tons of petrol and 52 tons of lubricating oil can be carried and these cargoes can be discharged through dedicated pumps at the rate of 50 tons per hour for petrol and 10 tons per hour for lubricating oil. They operate mostly around the coast of the UK and into the Mediterranean.

253

RFA Petrobus

PET CLASS

Ship	Completed	Builder
PETROBUS	00.02.18	Dunlop Bremner (Port Glasgow)

Displacement 1,024 tons Dimensions 164ft x 28ft x 11ft 6in Machinery Triple expansion steam engine, two SE cylindrical boilers, single shaft, 500 ihp Speed 9 knots Complement 16

Notes

One of 3 ships in the class that were completed for the Admiralty in 1918 and all 3 spent most of their lives in UK waters. Between 6 - 30 October she undertook a refit at Southampton.

RFA Bacchus

STORES SHIPS
BACCHUS CLASS

Ship	Completed	Builder
BACCHUS	20.09.36	Caledon SB & Eng Co Ltd (Dundee)

Displacement 5,150 tons (5,790 tons FL)   Dimensions 337ft 10in x 49ft x 18ft
Machinery Triple Expansion Steam Engine, single shaft, 2,000 ihp   Speed 12 knots
Complement 44

Notes

Equipped with a distilling plant for supplying naval vessels with fresh water. She conducts a regular UK - Mediterranean - Far East sea freighting service via the Suez Canal and Aden.

RFA Fort Beauharnois

FORT CLASS

Ship	Completed	Builder
FORT BEAUHARNOIS	29.10.44	West Coast Shipbuilders (Vancouver)
FORT CHARLOTTE	05.04.44	North Vancouver Ship Repair
FORT CONSTANTINE	25.04.44	Burrard (South Yard Vancouver)
FORT DUNVEGAN	14.04.44	Burrard (South Yard Vancouver)
FORT DUQUESNE	25.11.44	West Coast Shipbuilders (Vancouver)
FORT LANGLEY	28.12.44	Victoria MD (Victoria)
FORT ROSALIE	07.07.45	United Shipyards (Montreal)
FORT SANDUSKY	01.08.45	United Shipyards (Montreal)

Displacement 9,788 tons Dimensions 424ft 6in x 57ft x 27ft Machinery Triple Expansion Steam Reciprocating Engine, 2 Babcock & Wilcox Boilers, single shaft, 2,500 ihp Speed 11 knots Complement 115

Notes

The survivors of a group of ships known collectively as the Victory class, acquired from, and built in, Canada during the Second World War. As completed they were mercantile manned, but with a naval stores staff. It was not until after the war that those retained in RN service were operated by the RFA. Sixteen similar vessels were completed for the RN as Maintenance Ships (see page 214).

FORT BEAUHARNOIS, FORT CHARLOTTE, FORT DUNVEGAN and FORT DUSQUESNE are Victualing Store Issuing Ships. FORT ROSALIE and FORT SANDUSKY are Armament Store Ships. FORT LANGLEY is an Air Stores Ship. These ships are Royal Fleet Auxiliaries, except for FORT LANGLEY, which is officially listed as a Merchant Fleet Auxiliary.

In 1951 FORT DUQUESNE was fitted with a flight deck aft to carry out helicopter landing trials in the English Channel.

In October 1952 FORT BEAUHARNOIS, FORT CONSTANTINE and FORT ROSALIE were all deployed in support of Operation Hurricane 1, the British atomic weapon tests at Monte Bello off the west coast of Australia. FORT DUNVEGAN had been placed in reserve after the war, but was brought forward for further servce as a Victualling Stores Issue Ship in 1951. FORT LANGLEY has been operating in the Far East in support of operations off Korea.

Previous names

Several of the class were originally laid down as Park class vessels and were renamed on being taken over by the Ministry of War Transport in 1945.

FORT CHARLOTTE ex-BUFFALO PARK; FORT BEAUHARNOIS ex-CORNISH PARK, (launched as FORT GRAND RAPIDS), FORT LANGLEY ex-MONTEBELLO PARK and FORT DUNVEGAN ex-QUEENSBOROUGH PARK

RFA Robert Middleton

ROBERT DUNDAS CLASS

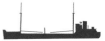

Ship	Completed	Builder
ROBERT DUNDAS	00.11.38	Grangemouth Dockyard Co
ROBERT MIDDLETON	25.08.38	Grangemouth Dockyard Co

Displacement 900 tons **Dimensions** 210ft x 35ft x 13ft 6in **Machinery** Atlas Polar Diesel, single shaft, 960 bhp **Speed** 10½ knots **Complement** 17

Notes

Small coastal stores carriers which operate mainly around the UK but have, on occasion, ventured into the Mediterranean. They have two holds, one of which can accommodate large items such as Landing Craft.

RFA Seafox

SKUA CLASS

Ship	Completed	Builder
SEAFOX	00.11.46	J. Pollock (Faversham)

Displacement 990 tons **Dimensions** 172ft 6in x 35ft x 13ft 6in **Machinery** Crossley 2-stroke diesels, 2 shaft, 960 bhp **Speed** 10½ knots

Notes

SEAFOX was withdrawn from RN service in May 1951 and is now a victualling store issuing ship in service with the RFA.

RFA Amherst

ARMAMENT CARRIERS
AMHERST TYPE

Ship	Completed	Builder
AMHERST	00.01.36	Blythswood SB & E Co (Scotstoun)

Displacement 5,337 tons **Dimensions** 341ft 9in x 45ft x 20ft **Machinery** Reciprocating Steam Engine, 1 shaft **Speed** 13½ knots

Notes

She was originally purposely designed as a small cargo passenger ship for the Red Cross Line, a subsidiary of Furness, Withy & Co Ltd and sailed between Newfoundland, Nova Scotia , New York and the British West Indies as FORT AMHERST. Purchased by the Admiralty, in December 1951, as a Naval Armaments Vessel to replace NAV BEDENHAM which had exploded at Gibraltar on 27 April 1951. On completion of a successful hull survey she entered RFA service on 15 July 1952.

NAV Kinterbury

KINTERBURY CLASS

Ship	Completed	Builder
KINTERBURY	00.04.43	Philip & Son (Dartmouth)
THROSK	00.12.43	Philip & Son (Dartmouth)

Displacement 1,488 tons   Dimensions 185ft x 33ft x 14ft 6in   Machinery Triple expansion steam engine; 900 ihp   Speed 11 knots   Complement 13

Notes

A similar vessel, CHATTENDEN, has been laid up in Portchester Creek since 1951.

NAV Snider

GATLING CLASS

Ship	Completed	Builder
ENFIELD	00.12.45	Lobnitz & Co Ltd (Renfrew)
GATLING	25.10.45	Lobnitz & Co Ltd (Renfrew)
MAXIM	14.11.45	Lobnitz & Co Ltd (Renfrew)
NORDENFELT	14.03.46	Lobnitz & Co Ltd (Renfrew)
SNIDER	00.00.46	Lobnitz & Co Ltd (Renfrew)

Displacement 604 tons Dimensions 134ft x 25ft 3in x 10ft 6in Machinery Reciprocating steam engine, one SE cylindrical boiler, single shaft, 500 ihp Speed 10½ knots Complement 13

Notes

Designed by the Director of Naval Construction they were intended for Pacific operations to carry ammunition from larger ships offshore to coastal areas or small harbours. GATLING and NORDENFELT were completed to mercantile standards while the others were on "Yard Craft" Dockyard agreements and were completed with naval style accommodation. Two similar vessels, FLINTLOCK and MATCHLOCK, built by Philip & Sons, Dartmouth, remain in service.

HMS Spa

WATER CARRIERS
SPA CLASS

Ship	Completed	Builder
SPA	24.04.42	Philip & Son (Dartmouth)
SPABECK (RFA)	03.09.43	Philip & Son (Dartmouth)
SPABROOK	12.12.44	Philip & Son (Dartmouth)
SPABURN	12.04.46	Philip & Son (Dartmouth)
SPALAKE	28.11.46	Charles Hill & Son (Bristol)
SPAPOOL	14.06.46	Charles Hill & Son (Bristol)

Displacement 719 tons (1,219 tons FL) Dimensions 163ft x 30ft x 12ft Machinery Three cylinder Triple Expansion steam engine, single shaft, 675 ihp Speed 9 knots

Notes

Small Admiralty designed water carriers designed to provide water to HM ships. Originally manned by the Royal Fleet Auxiliary, some have reverted to Dockyard management, their crews being sourced locally. SPABECK is to be converted to support the HTP experimental submarine programme.

SPA is dockyard manned at Greenock; SPABROOK at Malta; SPABURN at Sheerness and SPAPOOL at Mombasa (Kenya).

263

Freshspray

FRESH CLASS

Ship	Completed	Builder
FRESHBROOK	17.04.42	Lytham Shipbuilding
FRESHBURN	01.04.44	Lytham Shipbuilding
FRESHENER	22.07.42	Lytham Shipbuilding
FRESHET	10.12.40	Lytham Shipbuilding
FRESHFORD	18.07.44	Lytham Shipbuilding
FRESHLAKE	14.11.42	Lytham Shipbuilding
FRESHMERE	22.03.43	Lytham Shipbuilding
FRESHPOND	25.12.45	Lytham Shipbuilding
FRESHPOOL	03.07.43	Lytham Shipbuilding
FRESHSPRAY	07.08.46	Lytham Shipbuilding
FRESHSPRING	10.02.47	Lytham Shipbuilding

Ship	Completed	Builder
FRESHTARN	22.12.44	Lytham Shipbuilding
FRESHWATER	10.09.40	Lytham Shipbuilding
FRESHWELL	30.10.43	Lytham Shipbuilding

Displacement 230 tons (594 tons FL)   Dimensions 126ft 3in x 25ft 6in x 10ft 9in
Machinery   Vertical Triple Expansion Steam Engine, Scotch return tube boiler, single shaft, 450 ihp, coal fired   Speed 9½ knots   Complement 8

Notes

A class of 14 water carriers built for the Admiralty for coastal operations. They are also fitted with a salvage and fire-fighting capability.

Five vessels are operated by the Director of Victualling (FRESHBROOK, FRESHBURN, FRESHTARN, FRESHWATER and FRESHWELL). The remaining vessels are operated by the Director of Fuelling (FRESHENER at Gibraltar, FRESHET and FRESHLAKE at Portsmouth, FRESHLAKE and FRESHPOND at Devonport, FRESHMERE and FRESHPOOL at Greenock and FRESHSPRAY and FRESHSPRING at Malta).

RFA Maine

HOSPITAL SHIP
MAINE CLASS

Ship	Completed	Builder
MAINE	1925	Ansaldo San Giorgio (Muggiano)

Displacement 7,515 tons Dimensions 447ft x 52ft 6in x 36ft Machinery Six double reduction geared turbines, 2 shafts Speed 12 knots Complement 200

Notes

This is former Italian liner LEONARDO DA VINCI, captured at Massawa in 1943 and converted into the 300 bed hospital ship EMPIRE CLYDE. She was renamed MAINE in 1948. She is operating from Hong Kong, Sasebo and Kure in support of combat operations off Korea. There are plans to replace her with a modern vessel as she suffers from both age and inadequate ventilation.

RFA Mediator

TUGS
BUSTLER CLASS

Ship	Completed	Builder
BUSTLER	1942	Henry Robb (Leith)
GROWLER (RFA)	1943	Henry Robb (Leith)
MEDIATOR	1944	Henry Robb (Leith)
REWARD	1945	Henry Robb (Leith)
SAMSONIA	1942	Henry Robb (Leith)
TURMOIL	1945	Henry Robb (Leith)
WARDEN (RFA)	1945	Henry Robb (Leith)

Displacement 1,118 tons (1,630 FL) Dimensions 205ft x 41ft x 13ft Machinery 2 x Atlas Polar 8-cylinder diesels, 1 shaft, 4,000 bhp Speed 16 knots Complement 42

Notes

Originally a class of eight vessels, they were designed for ocean towing, salvage and rescue and were the first RN Fleet tugs to be powered by diesel. During the war trials had been carried out to test their suitability as influence minesweepers. The idea was that they would tow a barge to simulate a merchant ship in an effort to detonate mines. As it turned out the pressure wave from the tugs themselves, as they passed through the water, was sufficient to detonate an influence mine so the idea was abandoned.

Post war many of the class have been chartered to commercial operators. In 1946 BUSTLER was chartered to Metal Industries (Salvage) Ltd. GROWLER was on long term charter to Moller Towages Ltd (Shanghai) and renamed CAROLINE MOLLER (1947). In May this year she was rechartered to Hong Kong Salvage and Towing Co. Ltd and renamed CASTLE PEAK. In 1946 TURMOIL was chartered to Oversea Towage & Salvage Co. Ltd, who continue to operate her under her original name. Since 1947 SAM-SONIA had been on charter to Foundation Maritime Ltd of Nova Scotia and renamed FOUNDATION JOSEPHINE. She was returned to the Admiralty in November. WARDEN had been on charter to Risdon A. Beazeley Ltd since 1946 and renamed TWYFORD. She was returned to the Admiralty in 1951. REWARD is laid up at Chatham.

HM Tug Careful

NIMBLE CLASS

Ship	Completed	Builder
CAPABLE	1946	Fleming & Ferguson (Paisley)
CAREFUL	1946	Fleming & Ferguson (Paisley)
EXPERT	1945	Fleming & Ferguson (Paisley)
NIMBLE	1942	Fleming & Ferguson (Paisley)

Displacement 890 tons (1,190 tons FL) **Dimensions** 175ft x 35ft 9in x 13ft 9in
Machinery Triple expansion steam engine, 2 shafts, 3,500 ihp **Speed** 16 knots
Complement 30

Notes

Designed for sea towing, salvage and harbour work. Originally completed with open
bridges, but now have an enclosed wheelhouse. CAPABLE is allocated to Portsmouth,
CAREFUL to Devonport, EXPERT to Malta and NIMBLE is at Gibraltar.

HMT Freebooter

BRIGAND CLASS

Ship	Completed	Builder
BRIGAND	1937	Fleming & Ferguson (Paisley)
BRITON	1938	Fleming & Ferguson (Paisley)
FREEBOOTER	1940	Fleming & Ferguson (Paisley)
MARAUDER	1938	Fleming & Ferguson (Paisley)

Displacement 840 tons (1,190 tons FL)   Dimensions 174ft x 32ft x 10ft 7in
Machinery Triple expansion steam engine; 2 shafts; 3,000 ihp   Speed 15½ knots
Complement 43

Notes

Designed as Fleet tugs and fitted for firefighting, salvage, rescue and target towing duties.
BRIGAND & MARAUDER are based at Malta; BRITON at Simon's Town; FREEBOOT-
ER at Devonport.

HM Tug Retort

RESOLVE CLASS

Ship	Completed	Builder
RESPOND	1918	Ayrshire Dockyard (Irvine)
RETORT	1918	Day, Summers & Company
ROLLICKER	1918	Ferguson (Port Glasgow)
ROYSTERER	1919	J.I. Thornycroft & Co (Woolston)

Displacement 1,400 tons Dimensions 186ft x 36ft 2in x 17ft Machinery Steam reciprocating, four boilers, 2 shafts, 2,400 ihp Speed 14 knots Complement 30

Notes

RETORT was based at Devonport, but this year was refitted with new boilers and transferred to Gibraltar. RESPOND and ROYSTERER are at Malta. ROLLICKER was based at Gibraltar, but was withdrawn from service this year and sold for breaking up in June.

271

HMT Swarthy

ROBUST CLASS

Ship	Completed	Builder
CAMEL	1915	Bow McLachlan & Co (Paisley)
FIRM	1911	HM Dockyard (Chatham)
GRAPPLER	1908	HM Dockyard (Chatham)
RAMBLER	1909	J. Brown & Co (Clydebank)
ROBUST	1907	Bow McLachlan & Co (Paisley)
SPRITE	1915	Bow McLachlan & Co (Paisley)
SWARTHY (ex-STURDY)	1913	J.I. Thornycroft & Co (Woolston)
ANCIENT (ex-VETERAN)	1915	J.I. Thornycroft & Co (Woolston)

Displacement 625 tons (780 tons FL) Dimensions 152 ft 6in x 50ft 6in x 11ft
Machinery Steam reciprocating double expansion, 2 independent paddle wheels with feathering blades, 1,250 ihp Speed 12 knots Complement 17

Notes

CAMEL was based at Devonport; FIRM at Sheerness; GRAPPLER, SPRITE and SWARTHY at Portsmouth; RAMBLER at Rosyth, ROBUST and ANCIENT at Malta.

HMT Pert

PERT CLASS

Ship	Completed	Builder
PERT	1916	J.I. Thornycroft & Co (Woolston)

Displacement 1,023 tons Dimensions 179ft 6in x 59ft x 12ft Machinery Steam double expansion reciprocating engine; 3 boilers; 2 independent paddle wheels, feathering blades; 2000 ihp Speed 13 knots Complement 20

Notes

She was the largest paddle tug in Admiralty service and was based at Devonport. Paddle tugs were very versatile craft. When secured alongside another vessel for a cold move the tug would be firmly secured abeam of the vessel's natural turning point and a single tug could produce forward or reverse movement from the inboard paddle and influence direction from the outboard paddle.

RFA Enforcer

ENVOY CLASS

Ship	Completed	Builder
ENCORE	1944	Cochrane & Sons (Selby)
ENFORCER (RFA)	1944	Cochrane & Sons (Selby)
ENIGMA	1944	Cochrane & Sons (Selby)
ENVOY (RFA)	1944	Cochrane & Sons (Selby)

Displacement 868 tons (1,332 tons FL) Dimensions 174ft 6in x 36ft x 17ft Machinery Steam triple expansion engine, two SE cylindrical boilers, single shaft, 1,625 ihp Speed 13 knots Complement 33

Notes

Both ENFORCER and ENVOY are civilian manned under RFA conditions. ENCORE is Naval manned. ENIGMA is based at Singapore, originally as a Fleet Target Towing and Rescue Tug, but this year is being modified for harbour work. In 1950 ENFORCER was transferred to Rosyth for sea-going duties.

RFA Prosperous

ASSURANCE CLASS

Ship	Completed	Builder
ALLIGATOR	1941	Cochrane & Sons (Selby)
ANTIC (RFA)	1943	Cochrane & Sons (Selby)
ASSIDUOUS	1943	Cochrane & Sons (Selby)
CAUTIOUS (RFA)	1940	Cochrane & Sons (Selby)
EARNER (RFA)	1943	Cochrane & Sons (Selby)
HENGIST	1941	Cochrane & Sons (Selby)
JAUNTY (RFA)	1941	Cochrane & Sons (Selby)
PROSPEROUS (RFA)	1942	Cochrane & Sons (Selby)
RESTIVE	1940	Cochrane & Sons (Selby)
SAUCY (RFA)	1942	Cochrane & Sons (Selby)
TRYPHON	1942	Cochrane & Sons (Selby)

Displacement 630 tons Dimensions 156ft 6in x 35ft x 16ft 6in Machinery Steam triple expansion engine, single shaft, 1,350 ihp Speed 13 knots Complement 31

275

The 21 tugs originally in this class, 7 of which saw service as RFA's, were acquired during World War II. With a bollard pull of 13½ tons they were designed for escort/rescue work, although post war they have been employed on more general duties. ALLIGATOR, ANTIC, ASSIDIOUS, HENGIST, RESTIVE are naval manned, the remainder being civilian manned under RFA conditions. ANTIC operates with a naval crew as a tender to HMS Excellent. ASSIDUOUS and HENGIST are based at Trincomalee, Ceylon. PROSPEROUS is based at Portsmouth and RESTIVE at Bermuda. SAUCY is based at Portland for Target Towing duties. On 27 April 1951 CAUTIOUS sustained considerable damage at Gibraltar when RFA BEDENHAM blew up nearby.

Previous Names

ANTIC (ex-ANT); ALLIGATOR (ex-CHARON); HENGIST (ex-DECISION); EARNER (ex-EARNEST); CAUTIOUS (ex-PRUDENT); TRYPHON (ex-STORMKING, ex-STORM-COCK).

Fortitude

EMPIRE CLASS

Ship	Deployment
AID	Captain Superintendent Trincomalee (Ceylon)
DILIGENT	Captain of Dockyard (Malta)
EGERTON	Chatham
ELF	Naval Service (Singapore)
EMINENT	Captain of Dockyard (Portsmouth)
EMPHATIC	Captain of Dockyard (Chatham)
EMULOUS	Basin Tug (Chatham)
FIDGET	Captain of Dockyard (Singapore)
FORTITUDE	Portsmouth Dockyard - Civilian manned
INTEGRITY	Sheerness
MASTERFUL	Captain of Dockyard (Devonport)
PROMPT	Captain of Dockyard (Malta)
SECURITY	Captain in Charge (Portland)

Ship	Deployment
VAGRANT	Captain of Dockyard (Chatham)
WEASEL	Naval Service (Singapore)
EMPIRE DEMON (RFA)	NOIC (Londonderry) - Civilian manned/RFA conditions
EMPIRE EDWARD	Naval Service with Allied Military Govt (Trieste)
EMPIRE FRED	Naval Service with Allied Military Govt (Trieste)
EMPIRE IMP	Dockyard Service (Sheerness/Chatham)
EMPIRE LUCY	Harwich
EMPIRE NETTA (RFA)	Milford Haven - Civilian manned/RFA conditions
EMPIRE PLANE (RFA)	BDO (Clyde) - Civilian manned/RFA conditions
EMPIRE RITA (RFA)	BDO (Clyde) - Civilian manned/RFA conditions
EMPIRE ROSA (RFA)	BDO (Pembroke Dock) - Civilian manned/RFA conditions
EMPIRE ZONA (RFA)	BDO (Clyde) - Civilian manned/RFA conditions

All Empire tugs were of single screw steam tug design, both oil and coal fired. There were variations in size and power to cover a variety of roles. All built between 1941 and 1946. Approximately 144 were built of which about a half were in naval service.

Notes

The "Empires" comprised a number of vessels which fell into the category of Miscellaneous Harbour Tugs which all belonged to different Classes and which were based at various Naval Bases for general duties, either naval manned, or civilian manned under RFA conditions. Many were operated on charter to civilain companies.

Previous Names

AID (ex-EMPIRE JENNY); DILIGENT (ex-EMPIRE ACE); EGERTON (ex-EMPIRE DARBY); ELF (ex-EMPIRE BELLE); EMINENT (ex-EMPIRE TESSA); EMPHATIC (ex-EMPIRE JOAN); EMULOUS (ex-EMPIRE SPRUCE); FIDGET (ex-EMPIRE JOHNATHAN); FORTITUDE (ex-EMPIRE CHARLES); INTEGRITY (ex-EMPIRE CUPID); MASTERFUL (ex-EMPIRE LAWN); PROMPT (ex-EMPIRE SPITFIRE); SECURITY (ex-EMPIRE RODERICK); WEASEL (ex-EMPIRE MADGE); VAGRANT (ex-EMPIRE TITANIA).

HMT Energy

FLAMER CLASS

Ship	Completed	Builder
DRIVER	1943	Alexander Hall (Aberdeen)
ENERGY	1943	Alexander Hall (Aberdeen)
FLAMER	1940	Alexander Hall (Aberdeen)
HANDMAID (ex-FRESCO)	1940	Alexander Hall (Aberdeen)
IMPETUS	1940	Alexander Hall (Aberdeen)

Displacement 233.8 tons Dimensions 98ft x 29ft 2in x 14ft Machinery Steam reiprocating engine, single shaft, 850 ihp Speed 10 knots

Notes

All based at Rosyth under Captain of Dockyard control.

279

HMT Roundshot

MINION CLASS

Ship	Completed	Builder
BOMBSHELL	1945	Philip & Son (Dartmouth)
CHAINSHOT	1945	Philip & Son (Dartmouth)
GRAPESHOT	1945	Philip & Son (Dartmouth)
MINION	1940	Philip & Son (Dartmouth)
ROUNDSHOT	1945	Philip & Son (Dartmouth)

Displacement 56.41 tons Dimensions 71ft 6in x 19ft x 8ft 6in Machinery Diesel engine, single shaft, 350 bhp Speed 8 knots Complement 7

Notes

The design was produced in 1938 and a total of five tugs were built for harbour service work. BOMBSHELL based at RNAD Bull Point, Devonport; CHAINSHOT and GRAPESHOT based at RNAD Upnor, Chatham; MINION based at RNAD Priddys Hard, Portsmouth and ROUNDSHOT based at RNAD Singapore.

TANAC 56

TANAC CLASS

Ship	Deployment
TANAC 25	NASO Trincomalee (Ceylon)
TANAC 35	Captain of Dockyard (Malta)
TANAC 36	War Office (Marchwood)
TANAC 37	Captain of Dockyard (Malta)
TANAC 56	Captain of Dockyard (Malta)
TANAC 58	Captain of Dockyard (Malta)
TANAC 59	Director of Armament Supply (Malta)
TANAC 60	Director of Armament Supply (Malta)
TANAC 83	Captain of Dockyard (Malta)
TANAC 105	NASO Trincomalee (Ceylon)
TANAC 121	RNAD (Hong Kong)
TANAC 150 (C721)	Fleet Fuelling Service, Trincomalee (Ceylon)
TANAC 154 (C720)	Fleet Fuelling Service, Trincomalee (Ceylon)

Ship	Deployment
TANAC 157	VictuallingSupply Officer, Trincomalee (Ceylon)
TANAC 163	VictuallingSupply Officer, Trincomalee (Ceylon)

Displacement 67 tons Dimensions 65ft x 17ft x 6ft Machinery Diesel engine, single shaft, 220-270 BHP (depending on engine fitted) Speed 9 knots Complement 5

Notes

All built in Canada during 1944 to a similar design with minor varations.

TID 50

TID CLASS

Ship	Deployment
TID 2 (C677)	SNSO for Fleet Fuelling Service (Sheerness)
TID 3	RNAD Upnor (Chatham)
TID 4	Captain of Dockyard (Portsmouth)
TID 11	Gibraltar Dockyard
TID 32 (C702)	SNSO for Fleet Fuelling Service (Devonport)
TID 46	BDO for Mooring Duties (Devonport)
TID 50	Captain of Dockyard (Portsmouth)
TID 52	Captain of Dockyard (Chatham)
TID 56 (C688)	SNSO Gibraltar
TID 57	Captain of Dockyard (Rosyth)
TID 61	Captain of Dockyard (Chatham)
TID 68	SASO Bull Point (Devonport)
TID 71	SVSO (Deptford)
TID 75	Captain in Charge (Portland)
TID 76	Admiralty (Malta)

Ship	Deployment
TID 80	Captain in Charge (Portland)
TID 83	Captain of Dockyard (Chatham)
TID 97	Captain of Dockyard (Chatham)
TID 99	Portsmouth for towage outside port limits
TID 101	BDO (Malta)
TID 106	RNAD Priddy's Hard (Portsmouth)
TID 107	SORF (Harwich)
TID 122	SVSO (Hong Kong)
TID 123 (C742)	SNSO (Hong Kong)
TID 124	SNSO (Hong Kong)
TID 129	SNSO (Hong Kong)
TID 130	SNSO (Hong Kong)
TID 136	RNAD Kilindini (Mombasa)
TID 142	Singapore for Dockyard Service
TID 144	SASO (Singapore)
TID 145	SASO (Singapore)
TID 149	Captain of Dockyard (Singapore)
TID 164	HMS LOCHINVAR (Port Edgar)
TID 165	HMS SAFEGUARD (Rosyth)
TID 172	Civil Engineer in Chief (Chatham)

Displacement 54 tons Dimensions 65ft x 17ft x 6ft Machinery Compound Steam engine, single shaft, 220 IHP Speed 8½ knots

Notes
Small tugs built between 1943 and late 1946, initially to support invasion preparations. 182 vessels completed to the order of the Ministry of War Transport, with allocations being made for Naval Service, to various Army units and to civilian organisations. At the cessation of hostilities a number of tugs were designated for Admiralty use and transferred permanently to Naval Service.

THE DOMINION NAVIES
1952

It is an unavoidable fact that Britain and its interests spread far and wide around the globe. It is also obvious that our country relies heavily upon the sea and the trade which travels over it for its very survival. In 1919 Admiral of the Fleet, Lord Jellicoe toured, what was then the British Empire, to review and report on the defences around the world. It was becoming increasingly obvious that Britain alone could not carry the financial burden of providing fleets to protect the widely dispersed trade routes and it was recommended that each Dominion should have its own naval force, manned, trained and supplied by the Dominion. These forces should be able to patrol and protect their own waters and there would be a series of bases around the world able to support and service British warships in a time of crisis.

Since those early days and through World War II, these naval forces have, in many cases, grown beyond small patrol forces and have rapidly become navies in their own right able to operate beyond their national boundaries. Canada and Australia now have a full mix of fighting vessels, including aircraft carriers, while, India and New Zealand operate cruisers.

These navies now form a nucleus of efficiently operated warships capable looking after their own national interests in addition to supporting the Royal Navy in operations around the world if required.

Australia

The Australian Navy officially came into existence on 1 July 1911, when the Commonwealth Naval Forces became the Royal Australian Navy (RAN) and its ships carried the prefix HMAS. In January 1949 the RAN changed the title of His Majesty's Royal Australian Squadron to His Majesty's Australian Fleet. On the death of King George VI this year, and the accession of Queen Elizabeth II it was changed to Her Majesty's Australian Fleet.

Canada

Founded following the introduction of the Naval Service Bill of 1910, the Naval Service of Canada was intended as a distinct naval force for the Dominion, that, if necessary, could be placed under British control. The service was renamed Royal Canadian Navy by King George V on 29 August 1911. At the outbreak of the Second World War, the RCN had just warships, but expanded so rapidly that by the end of the war she was recognised as the third largest navy in the world after the United States Navy and the Royal Navy.

New Zealand

In October 1941, the New Zealand Division of the Royal Navy (which had been established by the Naval Defence Act of 1913) was, by Royal Decree, to be renamed the Royal New Zealand Navy and its warships prefixed by HMNZS.

India

The Indian Navy can trace its roots back to 1830 when the Bombay Marine was renamed Her Majesty's Indian Navy. It was later to be renamed the Royal Indian Marine prior to being renamed the Royal Indian Navy in 1934. Following India's independence in 1947 and the ensuing partition, the Royal Indian Navy was divided between India and Pakistan, and the Armed Forces Reconstitution Committee divided the ships and men of the Royal Indian Navy between India and Pakistan. The newly-formed Royal Pakistan Navy would receive three of the seven active sloops, four of the ten operational minesweepers, two frigates, two naval trawlers, four harbour launches and a number of harbour defence motor launches while India retained the remainder of the RIN's assets and personnel. On January 1950, when India became a republic, the Royal Indian Navy was succeeded by the Indian Navy and its vessels now carry the prefix INS (Indian Naval Ship).

Pakistan

As detailed above, the foundation of the Royal Pakistan Navy came a day after the independence of Pakistan on 15 August 1947. The Armed Forces Reconstitution Committee divided the Royal Indian Navy between both India and Pakistan. Although a young navy, many of its personnel transferred with the ships and therefore it lacks neither experience or ambition - indeed the Pakistan government are already in talks to expand their fleet.

South Africa

On 1 July 1913 the South African Division of the Royal Naval Volunteer Reserve (RNVR) was formed through the amalgamation of the Natal Naval Volunteers (1885) and the Cape Naval Volunteers (1905). In January 1940 the Seaward Defence Force, was formed, being responsible for operating minesweepers, anti-submarine ships, and other inspection and signaling duties in South African waters. The Seaward Defence Force and the South African RNVR were consolidated on 1 August 1942 to form the South African Naval Forces (SANF). At the end of the war the SANF was reformed as part of the Union Defence Force and in 1951 the South African Naval Forces became the South African Navy. This year it was announced that the prefix of HMSAS was to be changed to SAS (South African Ship) in 1952.

Ceylon

The roots of the modern Ceylon Navy dates back to 1937 when the Ceylon Naval Volunteer Force was established, which was renamed and absorbed into the Royal Navy as the Ceylon Royal Naval Volunteer Reserve during World War II. The current Sri Lankan Navy was established on 9 December 1950 when the Navy Act was passed for the formation of the Royal Ceylon Navy.

Malaya

The Malay Navy, which was the Malay Section of the Royal Navy, was reactivated on 24 December 1948 at the outbreak of the Communist Emergency, when the Malayan Naval Force regulation was officially gazetted on 4 March 1949. The main mission of the Malayan Naval Force (MNF) was coastal patrol in order to stop the communist terrorists from receiving supplies from the sea. In addition, the Force was tasked with guarding the approaches to Singapore and other ports. In August 1952 Her Majesty Queen Elizabeth II, bestowed the title Royal Malayan Navy Singapore to the Malayan Naval Force in recognition of their sterling service in action during the Malayan Emergency.

East Africa

Naval Volunteer Reserves were raised in Zanzibar (1938) and Tanganyika (1939). After 1942 all three local Reserves were treated as one organisation, and became known as the East African Naval Force (EANF). The Royal East African Navy is a naval force of the British colonies of Kenya, Tanganyika, Uganda and Zanzibar which was formed in 1952 to replace the EANF.

(The listings that follow present the major warships operated by the Dominion Navies. Many additionally operate a number of smaller MLs and SDMLs.)

SHIPS OF THE ROYAL AUSTRALIAN NAVY
Pennant Numbers

Penn	Ship Name	Penn	Ship Name
Aircraft Carriers		F442	MURCHISON
		F532	MACQUARIE
R17	SYDNEY	F535	SHOALHAVEN
R21	MELBOURNE	F698	CONDAMINE
R71	VENGEANCE		
		Minesweepers	
Cruisers			
		M05	COLAC
C63	HOBART	M34	ARARAT
C73	SHROPSHIRE	M183	WAGGA
C84	AUSTRALIA	M186	COOTAMUNDRA
		M203	ROCKHAMPTON
Destroyers		M204	KATOOMBA
		M205	TOWNSVILLE
D11	QUADRANT	M206	LITHGOW
D37	TOBRUK	M207	MILDURA
D59	ANZAC	M218	KAPUNDA
D123	WARRAMUNGA	M231	BUNDABERG
D130	ARUNTA	M232	DELORAINE
D191	BATAAN	M234	LATROBE
D262	QUALITY	M235	HORSHAM
D270	QUEENBOROUGH	M241	BUNBURY
D281	QUIBERON	M244	CASTLEMAINE
D292	QUICKMATCH	M238	GYMPIE
		M246	FREMANTLE
Frigates		M248	SHEPPARTON
		M251	DUBBO
F74	SWAN	M285	BOWEN
F354	GASCOYNE	M323	BENALLA
F363	HAWKESBURY	M324	GLADSTONE
F376	BURDEKIN	M326	GLENELG
F377	DIAMANTINA	M351	COWRA
F406	BARWON	M361	PARKES
F408	CULGOA	M362	JUNEE

Penn	Ship Name	Penn	Ship Name
M363	STRAHAN	A312	WARREGO

Landing Ships (Tank)		Boom Defence Vessels	
L3017	TARAKAN	P69	KOALA
L3035	LAE	P80	KANGAROO
L3501	LABUAN	P286	KARANGI

Survey Ships			
A175	BARCOO		

HMAS Sydney

AIRCRAFT CARRIERS

COLOSSUS CLASS

Ship	Completed	Builder
VENGEANCE	15.01.45	Swan Hunter & Wigham Richardson

Displacement 13,190 tons (18,040 tons FL) Dimensions 693ft 2in x 80ft x 23ft 6in Machinery Parsons SR Geared Turbines, Four Admiralty 3-drum boilers, 2 shafts, 42,000 shp Speed 24½ knots Armament 12 x 40mm, 32 x 20mm Complement 1,343

Notes

The ship is on loan to the RAN until the arrival of MAJESTIC which is under construction in Great Britain. VENGEANCE was handed over to the RAN at Devonport on 13 November 1952.

MAJESTIC CLASS

Ship	Completed	Builder
SYDNEY	05.02.49	HM Dockyard (Devonport)

Displacement 15,740 tons (19,550 tons FL) Dimensions 695ft x 112ft 6in x 25ft Machinery Parsons SR Geared Turbines, Four Admiralty 3-drum Boilers, 2 shafts, 40,000 SHP Speed 24½ knots Armament 12 x 40mm, 4 x 3-pdr Complement 1,300

Notes

Laid down as HMS TERRIBLE and commissioned at Devonport on 16.12.48 as HMAS SYDNEY. By January 1952 the ship had completed seven operational patrols off Korea.

A further Majestic class carrier, which has been laid up incomplete since 1946, is to be completed for service with the RAN. Work resumed on MAJESTIC in 1949 after the ship was purchased by the Australian Government. She will be completed to a modernised design to take into account post war developments.

CRUISERS

COUNTY CLASS

Ship	Completed	Builder
AUSTRALIA	24.04.28	J. Brown (Clydebank)

Displacement 10,000 tons (13,540 tons FL) **Dimensions** 630ft x 68ft 4in x 16ft 3in **Machinery** Four Brown Curtis SR Geared Turbines, Eight Admiralty three drum boilers, 4 shafts 80,000 shp **Speed** 31½ knots **Armament** 6 x 8in (3 x twin), 8 x 4in (4 x twin) 20 x 40mm, 16 x 2-pdr) **Complement** 679

Notes

Similar to HMS CUMBERLAND. She was refitted and upgraded in the UK in 1945. During 1952 the ship visited New Guinea, New Britain and the Solomon Islands, dropping a wreath at Savo Island to commemorate the sinking of her sister ship CANBERRA on 9 August 1942. A half sister ship, SHROPSHIRE, presented by the RN to replace CANBERRA, is now laid up.

IMPROVED LEANDER CLASS

Ship	Completed	Builder
HOBART	13.01.36	HM Dockyard (Devonport)

Displacement 7,105 tons (9,420 tons FL) **Dimensions** 555ft x 56ft 8in x 15ft 8 in **Machinery** Four Admiralty three drum boilers, 4 shafts; Four Parsons SR Geared Turbines; 72,000 shp **Speed** 32½ knots **Armament** 6 x 6in (3 x twin), 8 x 4in (4 x twin) 9 x 40mm, 2 x 20mm, 8 x 21-inch torpedo tubes) **Complement** 550

Notes

Formerly HMS APOLLO, she was acquired from the RN in 1938. She paid off into reserve in 1947 following operations off Japan in support of the Occupation Forces. She is scheduled to undergo a modernisation refit to and then operate as a fleet training ship.

DESTROYERS

DARING CLASS

Ship	Completed	Builder
VAMPIRE	01.07.52 (LD)	Williamstown Dockyard
VENDETTA	04.07.49 (LD)	Cockatoo Island Dockyard
VOYAGER	01.03.52 (L)	Cockatoo Island Dockyard
WATERHEN	00.02.52 (LD)	Williamstown Dockyard

Displacement 2,610 tons (3,700 tons FL) Dimensions 390ft x 43ft x 12ft 9in
Machinery English Electric SR geared turbines, 2 shafts, 54,000 shp Speed 33 knots
Armament 6 x 4.5in (3 x twin), 6 x 40mm (3 x twin), 10 x 21in TT Complement 314

Notes

Ordered in 1947 and similar in design to the RN Daring class, but modified to suit RAN
requirements.

BATTLE CLASS

Ship	Completed	Builder
ANZAC	22.03.51	Williamstown Dockyard
TOBRUK	08.05.50	Cockatoo Docks & Eng. Co.

Displacement 2,325 tons (3,300 tons FL) Dimensions 379ft x 41ft x 12ft 9in
Machinery Parsons SR geared turbines, 2 Admiralty 3-drum boilers, 2 shafts, 50,000
shp Speed 35½ knots Armament 4 x 4.5in, 12 x 40mm, 10 x 21in TT Complement
290

Notes

Very similar to the RN Battle class but with revised armament and improved accommodation arrangements. TOBRUK joined the fleet on 16 January 1951 and ANZAC 14 March
1951. The ships cost £2,470,000 and £2,500,000 respectively. Both vessels have been
operating off the coast of Korea, TOBRUK returning to Australia in February this year.
Following a short refit ANZAC sailed in September for a second tour of duty off Korea.

TRIBAL CLASS

Ship	Completed	Builder
ARUNTA	03.03.42	Cockatoo Docks & Eng. Co.
BATAAN	25.05.45	Cockatoo Docks & Eng. Co.
WARRAMUNGA	23.11.42	Cockatoo Docks & Eng. Co.

Displacement 1,970 tons (2,675 tons FL) Dimensions 377ft 6in x 36ft 6in x 15ft 6in
Machinery Parsons SR geared turbines, 3 Admiralty 3-drum boilers, 2 shafts, 44,000
shp Speed 36½ knots Armament 6 x 4.7in (4 x 4.7in in ARUNTA), 2 x 4in, 6 x 40mm,
4 x 21in TT, 2 x DCT (Squid in ARUNTA) Complement 250

Notes

BATAAN deployed from Sydney on 8 January for a second tour of duty in the Korean War
and relieved HMAS MURCHISON at Kure on 4 February. Following a refit and work up
period WARRAMUNGA sailed on 11 January for her second tour off Korean. ARUNTA
underwent a refit and modernisation and recommissioned in November. The after deckhouse was extended aft and 'X' turret replaced by a Squid A/S mortar. Reclassified as an
A/S destroyer. BATAAN and WARRAMUNGA likely to undergo a similar modernisation.

'Q' CLASS

Ship	Completed	Builder
QUALITY	07.09.42	Swan Hunter & Wigham Richardson
QUADRANT	26.11.42	Hawthorn Leslie & Co (Hebburn)
QUEENBOROUGH	10.12.42	Swan Hunter & Wigham Richardson
QUIBERON	22.07.42	J S White (Cowes)
QUICKMATCH	30.09.42	J S White (Cowes)

Displacement 1,705 tons (2,425 tons FL) Dimensions 358ft 9in x 35ft 9in x 9ft 6in
Machinery Parsons SR geared turbines, 2 Admiralty 3-drum boilers, 2 shafts, 40,000
shp Speed 36 knots Armament 4 x 4.7in, 6 x 20mm, 8 x 21in TT Complement 250

Notes

Ex-RN destroyers lent to the RAN between 1943-45 and transferred on a permanent
basis in June 1950. All to be converted to fast A/S frigates along similar lines to the RN
Type 15 conversions. Work being carried out by Cockatoo Island and Williamstown dock-

yards. Armament on completion of conversion expected to be a twin 4-inch mount, two 40mm Bofors, two single torpedo tubes and two Squid A/S mountings. QUADRANT, the first to undergo conversion, entered refit in April 1950 at Williamstown and is expected to recommission next year. QUEENBOROUGH was taken in hand by Cockatoo Island Dockyard in May 1950, and QUIBERON in November 1950 at the same yard. On 28 March 1951 QUICKMATCH was towed by the tug HMAS RESERVE to Williamstown Naval Dockyard where work commenced on her conversion. QUALITY remains in reserve and has not yet been allocated to the conversion programme.

FRIGATES

BAY CLASS

Ship	Completed	Builder
CONDAMINE	22.02.46	NSW Engineering (Newcastle)
CULGOA	01.04.47	Williamstown Dockyard
MURCHISON	17.12.45	Evans, Deakin & Co (Brisbane)
SHOALHAVEN	01.05.46	Walkers Ltd (Maryborough)

Displacement 1,537 tons (2,200 tons FL) Dimensions 301ft x 36ft 6in x 12ft Machinery Triple expansion, 2 shafts, 5,500 ihp Speed 19 knots Armament 4 x 4in, 3 x 40mm, 4 x 20mm, Hedgehog, 4 x DCT Complement 177

Notes

Built to the design of the RN's Bay Class Frigates, these ships were generally known as Modified River Class Frigates due to their names bing taken from Australian rivers, although they are sometimes referred to as Bay Class vessels. In June CONDAMINE sailed to join United Nations forces operating in Korean waters. She reached Singapore on 11 July and Japanese waters at the close of the month. Throughout 1952 both CULGOA and MURCHISON were used as training ships for National Service Trainees and in October 1952, together with SHOALHAVEN, supported the British atomic test at the Monte Bello Islands.

RIVER CLASS

Ship	Completed	Builder
BARCOO	17.08.44	Cockatoo Docks & Eng. Co.

Ship	Completed	Builder
BARWON	10.12.45	Cockatoo Docks & Eng. Co.
BURDEKIN	27.06.44	Walkers Ltd (Maryborough)
DIAMANTINA	27.04.45	Walkers Ltd (Maryborough)
GASCOYNE	18.11.43	Mort's Dock (Sydney)
HAWKESBURY	05.07.44	Mort's Dock (Sydney)
MACQUARIE	07.12.45	Mort's Dock (Sydney)

Displacement 1,420 tons (2,220 tons FL) Dimensions 301ft 4in x 36ft 8in x 12ft Machinery Triple expansion, 2 shafts, 5,500 ihp Speed 20 knots Armament 2 x 4in, 2 x 40mm, 4 x DCT, (Squid in BARCOO) Complement 140

Notes

Similar to the RN River class. BARCOO is employed on surveying duties. HAWKES-BURY recommissioned on 14 May this year after five years in reserve and transferred to the operational control of the Fourth Task Force of the Royal Navy as a unit of the First Frigate Squadron. MACQUARIE recommissioned at Melbourne on 15 August and after

working up, conducted surveillance activities and duties as the weather support ship for the British atomic test at Monte Bello. A sistership LACHLAN is on loan to New Zealand for three years for surveying and research work. BARWON, BURDEKIN, DIA-MANTINA and GASCOYNE are in reserve.

SWAN CLASS

Ship	Completed	Builder
SWAN	10.12.36	Cockatoo Docks & Eng. Co.
WARREGO	21.08.40	Cockatoo Docks & Eng. Co.

Displacement 1,060 tons (1,575 tons FL) Dimensions 250ft x 36ft x 7ft 6in Machinery Parsons SR geared turbines, 2 Admiralty 3-drum boilers, 2 shafts, 2,000 shp Speed 16½ knots Armament 4 x 4in (3 x 4-inch WARREGO), 1 x 40mm (2 x 40mm, 4 x 20mm WARREGO) Complement 160

Notes

WARREGO is employed on surveying duties but retains her full armament. She returned to active service in June 1951 following a period in reserve. She surveyed the Monte Bello Islands off Western Australian prior to this years British atomic test. SWAN paid off into reserve on 18 August 1950.

MINESWEEPERS

BATHURST CLASS

Ship	Completed	Builder
ARARAT	16.06.43	Evans Deakin (Brisbane)
BENALLA	28.04.43	Williamstown Dockyard
BOWEN	09.11.42	Walkers (Maryborough)
BUNBURY	03.01.43	Evans Deakin (Brisbane)
BUNDABERG	12.09.42	Evans Deakin (Brisbane)
CASTLEMAINE	17.02.42	Williamstown Dockyard
COLAC	06.01.42	Mort's Dock (Sydney)
COOTAMUNDRA	03.04.43	Poole & Steel (Sydney)
COWRA	08.10.43	Poole & Steel (Sydney)
DELORAINE	22.11.41	Mort's Dock (Sydney)
DUBBO	31.07.42	Mort's Dock (Sydney)
FREMANTLE	24.03.43	Evans Deakin (Brisbane)
GLADSTONE	22.03.43	Walkers (Maryborough)
GLENELG	16.11.42	Evans Deakin (Brisbane)
GYMPIE	04.11.42	Evans Deakin (Brisbane)
HORSHAM	18.11.42	Williamstown Dockyard
JUNEE	11.04.44	Poole & Steel (Sydney)
KAPUNDA	21.10.42	Poole & Steel (Sydney)
KATOOMBA	17.12.41	Poole & Steel (Sydney)
LATROBE	06.11.42	Mort's Dock (Sydney)

296

Ship	Completed	Builder
LITHGOW	14.06.41	Mort's Dock (Sydney)
MILDURA	22.07.41	Mort's Dock (Sydney)
PARKES	25.05.44	Evans Deakin (Brisbane)
ROCKHAMPTON	26.01.42	Walkers (Maryborough)
SHEPPARTON	01.02.43	Williamstown Dockyard
STRAHAN	14.03.44	State Dockyard (Newcastle)
TOWNSVILLE	19.12.41	Evans Deakin (Brisbane)
WAGGA	18.12.42	Mort's Dock (Sydney)

Displacement 760 tons (1,025 tons FL) Dimensions 186ft x 31ft x 8ft 6in Machinery Triple expansion, 2 Admiralty 3-drum small tube boilers, 2 shafts, 1,800 ihp Speed 15½ knots Armament 1 x 4in, 1 x 40mm Complement 70

Notes

Design similar to the RN Bangor class. Sixty of the type were built in Australia, including four for the Indian Navy and 20 for the Royal Navy, however, all twenty were operated and manned by the RAN. Four ships (ECHUCA, INVERELL, KIAMA and STAWELL) were transferred to New Zealand in 1952. COOTAMUNDRA, COWRA, FREMANTLE, GLADSTONE, JUNEE, MILDURA and WAGGA are used as training ships for Permanent Service, Reserve and National Service personnel. The remaining vessels are in reserve.

AUXILIARIES

BAR CLASS

Ship	Completed	Builder
KANGAROO	27.09.40	Cockatoo Docks & Eng. Co.
KARANGI	23.12.41	Cockatoo Docks & Eng. Co.
KOALA	07.02.40	Cockatoo Docks & Eng. Co.

Displacement 768 tons Dimensions 164ft x 32ft 2in x 9ft 9in Machinery Triple expansion, single screw, 850 ihp Speed 11½ knots Complement 32

These vessels are constructed to a design similar to that of the Royal Navy's Bar class vessels. On 5 September 1952 KARANGI arrived at Sydney to begin a refit.

LANDING SHIP TANK (LST 3)

Ship	Completed	Builder
LABUAN	19.05.45	Vickers Armstrong (Walker)
LAE	10.03.45	Wm Denny & Bros (Dumbarton)
TARAKAN	09.06.45	Hawthorn Leslie (Hebburn)

Displacement 3,065 tons (3,114 tons FL) Dimensions 345ft 9in x 54ft x 11ft 6in Machinery Steam reciprocating engine, Admiralty three-drum boiler, 2 shafts, 5,500 ihp Speed 13½ knots Armament 4 x 40mm, 16 x 20mm Complement 104

Notes

Each ship can transport 18 tanks, 27 trucks, 7 LCMs and 168 troops. LAE and TARAKAN are laid up in reserve. LABUAN operates as a supply vessel for the Australian Antarctic bases.

DEPOT SHIP

Ship	Completed	Builder
PLATYPUS	21.03.17	John Brown (Clydebank)

Displacement 3,476 tons Dimensions 325ft x 44ft x 15ft 6in Machinery Two sets triple expansion, 4 cylindrical return-tube boilers, 2 shafts, 850 ihp Speed 11½ knots Armament 1 x 12-pdr Complement 32

Notes

Originally constructed as a Submarine Depot ship she served throughout the Second World War as a Repair and Mainetnance ship. She was paid off in May 1946 but continues to give service as a HQ and accommodation ship for vessels in reserve at Sydney.

SHIPS OF THE ROYAL CANADIAN NAVY
Pennant Numbers

Penn	Ship Name	Penn	Ship Name
Aircraft Carriers		309	STE THERESE
		310	OUTREMONT
21	MAGNIFICENT	311	STETTLER
		312	FORT EIRE
Cruisers		313	SUSSEXVALE
		314	BUCKINGHAM
31	QUEBEC	315	NEW GLASGOW
32	ONTARIO	316	PENETANG
		317	CAP DE LA MADELEINE
Destroyers		318	JONQUIERE
		319	TORONTO
		320	VICTORIAVILLE
213	NOOTKA	321	LANARK
214	MICMAC	322	LAUZON
215	HAIDA	323	ST STEPHEN
216	HURON	324	ST CATHERINES
217	IROQUOIS		
218	CAYUGA	**Minelayers**	
219	ATHABASKAN		
224	ALGONQUIN	113	WHITETHROAT
225	SIOUX		
226	CRESCENT	**Minesweepers**	
228	CRUSADER		
		143	GASPE
Frigates		144	CHALEUR
		145	FUNDY
301	ANTIGONISH	146	COMOX
302	STONETOWN	147	COWICHAN
303	BEACON HILL	148	UNGAVA
304	NEW WATERFORD	149	QUINTE
305	LA HULLOISE	150	MIRAMICHI
306	SWANSEA	151	FORTUNE
307	PRESTONIAN	152	JAMES BAY
308	INCH ARRAN	153	THUNDER

Penn	Ship Name	Penn	Ship Name
154	RESOLUTE	187	WESTMOUNT
156	CHIGNECTO	188	NIPIGON
157	TRINITY	189	MINAS
168	NEW LISKEARD	190	SARNIA
169	PORTAGE	191	KENORA
170	FORT FRANCES	192	MAHONE
171	KAPUSKASING	193	BLAIRMORE
172	WALLACEBURG	194	MILLTOWN
173	ROCKCLIFFE	195	FORT WILLIAM
174	OSHAWA	196	RED DEER
176	SAULT STE MARIE	197	MEDICINE HAT
177	WINNIPEG	198	GODERICH
182	KENTVILLE		
183	PORT HOPE	**Survey Ships**	
184	GANANOQUE		
185	SWIFT CURRENT	532	SACKVILLE
186	MALPEQUE		

HMCS Cayuga

AIRCRAFT CARRIERS

MAJESTIC CLASS

Ship	Completed	Builder
MAGNIFICENT	21.05.48	Harland & Wolff (Belfast)

Displacement 15,740 tons (19,550 tons FL) **Dimensions** 695ft x 112ft 6in x 25ft **Machinery** Parsons SR Geared Turbines, Four Admiralty 3-drum Boilers, 2 shafts, 40,000 shp **Speed** 24½ knots **Armament** 16 x 40mm (twin), 14 x 40mm (single) **Complement** 1,350

Notes

Completed to the original design, except for a reduced close range armament, she is on loan to the RCN until the completion of POWERFUL, another Majestic class carrier, on which all work was suspended at the end of the Second World War. She was purchased in 1952 by Canada and renamed BONAVENTURE.

CRUISERS

MINOTAUR CLASS

Ship	Completed	Builder
ONTARIO	25.05.45	Harland & Wolff (Belfast)

Displacement 8,700 tons (11,480 tons FL) **Dimensions** 555ft 6in x 63ft x 16ft 6in **Machinery** Parsons SR geared turbines, 4 Admiralty 3-drum boilers, 4 shafts, 72,500 shp **Speed** 31½ knots **Armament** 9 x 6in, 10 x 4in, 20 x 40mm, 6 x TT **Complement** 730

Notes

A Minotaur class light cruiser built for the Royal Navy as HMS MINOTAUR, but transferred to the Royal Canadian Navy on completion and renamed ONTARIO. Operated as a training cruiser.

COLONY CLASS

Ship	Completed	Builder
QUEBEC	03.01.43	Vickers-Armstrong (Tyne)

Displacement 8,000 tons (10,840 tons FL) Dimensions 555ft 6in x 61ft 8in x 17ft Machinery Parsons SR geared turbines, 4 Admiralty 3-drum boilers, 4 shafts, 72,000 shp Speed 31 knots Armament 9 x 6in, 8 x 4in, 8 x 40mm, 12 x 20mm, 6 x TT Complement 730

Notes

HMS UGANDA was transferred to the Royal Canadian Navy on Trafalgar Day, 21 October 1944 and was recommissioned as HMCS UGANDA. Following a period of reserve post war, the ship was recommissioned and renamed QUEBEC on 14 January and transferred from the Pacific fleet to the Atlantic to replace vessels deployed for the Korean War.

DESTROYERS

TRIBAL CLASS

Ship	Completed	Builder
HAIDA	18.09.43	Vickers-Armstrong (Tyne)
HURON	28.07.43	Vickers-Armstrong (Tyne)
IROQUOIS	10.12.42	Vickers-Armstrong (Tyne)
ATHABASKAN	20.01.48	Halifax Shipyards Ltd (Halifax)
CAYUGA	20.10.47	Halifax Shipyards Ltd (Halifax)
MICMAC	12.09.45	Halifax Shipyards Ltd (Halifax)
NOOTKA	08.10.46	Halifax Shipyards Ltd (Halifax)

Displacement 1,927 tons (2,745 tons) Dimensions 355ft 6in x 37ft 6in x 9ft 6in Machinery Parsons SR geared turbines, 3 Admiralty 3-drum boilers, 2 shafts, 44,000 shp Speed 36½ knots Armament 4 x 4in, 2 x 3in, 4 x 40mm, 2 x Squid, 4 x 21in TT (ATHABASKAN: 8 x 4in, 2 x 3in, 6 x 40mm, 4 x 21-in TT) (NOOTKA: 6 x 4in, 4 x 40mm, 4 x 20mm, 4 x 21in TT) Complement 240

All are to be modernised and their role changed to that of A/S escort. HAIDA, HURON and IROQUOIS have completed thier refits with ATHABASKAN, CAYUGA, MICMAC and NOOTKA expected to complete theirs by 1954. On completion all will have a uniform armament fit and a new shorter foremast. ATHABASKAN spent the first half of 1952 on combat operations off Korea, as did CAYUGA. On completion of her modernisation refit in March HAIDA undertook a shakedown cruise to Europe before deploying to Korea in September. IROQUOIS also conducted operations off Korea for the second half of the year. NOOTKA spent all of 1952 on operations off Korea arriving back at Halifax in December.

'CR' CLASS

Ship	Completed	Builder
CRESCENT	21.09.45	John Brown (Clydebank)
CRUSADER	26.11.45	John Brown (Clydebank)

Displacement 1,710 tons (2,560 tons FL) Dimensions 362ft 9in x 35ft 9in x 13ft 10in Machinery Parsons SR geared turbines, 2 Admiralty 3-drum boilers, two shafts, 40,000 shp Speed 33 knots Armament 2 x 4in, 2 x 3in, 4 x 40mm, 4 x 21in TT Complement 165

Notes

Both ships were lent to the RCN by Great Britain in 1945 and permanently transferred in 1951. CRESCENT operating as a training ship from Halifax while CRUSADER similarly operated from Esquimalt. Following a short refit CRUSADER sailed for operations off Korea in May. CRESCENT is to undergo a conversion to a Fast A/S escort along the lines of the RNs Type 15 programme.

'V' CLASS

Ship	Completed	Builder
ALGONQUIN	28.02.44	John Brown (Clydebank)
SIOUX	05.03.44	J S White (Cowes)

Displacement 1,710 tons (2,530 tons FL) Dimensions 362ft 9in x 35ft 9in x 10ft Machinery Parsons SR geared turbines, 2 Admiralty 3-drum boilers, two shafts,

40,000 shp Speed 34 knots Armament 2 x 4in, 2 x 3in, 4 x 40mm, 2 x Squid
Complement 230

Notes

The former RN destroyers VALENTINE and VIXEN transferred to the RCN in 1944. In
1951 ALGONQUIN entered refit at Yarrow Ltd to undergo conversion in to a Fast A/S
frigate similar to the RN Type 15 programme and is scheduled to re-enter service in 1953.
SIOUX returned from operations off Korea in 1951 and is also scheduled to undergo a
similar conversion to her sister.

DESTROYER ESCORTS

ST LAURENT CLASS

Ship	Completed	Builder
ST LAURENT	30.11.51(L)	Canadian Vickers Ltd
SAGUENAY	04.04.51(LD)	Halifax Shipyards
SKEENA	19.08.52(L)	Burrard DD & SB
OTTAWA	08.06.51(LD)	Canadian Vickers Ltd
MARGAREE	24.09.51(LD)	Halifax Shipyards
FRASER	11.12.51(LD)	Burrard DD & SB
ASSINIBOINE	19.05.52(LD)	Marine Industries Ltd

Displacement 2,263 tons (2,800 tons FL) Dimensions 366ft x 42ft x 13ft 2in
Machinery Geared steam turbines, 2 water tube boilers, two shafts, 20,000 shp
Speed 25+ knots Armament 4 x 3in (2 x twin), 2 x 40mm, 2 x A/S mortar
Complement 290

Notes

Design work for these ships began in 1949 and they will be the first class of major warship to be designed and built in Canada. The design incorporates a flush deck and low
bridge and a considerable use of aluminium instead of steel for the superstructure.
Propelling machinery is of British design. Yarrow & Co (Scotstoun) received an order from
Canadian Vickers for the supply of a complete set of machinery for the first vessel, the
remainder being supplied with similar machinery but produced in Canada. The main turbines are of English Electric design. The first ship is scheduled to begin sea trials in 1953.

RESTIGOUCHE CLASS

Ship	Completed	Builder
CHAUDIERE	Ordered	Halifax Shipyards
COLUMBIA	Ordered	Burrard DD & SB
GATINEAU	Ordered	Davie Shipbuilding & Repairing
KOOTENAY	21.08.52(LD)	Burrard DD & SB
RESTIGOUCHE	Ordered	Canadian Vickers Ltd
ST CROIX	Ordered	Marine Industries Ltd
TERRA NOVA	Ordered	Victoria Machinery Depot Co.

Displacement 2,365 tons (2,900 tons FL) **Dimensions** 366ft x 42ft x 13ft 6in
Machinery Geared steam turbines, 2 water tube boilers, two shafts, 30,000 shp
Speed 28 knots **Armament** 4 x 3in (2 x twin), 2 x 40mm, 2 x A/S mortar **Complement**
290

Notes

Ordered in 1952 as part of the 1951 re-equipment programme. The design of these ships
is derived from the St Laurent class, using the same hull form but with differing bridge
details.

FRIGATES

RIVER CLASS

Ship	Completed	Builder
ANTIGONISH	04.07.44	Yarrows Ltd (Esquimalt)
BEACON HILL	16.05.44	Yarrows Ltd (Esquimalt)
BUCKINGHAM	02.11.44	Davie SB & Repair Co (Quebec)
CAP DE LA MADELEINE	30.09.44	Morton Eng & DD Co (Quebec)
FORT EIRE	27.10.44	George T Davie & Sons (Quebec)
INCH ARRAN	18.11.44	George T Davie & Sons (Quebec)
JONQUIERE	10.05.44	Davie SB & Repair Co (Quebec)

Ship	Completed	Builder
LA HULLOISE	20.05.44	Canadian Vickers Ltd (Montreal)
LANARK	06.07.44	Canadian Vickers Ltd (Montreal)
LAUZON	30.08.44	George T Davie & Sons (Quebec)
NEW GLASGOW	23.12.43	Yarrows Ltd (Esquimalt)
NEW WATERFORD	21.01.44	Yarrows Ltd (Esquimalt)
OUTREMONT	27.11.43	Morton Eng & DD Co (Quebec)
PENETANG	19.10.44	Davie SB & Repair Co (Quebec)
PRESTONIAN	13.09.44	Davie SB & Repair Co (Quebec)
ST CATHERINES	31.07.43	Yarrows Ltd (Esquimalt)
ST STEPHEN	28.07.44	Yarrows Ltd (Esquimalt)
STE THERESE	28.05.44	Davie SB & Repair Co (Quebec)
STETTLER	07.05.44	Canadian Vickers Ltd (Montreal)
STONETOWN	21.07.44	Canadian Vickers Ltd (Montreal)
SUSSEXVALE	29.11.44	Davie SB & Repair Co (Quebec)
SWANSEA	24.10.43	Yarrows Ltd (Esquimalt)
TORONTO	06.05.44	Davie SB & Repair Co (Quebec)
VICTORIAVILLE	11.11.44	George T Davie & Sons (Quebec)

Displacement 1,445 tons (2,216 tons FL) Dimensions 301ft 6in x 36ft 6in x 12ft Machinery Triple expansion, 2 Admiralty 3-drum boilers, 2 shafts, 5,500 shp Speed 20 knots Armament 2 x 4in (1 x twin), 8 x 20mm (4 x twin), A/S mortars Complement 141

Notes

Of similar design to the RN River class, these remaining ships have, since the end of the war, been placed in reserve, although some have been returned to service for short periods to act as training ships. There are plans in hand to convert the majority into modern A/S frigates with the first PRESTONIAN expected to re-enter service in 1953. The conversion includes the rebuilding of the superstructure to a revised design, and the extension of the forecastle right aft creating a flushdeck. The new armament will comprise 2 x 4-in guns, 6 x 40mm and two Squid mountings.

MINESWEEPERS

GASPE CLASS

Ship	Completed	Builder
CHALEUR	21.06.52(L)	Port Arthur SB Co Ltd
CHIGNECTO	12.05.52(L)	Marine Industries Ltd (Quebec)
COMOX	24.04.52(L)	Victoria Machinery
COWICHAN	12.11.51(L)	Davie SB & Repair Co (Quebec)
FORTUNE	24.04.52(LD)	Victoria Machinery
FUNDY	19.06.51(LD)	St John Dry Dock
GASPE	12.11.51(L)	Davie SB & Repair Co (Quebec)
JAMES BAY	16.08.51(LD)	Yarrows Ltd (Esquimalt)
MIRAMICHI	15.05.52(LD)	St John Dry Dock
QUINTE	02.05.52(LD)	Port Arthur SB Co Ltd
RESOLUTE	29.08.51(LD)	Kingston Shipyard
THUNDER	17.07.52(L)	Canadian Vickers Ltd (Montreal)
TRINITY	31.01.52(LD)	George T Davie & Sons (Quebec)
UNGAVA	17.12.51(LD)	Davie SB & Repair Co (Quebec)

Displacement 370 tons (410 tons FL) Dimensions 152ft x 28ft x 8ft 7in Machinery 2 General Motors V12 diesels, two shafts, 2,400 bhp Speed 16 knots Armament 1 x 40mm Complement 44

Notes

A new class of coastal minesweeper, similar in appearance to the RN CMS class, but extensively built of aluminium, including frames and decks. Four were ordered under the 1950 programme and a further ten under the 1951 programme.

ALGERINE CLASS

Ship	Completed	Builder
FORT FRANCES	28.10.44	Port Arthur SB Co Ltd

Ship	Completed	Builder
KAPUSKASING	17.08.44	Port Arthur SB Co Ltd
NEW LISKEARD	21.11.44	Port Arthur SB Co Ltd
OSHAWA	06.07.44	Port Arthur SB Co Ltd
PORTAGE	22.10.43	Port Arthur SB Co Ltd
ROCKCLIFFE	30.09.44	Port Arthur SB Co Ltd
SAULT STE MARIE	24.06.44	Port Arthur SB Co Ltd
WALLACEBURG	18.11.43	Port Arthur SB Co Ltd
WINNIPEG	29.07.43	Port Arthur SB Co Ltd

Displacement 1,040 tons (1,335 tons FL) Dimensions 235ft 6in x 35ft 6in x 11ft Machinery Triple expansion steam, 2 Admiralty 3-drum boilers, 2 shafts, 2,000 ihp Speed 16½ knots Armament 1 x 4in, 1 x 40mm, 1 x Hedgehog Complement 85

Notes

Of the same type as the British Algerine class. FORT FRANCIS and KAPUSKASING are operated by the Department of Mines and Technical Surveys and modified for hydrographic work. PORTAGE, SAULT STE MARIE and WALLACEBURG are employed on training duites. The remaining vessels are in reserve.

BANGOR CLASS

Ship	Completed	Builder
BLAIRMORE	17.11.42	Port Arthur SB Co Ltd
BROCKVILLE	19.09.42	Marine Industries Ltd (Quebec)
DIGBY	26.07.42	Davie SB & Repair Co (Quebec)
FORT WILLIAM	25.08.42	Port Arthur SB Co Ltd
GANANOQUE	08.11.41	Dufferin SB Co (Toronto)
GODERICH	23.11.41	Dufferin SB Co (Toronto)
GRANBY	20.06.42	Davie SB & Repair Co (Quebec)
KENORA	06.12.42	Port Arthur SB Co Ltd

Ship	Completed	Builder
KENTVILLE	10.10.42	Port Arthur SB Co Ltd
MAHONE	29.09.41	North Vancouver SR Ltd
MALPEQUE	04.08.41	North Vancouver SR Ltd
MEDICINE HAT	04.12.41	Canadian Vickers Ltd (Montreal)
MILLTOWN	18.09.42	Port Arthur SB Co Ltd
MINAS	02.08.41	Burrard DD Co Ltd (Vancouver)
NIPIGON	11.08.41	Dufferin SB Co (Toronto)
PORT HOPE	30.07.42	Dufferin SB Co (Toronto)
RED DEER	24.11.41	Canadian Vickers Ltd (Montreal)
SARNIA	13.08.42	Dufferin SB Co (Toronto)
SWIFT CURRENT	11.11.41	Canadian Vickers Ltd (Montreal)
WESTMOUNT	10.12.42	Dufferin SB Co (Toronto)

Displacement 672 tons (900 tons FL)   Dimensions 180ft x 28ft 6in x 9ft 6in
Machinery Triple expansion steam, 2 Admiralty 3-drum boilers, 2 shafts Speed 16½
knots Armament 1 x 4in, 2 x 20mm Complement 70

Notes

All had been discarded after the Second World War. BROCKVILLE, DIGBY and
GRANBY were allocated to the Royal Canadian Mounted Police, but only
BROCKVILLE was taken over. She was reacquired by the RCN in 1951. All three were
subsequently employed as tenders to the Naval Reserve Divisions at Halifax, St John
and Cornerbrook. In 1951 BLAIRMORE, FORT WILLIAM, GODERICH, MEDICINE
HAT, MAHONE, SARNIA, SWIFT CURRENT and WESTMOUNT were reacquired by
the RCN owing to the Korean War. The remaining vessels were reacquired in 1952. It
is not yet known what role they will play.

RESEARCH VESSELS

ISLES CLASS

Ship	Completed	Builder
WHITETHROAT	07.12.44	Cook, Welton & Gemmell

Displacement 545 tons (735 tons FL) Dimensions 164ft x 27ft 6in x 12ft 6in
Machinery Triple expansion, one cylindrical boiler, 1 shaft, 850 ihp Speed 12½ knots
Armament 1 x 20mm Complement 40

Notes

Built as a controlled minelayer for the Royal Navy she was transferred to the RCN in
1944. After the war she was converted to act as a tender for naval experimental estab-
lishments.

RESEARCH VESSELS

FLOWER CLASS

Ship	Completed	Builder
SACKVILLE	30.12.41	St John DD & SB Co Ltd

Displacement 950 tons (1,350 tons FL) Dimensions 205ft x 33ft x 11ft 6in
Machinery Triple expansion steam, 2 fire tube Scotch boilers, single shaft, 2,750 ihp
Speed 16 knots Complement 85

Notes

SACKVILLE was laid up in reserve after the war, but reactivated in 1952 and converted to a research vessel for the Department of Marine and Fisheries. All armament was
removed and the hull painted black.

ESCORT MAINTENANCE SHIPS

CAPE CLASS

Ship	Completed	Builder
FLAMBOROUGH HEAD	25.04.45	Burrard South Yard (Vancouver)
BEACHY HEAD	20.03.45	Burrard DD (North Vancouver)

Displacement 8,580 tons (11,270 tons FL) Dimensions 439ft x 62ft x 29ft Machinery
Geared turbines, 2 Foster Wheeler water tube boilers, single shaft, 2,500 ihp Speed
17 knots Armament 16 x 20mm Complement 445

FLAMBOROUGH HEAD was returned to the RCN from the UK in 1951. She is used as a training ship for Artificers. BEACHY HEAD served with the Royal Navy until 1947, at which point she was lent to the Royal Netherlands Navy where she served as VULKAAN. She was returned to the Royal Navy in 1950 and acquired by the RCN in 1952.

TENDERS

LLEWELLYN CLASS

Ship	Completed	Builder
LLEWELLYN	24.08.42	Chantier Maritime de St. Laurent
REVELSTOKE	04.07.44	Star Shipbuilders Ltd (BC)

Displacement 255 tons (360 tons FL) **Dimensions** 119ft x 23ft x 10ft 6in **Machinery** Diesel, single shaft, 500 bhp **Speed** 10 knots **Complement** 20

Notes

Similar to the smaller Motor Minesweepers in the RN. Employed as tenders at St John (NB) and St John's (Newfoundland).

YMS CLASS

Ship	Completed	Builder
CORDOVA	05.02.45	Harry C Grebe (Chicago, Illinois)

Displacement 270 tons (325 tons FL) **Dimensions** 136ft x 24ft 6in x 8ft **Machinery** 2 General Motors diesels, 2 shafts, 1,000 bhp **Speed** 15 knots **Complement** 30

Notes

A former US Auxiliary Motor Minesweeper (YMS-420) sold to Canada on 3 December 1951 as HMCS CORDOVA (MCA 158). She was commissioned on 9 August and is employed as a tender to the Vancouver Naval Reserve Division.

SHIPS OF THE INDIAN NAVY
Pennant Numbers

Penn	Ship Name	Penn	Ship Name
Cruisers		**Minesweepers**	
C70	DELHI	M197	RAJPUTANA
		M228	KONKAN
Destroyers		M237	MADRAS
		M243	BENGAL
D115	RANA	M249	BOMBAY
D141	RANJIT		
D209	RAJPUT	**Survey Ships**	
		F243	INVESTIGATOR
Frigates		M180	ROHILKAND
F11	JUMNA	**LST**	
F46	KISTNA	L11	MAGAR
F95	SUTLEJ		
F110	CAUVERY		
F256	TIR		

INS Delhi

CRUISERS

LEANDER CLASS

Ship	Completed	Builder
DELHI (ex-ACHILLES)	06.10.33	Cammell & Laird (Birkenhead)

Displacement 7,030 tons (9,740 tons FL) Dimensions 554ft 6in x 55ft 2in x 16ft
Machinery Parsons geared turbines, 4 Admiralty 3-drum boilers, 4 shafts, 72,000 shp
Speed 32 knots Armament 6 x 6in, 8 x 4in, 15 x 40mm, 8 x 21in TT Complement 680

Notes

The former RN Leander class cruiser ACHILLES, she was sold to India in 1948. After India became a Republic in January 1950, she was renamed INS DELHI.

DESTROYERS

'R' CLASS

Ship	Completed	Builder
RANA	12.11.42	Cammell Laird (Birkenhead)
RAJPUT	27.08.42	John Brown (Clydebank)
RANJIT	01.10.42	John Brown (Clydebank)

Displacement 1,705 tons (2,425 tons FL) Dimensions 358ft 3in x 35ft 8in x 9ft 6in
Machinery Parsons geared turbines, 2 Admiralty 3-drum boilers, 2 shafts, 40,000 shp
Speed 34 knots Armament 4 x 4.7in, 4 x 2-pdr, 6 x 20mm (4 x 40mm RANJIT & RANA), 8 x 21-inch TT Complement 200

Notes

The former RN destroyers RAIDER, ROTHERHAM and REDOUBT transferred to India in 1949, arriving in India in 1950 where they now constitute the 11th Destroyer Squadron (RAJPUT as Senior Ship). Prior to transfer the ships had been refitted in the UK to bring them up to date - tripod masts were replaced with lattice masts and radar installed. Boilers were retubed and new ventilating trunks fitted throughout the ship for operations in tropical waters.

In June it was announced that approval has been given to loan three Hunt class destroyers from the RN to India for a period of three years. BEDALE is to be refitted at Cammell Lairds, at Indian expense, where, in November, she received the name GODAVARI. The second vessel CHIDDINGFOLD was towed to Messrs Crichton at Liverpool for refitting in July. She was renamed GANGA in November. The final ship has been identified as LAMERTON and is to be renamed GOMATI. All are expected to arrive in India in 1953.

FRIGATES

MODIFIED BLACK SWAN CLASS

Ship	Completed	Builder
CAUVERY	21.10.43	Yarrow & Co Ltd (Scotstoun)
KISTNA	26.08.43	Yarrow & Co Ltd (Scotstoun)

Displacement 1,470 tons (1,925 tons FL) Dimensions 292ft 6in x 38ft 6in x 11ft 3in
Machinery Parsons geared turbines, 2 Admiralty 3-drum boilers, 2 shafts, 4,300 shp
Speed 19 knots Armament 6 x 4in, 2 x 40mm, 2 x 20mm, DC Complement 214

Notes

The survivors of four such vessels built for the Indian Navy in World War II. The other two ships (GODAVARI and NARBADA) were handed over to Pakistan during the partition of the two countries in 1948, where they now operate as SIND and JHELUM respectively.

JUMNA CLASS

Ship	Completed	Builder
JUMNA	13.05.41	Wm. Denny (Dumbarton)
SUTLEJ	23.04.41	Wm. Denny (Dumbarton)

Displacement 1,300 tons (1,735 tons FL) Dimensions 292ft 6in x 37ft 6in x 10ft 10in
Machinery Parsons geared turbines, 2 Admiralty 3-drum boilers, 2 shafts, 3,600 shp
Speed 18 knots Armament 6 x 4in, 6 x 20mm, 4 x DCT Complement 160-197

Notes

These two ships, together with CAUVERY and KISTNA form the 12th Frigate Squadron. Consideration is being given to converting one of these ships for survey duties.

314

RIVER CLASS

Ship	Completed	Builder
TIR	07.07.43	C Hill & Sons Ltd (Bristol)

Displacement 1,460 tons (2,000 tons FL)   Dimensions 301ft 4in x 36ft 8in x 14ft
Machinery Reciprocating vertical 4-cylinder triple expansion, 2 Admiralty 3-drum boilers, 2 shafts, 5,500 shp   Speed 18 knots   Armament 2 x 4in   Complement 118

Notes

The former RN River class frigate BANN, she was transferred to the Indian Navy in December 1945. She was converted at Bombay in 1948 to a Midshipman training Vessel.

RIVER CLASS

Ship	Completed	Builder
INVESTIGATOR	27.02.43	C Hill & Sons Ltd (Bristol)

Displacement 1,460 tons (2,000 tons FL)   Dimensions 301ft 4in x 36ft 8in x 14ft
Machinery Reciprocating vertical 4-cylinder triple expansion, 2 Admiralty 3-drum boilers, 2 shafts, 5,500 shp   Speed 18 knots   Complement 118

Notes

The former RN River class frigate TRENT she was transferred to India in May 1946 for use as a Survey Ship. Following conversion she served as KUKRI until 1951 when she was renamed INS INVESTIGATOR.

FLEET MINESWEEPERS

BATHURST CLASS

Ship	Completed	Builder
BENGAL	4.08.42	Cockatoo Dockyard (Sydney)
BOMBAY	25.04.42	Mort's Dock (Sydney)
MADRAS	19.05.42	Cockatoo Dockyard (Sydney)

315

Displacement 790 tons (1,025 tons FL) Dimensions 186ft 6in x 31ft x 8ft 4in
Machinery Triple expansion steam engine, 2 Admiralty 3-drum boilers, 2 shafts, 2,000
shp Speed 15 knots Armament 1 x 40mm, 2 x 20mm, 1 x 12pdr Complement 87

Notes

Four such vessels were built, in Australia, for the Indian Navy during World War II. The
fourth (PUNJAB) was transferred to Pakistan.

BANGOR CLASS

Ship	Completed	Builder
ROHILKHAND	05.02.43	William Hamilton & Co.
KONKAN	12.06.42	Lobnitz (Renfrew)
RAJPUTANA	30.04.42	Lobnitz (Renfrew)

Displacement 656 tons (825 tons FL) (ROHILKHAND: 605 tons (780 tons FL))
Dimensions 180ft x 28ft 6in x 9ft 6in (ROHILKHAND: 174ft x 28ft 6in x 10ft 6in
Machinery Triple expansion steam engine (ROHILKHAND: Parsons geared turbines),
2 Admiralty 3-drum boilers, 2 shafts, 2,000 shp Speed 16½ knots (ROHILKHAND:
15½ knots Armament ROHILKHAND: 3 x 20mm, KONKAN: 1 x 2pdr, 4 x MG,
RAJPUTANA: 1 x 12pdr, 1 x 2pdr, 2 x 20mm Complement 87

Notes

All vessels originally intended for the RN and transferred to India ROHILKHAND (ex-
PADSTOW), KONKAN (ex-TILBURY) and RAJPUTANA (ex-LYME REGIS). Together
with the three Bathurst class they constitue the 37th Minesweeping Squadron. In order
to assist the survey ship INVESTIGATOR in the mammoth task of surveying India's 6,000
mile coastline it has been decided that ROHILKIND will be converted for survey operations. Work is scheduled to begin this year.

LST(3) CLASS

Ship	Completed	Builder
MAGAR (ex-AVENGER)	14.08.45	Fairfield SB & Eng Co (Govan)

Displacement 2,256 tons (4,980 tons FL) Dimensions 345ft 9in x 54ft x 11ft 6in (aft);
4ft 7in (forward) Machinery Steam reciprocating engine, Admiralty three-drum boiler, 2
shafts, 5,500 shp Speed 13 knots Armament 2 x 40mm, 6 x 20mm Complement 180

At the time of independence four landing ships tanks (LSTs) on loan from the RN, (SMITER, THRASHER, BRUISER and AVENGER) were in India, having been borrowed for dumping surplus ammunition into the sea. Since there was an immediate need to transport large quantities of stores and equipment from Bombay and Calcutta to Cochin and Vishakhapatnam for the development of the latter as fully-fledged naval bases, it had been decided to acquire one of these landing ships for the purpose and thus AVENGER was transferred to the RIN and recommissioned as HMIS MAGAR on 11 April 1949.

SHIPS OF THE ROYAL NEW ZEALAND NAVY
Pennant Numbers

Penn	Ship Name	Penn	Ship Name
Cruisers		F421	TAUPO
C63	BELLONA	**Minesweepers**	
C81	BLACK PRINCE	M252	ECHUCA
Frigates		M233	INVERELL
		M353	KIAMA
F422	HAWEA	M348	STAWELL
F625	ROTOITI		
F426	KANIERE	**Survey Ships**	
F424	PUKAKI		
F517	TUTIRA	F364	LACHLAN

HMNZS Kaniere

AUTHOR'S COLLECTION

318

CRUISERS

MODIFIED DIDO CLASS

Ship	Completed	Builder
BELLONA	29.10.43	Fairfield SB & Eng (Fairfield)
BLACK PRINCE	20.11.43	Harland & Wolff (Belfast)

Displacement 5,900 tons (7,410 tons FL) Dimensions 512ft x 50ft 6in x 18ft 6in Machinery Parsons SR geared turbines, 4 Admiralty 3-drum boilers, 4 shafts, 62,000 shp Speed 32 knots Armament 8 x 5.25in, 4 x 40mm, 12 x 2pdr, 3 x 20mm, 6 x 21-in TT Complement 535-551

Notes

Both ships lent by the Admiralty to New Zealand who pay for their annual maintenance. BLACK PRINCE was in reserve until January 1952 when she entered major refit, scheduled to complete next year. BELLONA underwent a refit from Aug-Nov 1951at Auckland Naval Dockyard. She took part in Exercise Mainbrace in the North Sea this year, but is expected to be reduced to reserve on her return to New Zealand at the end of the year.

FRIGATES

LAKE CLASS

Ship	Completed	Builder
HAWEA	07.11.44	Smith's Dock Co Ltd
KANIERE	01.02.45	Smith's Dock Co Ltd
PUKAKI	11.08.44	Henry Robb (Leith)
ROTOITI	29.12.44	Henry Robb (Leith)
TAUPO	10.10.44	Swan Hunter & Wigham Richardson
TUTIRA	02.08.44	Swan Hunter & Wigham Richardson

Displacement 1,435 tons (2,260 tons FL) Dimensions 307ft 6in x 38ft 8in x 14ft 3in Machinery Vertical reciprocating 4-cylinder triple expansion, 2 Admiralty 3-drum boilers, 2 shafts, 5,500 shp Speed 19½ knots Armament 1 x 4-in, 4 x 2pdr, 6 x 20mm, 2 x Squid Complement 114

Notes

Former RN Loch class frigates purchased from the RN in 1948 (HAWEA (ex-LOCH ECK); KANIERE (ex-LOCH ACHRAY); PUKAKI (ex-LOCH ACHANALT); ROTOITI (ex-LOCH KATRINE), TAUPO (ex-LOCH SHIN) and TUTIRA (ex-LOCH MORLICH)) and named after New Zealand lakes. KANIERE operated as a training frigate until paying off into reserve in November 1951. PUKAKI entered refit in 1951 to undergo a modernisation refit. She is scheduled to re-enter service in late 1953. TUTIRA and TAUPO paid off into reserve in May 1951 and October 1952 respectively following active service off Korea.

MINESWEEPERS

BATHURST CLASS

Ship	Completed	Builder
ECHUCA	07.09.42	Williamstown Dockyard
INVERELL	22.09.42	Mort's Dock (Sydney)
KIAMA	00.10.43	Evans Dewson (Brisbane)
STAWELL	23.08.43	Williamstown Dockyard

Displacement 790 tons (1,025 tons FL) Dimensions 186ft x 31ft x 8ft 6in Machinery Triple expansion, 2 Admiralty 3-drum boilers, 2 shafts, 1,800 shp Speed 15 knots Armament 1 x 4-inch, 1 x 40mm Complement 71

Notes

A plan to purchase four minesweepers from Australia was approved in October 1951, but in the event they were offerd as a gift and accepted on 28 Jaunaury 1952. INVERELL was handed over at Garden Island on 10 April 1952 from where she sailed for Port Chalmers to be refitted by Stevenson & Cook Eng. Co. KIAMA was commissioned on 24 April and sailed for Auckland on 1 May. She was delivered to Mason Bros Eng. Co. Ltd for refitting. STAWELL was commissioned on 8 May, also going to Mason Bros fro refit. ECHUCA was commissioned on 7 June and sailed for NZ on 14 June. Following an extended voyage due to machinery breakdowns she was eventually handed over to Stevenson & Cook for refit on 8 July.

CASTLE CLASS

Ship	Completed	Builder
HINAU	27.06.42	Senior Foundry Ltd (Auckland)
RIMU	27.06.42	Seagar Bros. Ltd (Auckland)

Displacement 625 tons Dimensions 126ft x 23ft 6in x 14ft Machinery Triple expansion, 1 shaft, 720 ihp Speed 10½ knots Armament 1 x 12pdr Complement 26

Notes

Retained in reserve with most of their minesweeping gear removed.

ISLES CLASS

Ship	Completed	Builder
INCHKEITH	24.10.41	John Lewis & Sons (Aberdeen)
KILLEGRAY	07.11.41	Cook, Welton & Gemmell Ltd
SANDA	04.11.41	Goole SB & Repairing Co. Ltd
SCARBA	25.11.41	Cook, Welton & Gemmell Ltd

Displacement 545 tons (770 tons FL) Dimensions 164ft x 27ft 6in x 10ft 6in Machinery Triple expansion, 1 cylindrical boiler; 1 shaft, 800 ihp Speed 12 knots Armament 1 x 12pdr, 3 x 20mm Complement 40

Notes

All paid off into reserve at Auckland in 1946, where they remain.

BIRD CLASS

Ship	Completed	Builder
KIWI	28.10.41	Henry Robb Ltd (Leith)
TUI	05.12.41	Henry Robb Ltd (Leith)

Displacement 600 tons (825 tons FL) Dimensions 156ft x 30ft x 14ft Machinery Triple expansion, 1 cylindrical boiler; 1 shaft, 1,000 ihp Speed 14 knots Armament 1 x 4-in, 1 x 2pdr Complement 33-35

Notes

Both ships brought forward from reserve in April 1951 and February 1952 respectively to fulfil training ship roles in order to release the Lake class frigates for operations off Korea.

SHIPS OF THE ROYAL PAKISTAN NAVY
Pennant Numbers

Penn	Ship Name	Penn	Ship Name
Destroyers		**Minesweepers**	
D49	TIPPU SULTAN	M55	PESHAWAR
D129	TARIQ	M129	DACCA
D204	TUGHRIL	M155	CHITTAGONG
		M182	BALUCHISTAN
Frigates		**Survey Ships**	
F40	JHELUM	F265	ZULFIQUAR
F52	SIND		
F392	SHAMSHER		

PNS Shamsher

DESTROYERS

'O' CLASS

Ship	Completed	Builder
TARIQ	20.09.41	Fairfield (Glasgow)
TIPPU SULTAN	08.10.41	J. Brown (Clydebank)
TUGHRIL	19.06.42	Fairfield (Glasgow)

Displacement 1,610 tons (2,270 tons FL) Dimensions 345ft x 35ft x 15ft 9in
Machinery Parsons SR geared turbines, 2 Admiralty 3-drum boilers, 2 shafts, 36,000
shp Speed 31 knots Armament 4 x 4in, 4 x 2pdr, 6 x 20mm Complement 175

Notes

Three fromer RN 'O' class destroyers, the first pair of which, OFFA and ONSLOW were
transferred in 1949 becoming TARIQ and TIPPU SULTAN respectively. The third ship,
ONSLAUGHT, was commissioned in March 1951 as TUGHRIL following refit and tropi-
calisation in the UK. All three comprise the 25th Destroyer Flotilla.

FRIGATES

MODIFIED BLACK SWAN CLASS

Ship	Completed	Builder
JHELUM (ex-NARBADA)	29.04.43	J I Thornycroft (Woolston)
SIND (ex-GODAVARI)	28.06.43	J I Thornycroft (Woolston)

Displacement 1,475 tons (1,925 tons FL) Dimensions 299ft 6in x 38ft 6in x 8ft 9in
Machinery Parsons geared turbines, Admiralty 3-drum boilers, 2 shafts, 4,300 shp
Speed 18½ knots Armament 6 x 4in, 6 x 40mm, Hedgehog Complement 192

Notes

Two former Indian Navy frigates ceded to Pakistan following partition. They form the 25th
Frigate Squadron. In 1951 JHELUM refitted in the UK at Southampton and on return to
Pakistan took part in exercise JET 01 (Joint Exercise Trincomalee) off Ceylon.

RIVER CLASS

Ship	Completed	Builder
SHAMSHER	20.01.44	Smith's Dock (Middlesborough)
ZULFIQUAR	02.03.43	Smith's Dock (Middlesborough)

Displacement 1,370 tons (1,830 tons FL)   Dimensions 283ft x 36ft 6in x 13ft
Machinery Reciprocating steam engine, Two Admiralty 3-drum boilers, 2 shafts, 5,500 shp Speed 20 knots Armament 2 x 4in, 3 x 40mm, Hedgehog Complement 177

Notes

Both vessels ceded to Pakistan on partition. The former HMS DEVERON had been commissioned as HIMS DHANUSH on 10 November 1945 and as HMPS ZULFI-QUAR on 14 August 1947. In October, 1948 she was converted to a Survey Ship. The former HMS NADDER was transferred into Royal Indian Navy and renamed HMIS SHAMSHER In 1945, before passing to the Pakistani Navy in 1947 where she retained the same name.

MINESWEEPERS

BANGOR CLASS

Ship	Completed	Builder
BALUCHISTAN	20.10.42	Blyth Dry Dock & SB Co Ltd
CHITTAGONG	23.12.42	Blyth Dry Dock & SB Co Ltd
DACCA(ex-OUDH)	21.10.43	Garden Reach (Calcutta)
PESHAWAR (ex-MALWA)	21.06.44	Garden Reach (Calcutta)

Displacement 673 tons (860 tond FL) Dimensions 189ft x 28ft 6in x 8ft 3in
Machinery Reciprocating steam engine, Two Admiralty 3-drum boilers, 2 shafts, 2,400 shp Speed 16 knots Armament 1 x 12-pdr, 1 x 2-pdr Complement 87

Notes

Two vessels were transferred from India and all four comprise the 33rd Minesweeping Squadron.

LAHORE CLASS

Ship	Completed	Builder
BAHAWALPUR	22.10.41	Shalimar
LAHORE	18.0742	Burns

Displacement 545 tons Dimensions 163ft 6in x 27ft 6in x 10ft 6in Machinery Reciprocating steam engine, single shaft, 850 ihp Speed 12 knots Armament 1 x 12-pdr, 1 x 20mm Complement 33

Notes

These are trawlers of the Bassett type formerly operated by India as BARODA and RAMPUR respectively. HMPS BAHAWALPUR which had been recommissioned in July 1951 was placed in the Reserve Fleet in January 1952.

SHIPS OF THE SOUTH AFRICAN NAVY
Pennant Numbers

Penn	Ship Name	Penn	Ship Name
Destroyers		M 439	BLOEMFONTEIN
D 237	SIMON VAN DER STEL	**Survey Ships**	
D 278	JAN VAN RIEBEECK		
		A321	PROTEA
Frigates		**Boom Defence Vessels**	
F 10	NATAL		
F 432	GOOD HOPE	P273	FLEUR
F 602	TRANSVAAL	P285	SOMERSET
Minesweepers			
M 291	PIETERMARITZBURG		

SAS Transvaal

327

DESTROYERS

'W' CLASS

Ship	Completed	Builder
JAN VAN RIEBEECK	11.05.44	Fairfield (Glasgow)
SIMON VAN DER STEL	25.04.44	Hawthorn Leslie & Co (Hebburn)

Displacement 1,710 tons (2,530 tons FL) Dimensions 362ft 9in x 35ft 9in x 16ft Machinery Parsons SR geared turbines, 2 Admiralty 3-drum boilers, 2 shafts, 40,000 shp Speed 33 knots Armament 4 x 4.7in, 5 x 40mm, 4 x 20mm, 8 x TT Complement 186

Notes

The former RN destroyers WHELP and WESSEX had been laid up at Simon's Town as part of the South Atlantic Reserve Fleet (together with KEMPENFELT and WAGER) and are to be acquired over a three-year period. JAN VAN RIEBEECK was handed over at Simon's Town in March 1950, with SIMON VAN DER STEL due to be delivered in February 1953. There is talk of a third vessel, KEMPENFELT, being requested for transfer but this has not yet been confirmed.

FRIGATES

LOCH CLASS

Ship	Completed	Builder
GOOD HOPE	01.12.44	Blyth DD & SB Co. Ltd
NATAL	08.03.45	Swan Hunter & Wigham Richardson
TRANSVAAL	21.05.45	Harland & Wolff (Belfast)

Displacement 1,435 tons (2,260 tons FL) Dimensions 307ft x 38ft 6in x 12ft Machinery Triple expansion, 2 Admiralty 3-drum boilers, 2 shafts, 5,500 ihp Speed 19½ knots Armament 1 x 4in, 4 x 2pdr, 10 x 20mm, 2 x Squid Complement 103

The three vessels were laid down during World War II as Loch class frigates for the RN (LOCH BOISDALE, LOCH CREE and LOCH ARD respectively), but were presented to South Africa, by the Admiralty, prior to completion, in recognition of the valiant part played by South African sailors in the war at sea. 400 officers and men of the South African Naval Forces arrived in the UK at the end of 1944 to commission the three new ships which served alongside their RN counterparts for the remainder of the war. NATAL was the first British-built ship to be fitted with internal strip lighting and her internal decoration comprised pastel shades of blue, green and pink paintwork, in place of the more standard all-over white. TRANSVAAL and NATAL remain in operation, whereas GOOD HOPE, since 1948 has been laid up on a care and maintenance basis.

MINESWEEPERS

ALGERINE CLASS

Ship	Completed	Builder
BLOEMFONTEIN	16.07.45	Port Arthur Shipyards
PIETERMARITZBURG	07.10.43	Lobnitz & Co. (Renfrew)

Displacement Turbine Group: 850 tons (1,125 tons FL), Reciprocating Group: 1,010 tons (1,305 tons FL) Dimensions 235ft x 35ft 6in x 10ft 6in Machinery Reciprocating triple expansion steam, 2 Admiralty 3-drum boilers, 2 shafts, 2,400 shp Speed 16½ knots Armament 1 x 4in, 4-6 x 20mm Complement 85

Notes

The first vessels acquired by the South African Naval Forces since the end of the war, the former HMS ROSAMUND was commissioned at Devonport as HMSAS ROSAMUND on 8 September 1947 while HMSAS PELORUS was commissioned the following day at Chatham. However, before departing for South Africa at the end of the year the ships had been renamed BLOEMFONTEIN and PIETERMARITZBURG respectively. Of note the prefix HMSAS was dropped in June this year in favour of SAS.

SURVEY VESSELS

FLOWER CLASS

Ship	Completed	Builder
PROTEA	04.11.41	C Hill & Sons Ltd (Bristol)

Displacement 940 tons (1,180 tons FL) Dimensions 205ft 3in x 33ft x 13ft 3in Machinery Triple steam expansion engine, Two cylindrical single ended boilers, single shaft, 2,750 ihp Speed 16 knots Complement 82

Notes

The former corvette HMS ROCKROSE was acquired in 1947 to continue the hydrographic survey of the South African coast which had been suspended during the war. Her conversion commenced in mid-1949 which involved significant internal and external alterations. She is equipped with dual echo-sounders, radar and direction-finding gear. Special derricks and davits for working dan buoys and floating beacons are fitted, together with handling equipment amidships for the operation of two motor survey launches. The opportunity was also taken to improve the accommodation, which resulted in bunks being fitted for every member of the crew.

BOOM DEFENCE VESSELS

FLOWER CLASS

Ship	Completed	Builder
SOMERSET	14.04.42	Blyth DD & SB Co Ltd
FLEUR	15.07.42	Wm Simons & Co Ltd (Renfrew)

Displacement 730 tons (875 tons FL) Dimensions 173ft 9in x 32ft 3in x 9ft 6in Machinery Triple expansion steam engine, 2 SE boilers, 850 ihp Speed 11¾ knots Complement 32

Notes

The former RN Bar class vessels BARCROSS and BARBRAKE (SOMERSET and FLEUR) arrived at the Cape in 1942 to assist in laying and maintaining the extensive A/S boom defences at Saldanha Bay. They were transferred shortly afterwards and were renamed in 1951.

SHIPS OF THE ROYAL CEYLON NAVY

MINESWEEPERS

ALGERINE CLASS

Ship	Completed	Builder
VIJAYA	14.10.44	Redfern (Toronto)

Displacement 1,010 tons (1,305 tons FL) Dimensions 235ft x 35ft 6in x 10ft 6in
Machinery Reciprocating triple expansion steam, 2 Admiralty 3-drum boilers, 2 shafts,
2,400 shp Speed 16½ knots Armament 1 x 4in, 4-6 x 20mm Complement 85

Notes

The former RN Algerine class minesweeper FLYING FISH was transferred in 1949.
She is employed as a training ship.

SHIPS OF THE ROYAL MALAYAN NAVY

FRIGATES

RIVER CLASS

Ship	Completed	Builder
TEST	12.10.42	Hall Russell (Aberdeen)

Displacement 1,370 tons (1,830 tons FL) Dimensions 301ft 6in x 36ft 9in x 14ft
Machinery Triple expansion, 2 Admiralty 3-drum boilers, 2 shafts, 5,500 ihp Speed 20
knots Armament 2 x 4in, 10 x 20mm, Hedgehog Complement 140

Notes

The former RN River-class frigate was used as a training ship but by 1950 was joined
by an ex-Japanese minelayer, a Landing Craft Tank (HMS PELANDOK), motor fish-
ing vessel (PANGLIMA) and several seaward defence motor launches (SDML).

SHIPS OF THE ROYAL EAST AFRICAN NAVY

TRAWLERS

SHAKESPEARE CLASS

Ship	Completed	Builder
ROSALIND	18.10.41	A. & J. Inglis (Pointhouse)

Displacement 545 tons (770 tons FL) Dimensions 164ft x 27ft 9in x 11ft Machinery Reciprocating steam engine, 1 SE cylindrical boiler, 950 ihp Speed 12 knots Complement 35

Notes

The East African Naval Force was inaugurated by the Governor of Tanganyika and the Acting Governor of Kenya, at Mombasa, in July 1950, but this year was renamed the Royal East African Navy (REAN). The ship could be used for either A/S or M/S operations, but in service with REAN is more likely to be employed on patrol duties.

NAVAL AVIATION
1952

Naval Aviation is the term used to describe that branch within the Royal Navy that is concerned with flying. It is now, by far, the largest single branch within the service and despite the demands it makes in terms of specialised training, ships, equipment and shore training it is fundamentally and essentially part of the Naval Service. The Fifth Sea Lord is the Admiralty Board member responsible for air matters and within the Admiralty there are several departments concerned with the organisational requirements of the air branch. Among their tasks is the need to maintain a close liaison with the Ministry of Supply for the procurement of aircraft and specialist equipment. Implementation of the Admiralty Board's air policy is vested in the Commanders-in-Chief of the various Fleets and in the Flag Officer Air (Home). The fighting capability of the aircraft carriers and the work of their air groups, whilst embarked, is the responsibility of the C-in-C of the Fleet in which they are serving but the onus for supplying air groups in fully operational condition to equip the carriers is that of the FO Air (Home) who is, in effect, the C-in-C of a reserve air arm. The operational strength of Naval Aviation is distributed among the Home and Mediterranean Fleets and the Far East Station under their individual Cs-in-C. The carrier task groups themselves are each commanded by a subordinate Admiral at sea. FO Air (Home) has three subordinate Rear Admirals, each with their own department, to carry out specific tasks under his overall command. These are the Flag Officer Flying Training (FOFT), Flag Officer Ground Training (FOGT) and Rear Admiral Reserve Aircraft (RARA) whose titles speak for themselves.

At the end of the Second World War the Royal Navy deployed some 1,300 operational aircraft in the front line with considerably more in training, trials, storage and distribution to replace losses. Post war economic issues and the need to reduce the size of the fleet, its manpower and the need to manufacture new aircraft that incorporate the latest technology have dramatically reduced the size of the front line. Thus in the spring of 1951 when manpower was the limiting factor, there were only 144 aircraft in operational squadrons due to the lack of aircrew. The number has now risen to 208 and the limiting factor is the shortage of effective aircraft. By next year the aim is to have about 225 aircraft in front line squadrons but from then onwards the amount of money available in the naval estimates is likely to be the limiting factor.

The development and introduction of the new generation of aircraft into service has proved unexpectedly difficult and there have been a number of setbacks. It is hoped that these will be resolved within the next year and the Mutual Defence Aid Programme (MDAP) is helping with the provision of Skyraiders, Avengers and helicopters from USN stock. The shortage of effective aircraft is bound to be serious for some time, however, and the RN is looking for an improved utilisation rate in second line tasks and a significant pruning of the tasks themselves in order to expand both the front line and the strength of the RNVR Air Branch. Another area being examined is the possibility of closing down some air stations and adding their tasks to others. This concentration of tasks and greater use of 'satellite' airfields would save both money and manpower but would require initial expenditure to provide the added facilities needed at the air stations selected for expansion. A reduction of Rear Admiral Reserve Aircraft's holdings of second line aircraft and greater use of the civilian aircraft industry are possibilities that are also under consideration.

Naval aircraft continue to do good work in the Korean conflict and HMS GLORY has had a number of visitors from NATO to see just how effective the light fleet carriers and their aircraft can be. The RAN has made its debut in naval air operations with HMAS SYDNEY and her air group replacing GLORY for a spell off Korea; an official Admiralty communiqué described her performance as "very effective indeed". The RN continues to provide the only British contribution to tactical air operations over Korea and a growing number of aircrew have gained valuable experience as have the carrier's ship's companies but naval air work in the main fleets has had to be reduced significantly to support the scale of effort in the Far East.

The continuing growth of the RNVR Air Branch has led to approval being given to expand the organisation into Divisions with an increased number of squadrons. On mobilisation some of the RNVR squadrons will retain their identity and, after a suitable work-up period, take their place in the front line on a basis of equality with RN squadrons. At present the total number of aircraft available for this plan is 43 in five squadrons, three fighter and two A/S, each with 12 pilots. The remaining RNVR aircrew are available to provide the planned overbearing of RN squadrons and instructors for refresher flying training either directly or by relief of suitable serving officers.

FRONT LINE AIRCRAFT TYPES

DAVID HOBBS COLLECTION

Blackburn FIREBRAND

Variants TF5
Role Strike
Engine 1 x Bristol Centaurus IX developing 2,520hp
Span 51ft 3½in (16ft 10in folded) **Length** 38ft 9in **Height** 13ft 3in
Max weight 17,500lb **Max speed** 295 knots **Crew** 1 pilot
Equipment VHF radio; attack-recording camera
Armament 4 x 20mm cannon in wings, each with 200 rpg; 1 x Mark 15 or 17 torpedo, 1 x 2,000lb or 1 x 1,000lb bomb, 1 x Mark 6, 7 or 9 mine or 1 x 100 gallon drop tank on centreline; 2 x 500lb or 250lb bombs, depth charges, up to 8 x 60lb or 12 x 25lb rockets, 45 gallon drop tanks, flares or markers under the wings.
Squadron Service 813, 827, 759 Naval Air Squadrons

Notes
A large aircraft that has not proved popular with pilots, the Firebrand was originally conceived as a fighter in 1939. After protracted development and a change of role, it entered operational service as a strike aircraft in 1945. The two front line units give an interim capability while delays developing the Wyvern are overcome; during 1952 813 NAS operated ashore from RNAS Ford and 827 NAS from HMS EAGLE. The latter is due to disband in December. The training unit, 759 NAS is expected to disband shortly afterwards.

335

De Havilland SEA VAMPIRE

Variants F20, F21, T22
Role Fighter, pilot conversion trainer
Engine 1 x de Havilland Goblin 2 delivering 3,000lb thrust
Span 38ft **Length** 30ft 9in **Height** 8ft 10in **Max weight** 12,660lb
Max speed 500 knots **Crew** 1 pilot (T22 – 2 pilots)
Equipment VHF radio
Armament 4 x 20mm cannon
Squadron Service 702, 703, 759, 771 Naval Air Squadrons

Notes
A prototype Sea Vampire, LZ551, was the first jet aircraft in the world to land on an air-craft carrier, HMS OCEAN in December 1945. F21s carried out landing experiments without undercarriages onto a rubber deck fitted on HMS WARRIOR during 1948/49. Sea Vampires have only spent limited periods embarked due to concerns that the engine's slow acceleration would make overshooting from a baulked approach difficult. They are used mainly to train the new generation of jet fighter pilots that will be need-ed to equip front line squadrons and for fleet requirements tasks. Sea Vampires embarked in HMS VENGEANCE during 1949 for Operation 'Rusty', an evaluation of Arctic operations, and are often seen embarked for trials.

De Havilland SEA HORNET

Variants F20, NF21, PR22
Role Fighter, night fighter and photographic reconnaissance
Details are for NF21
Engines 2 x Rolls Royce Merlin 130 series (134 port/135 starboard) Each developing 2,030hp
Span 45ft (27ft 6in folded) **Length** 36ft 8in **Height** 14ft **Max weight** 19,530lb
Max speed 402 knots **Crew** 1 pilot + 1 observer
Equipment AN/APS4 AI radar, VHF radio
Armament 4 x Hispano 20mm cannon, each with 180 rpg. Provision under wings for up to 8 x 60lb rockets or 2 x 500lb or 1,000lb bombs.
Squadron Service 809, 703, 728 Naval Air Squadrons

Notes
809 NAS' NF21s embarked in HMS INDOMITABLE during 1952 are the fleet's only night fighters; its aircraft are due to be replaced by Sea Venoms as soon as they become available. The other two variants are used by fleet requirements units in the UK and Malta for a variety of tasks in support of ships that are working up or undergoing trials.

De Havilland SEA VENOM

Variants NF20
Role Night fighter
Engine 1 x de Havilland Ghost 5 delivering 5,300lb thrust.
Span 42ft 10in **Length** 36ft 4in **Height** 7ft 6in **Max weight** 14,270lb
Max speed 522 knots **Crew** 1 pilot + 1 observer
Equipment AI Mark 10 radar, VHF radio
Armament 4 x 20mm Hispano cannon
Squadron Service Scheduled to enter service in 1953

Notes
Developed from the RAF's Venom NF2, the first prototype Sea Venom, WK376, carried out deck landing trials in 1951 which showed it to be extremely well suited to carrier operations. Delivery of Sea Venoms to replace Sea Hornets and form new operational squadrons is scheduled to commence in 1953, with the first 50 aircraft to NF20 standard and subsequent aircraft to an improved NF21 standard with USN-supplied AN/APS 57 radar and a more resilient undercarriage.

338

Douglas SKYRAIDER

Variants AEW1
Role Airborne early warning
Engine 1 x Wright Cyclone R-3350-26WA developing 2,700hp
Span 50ft **Length** 38ft 10in **Height** 15ft 8in **Max weight** 24,000lb
Max speed 305 knots **Crew** 1 pilot + 2 observers
Equipment AN/APS 20C radar, 2 VHF radios
Armament Provision for flares and markers
Squadron Service 849 Naval Air squadron

Notes
USN AD-4W Skyraider aircraft have been provided to the RN under the MDAP and have proved to be extremely efficient and effective aircraft. Trials were carried by 778 NAS which disbanded last July when 849 NAS was commissioned. The way the RN uses the Skyraider differs from American practice in that 2 observers are carried in the rear seats, each capable of interpreting the radar picture and controlling other aircraft and ships, in effect acting as an airborne operations room. The USN uses the type as an airborne radar relay with mechanics in the rear seats trained only to transmit the strongest signal to the parent carrier. 849 NAS is to act as the headquarters unit, deploying 4-aircraft flights, beginning with 849A, to each operational carrier.

Fairey BARRACUDA

Variants AS3
Role Anti-submarine search and strike
Engine 1 x Rolls Royce Merlin 32 developing 1,640hp
Span 49ft 2in **Length** 39ft 9in **Height** 15ft 1in **Max weight** 14,250lb
Max speed 205 knots **Crew** 1 pilot + 1 observer + 1 TAG
Equipment ASV Mark X radar, VHF radio, ARI 5206 HF W/T
Armament Up to 4 x 250lb depth charges, flares and markers. The ability to carry a Mark 15 or 17 torpedo is retained but no longer used. 500lb bombs could be carried instead of depth charges.
Squadron Service 815, 744, 750 Naval Air Squadrons

Notes
A number of Barracudas continue to be used for a variety of second line duties mainly concerned with observer training and the development of airborne anti-submarine equipment. 815 NAS, part of the Air A/S School at RNAS Eglinton is the only front-line unit now operating the type. Its aircraft are due to be replaced by Fairey Gannets next year. Whilst it operates mainly ashore, some of 815 NAS' aircraft embarked in HMS ILLUSTRIOUS in 1951 during exercises with the new NATO alliance.

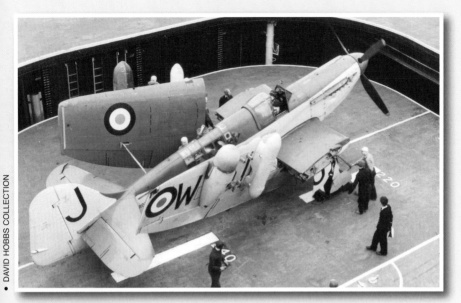

Fairey FIREFLY

Variants F1, FR4, FR5, AS4, AS5, AS6, AS7, T1, T2, T3, TT4, TT6 (RAN)
Role Strike, fighter-reconnaissance, night fighter, anti-submarine search or strike,
conversion training, target-towing
Engine 1 x Rolls Royce Griffon 74 developing 2,250hp
Span 41ft 2in (13ft 6in folded) **Length** 37ft 11in **Height** 13ft 11in
Max Weight 14,020lb **Max speed** 285 knots **Crew** 1 pilot + 1 observer
Equipment AN/APS4 radar, VHF radio, target winch in TT versions
Armament 4 x 20mm cannon with 160 rpg (not in AS6, AS7 and trainers), provision for
2 x 1,000lb or 500lb bombs underwing or 8 x 60lb or 25lb rocket-projectiles or mines
or depth charges. AS versions flares, marine markers and sonobuoys.
Squadron Service 810, 812, 814, 816(RAN), 817(RAN), 820, 821, 824, 825, 826,
1830(RNVR), 1833(RNVR), 1840(RNVR), 1841(RNVR), 1842(RNVR), 1843(RNVR),
703, 719, 723(RAN), 737, 744, 751, 766, 767, 771, 781, 782, 796 Naval Air squadrons

Notes
The ubiquitous Firefly is heavily involved with strike operations in the Korean conflict,
operating from RN and RAN light fleet carriers. The type continues in production
although it is expected to be replaced in the anti-submarine role from next year by the
Gannet and by other new types in its many operational roles. RNVR Fireflies operate
in the A/S and reconnaissance roles and are able to reinforce the front line at short
notice in an emergency. Second line Fireflies operate in a variety of training and operational development roles too numerous to list in the short space available.

Fairey GANNET

Variants AS1
Role Anti-submarine search and strike
Engines 1 x Armstrong-Siddeley Double Mamba 101 rated at 2,750shp
Span 54ft 4in (19ft 11in folded) **Length** 43ft **Height** 13ft 8½in **Max weight** 23,700lb
Max speed 360 knots **Crew** 1 pilot + 1 observer + 1 TAG
Equipment ASV19B radar, VHF/sonobuoy homer, V/UHF homing, VHF radio
Armament Large bomb bay is capable of carrying 2 Mark 30 'Dealer B' homing torpedoes or 1 x 2,000lb, 2x 1,000lb, 4 x 500lb bombs or 6 x depth charges, mines, flares or markers together with sonobuoys. Under-wing provision for up to 16 x 3" rocket projectiles. 2 x 81 gallon fuel tanks can be carried in the bomb bay instead of weapons to increase radius of action and/or endurance
Squadron Service Scheduled to enter service in 1953

Notes
The Gannet is a 'single package' anti-submarine aircraft capable of combining search and strike in a single sortie. Potentially up to 2,357lb of weapons and sonobuoys can be carried. VR546, the first prototype, made the world's first deck landing by a turboprop aircraft flown by Lt Cdr G R Callingham during carrier compatibility trials on HMS ILLUSTRIOUS. 210 Gannets are on 'super priority' order for the RN. 40 more have recently been ordered for the RAN.

The Gannet is designed to minimise fuel consumption by flying on patrol with one of its Double Mamba engine units shut down and its propeller stopped; the other unit continues to run at the most economical setting. The radome, seen in the lowered position to give 360 degree coverage, is raised before landing.

Hawker SEA FURY

Variants F10, FB11, T20
Role Fighter, fighter-bomber
Engine 1 x Bristol Centaurus developing 2,480hp
Span 38ft 4¾in (16ft 1in folded) **Length** 34ft 8in **Height** 15ft 10½in
Max weight 14,650lb **Max speed** 425 knots **Crew** 1 pilot (T20 - 2)
Equipment VHF radio
Armament 4 x 20mm cannon plus underwing variations of 2x 1,000lb or 500lb bombs, up to 12 x 60lb rocket projectiles, 2 x 90 or 45 gallon drop tanks, mines, depth charges, flares or markers.
Squadron Service 801, 802, 804, 805(RAN), 807, 808(RAN), 850(RAN), 870(RCN), 871(RCN), 898, 1831(RNVR), 1832(RNVR), 703, 723(RAN), 738, 759, 781 Naval Air squadrons

Notes

Extensively involved in carrier-borne operations off Korea alongside the Firefly, the Sea Fury is the principal fighter in service with the RN, RAN and RCN. Many more are employed in second line training and development tasks in the UK and around the world. On 9 August 1952 Lt P Carmichael in a Sea Fury of 802 NAS from HMS OCEAN shot down a MiG-15 over Korea. The Sea Fury is the first British-built RN aircraft to have power-folding wings. Sea Furies are gradually being replaced in operational squadrons by jet fighters.

343

Hawker SEA HAWK

Variants F1
Role Fighter
Engine 1 x Rolls Royce Nene 101 rated at 5,000lb thrust
Span 39ft (13ft 4in folded) **Length** 39ft 10in **Height** 8ft 8in **Max weight** 13,200lb
Max speed 520 knots **Crew** 1 pilot
Equipment VHF radio
Armament 4 x 20mm cannon with 200 rpg; wing hard-points for 2 x 1,000lb bombs or rocket projectiles.
Squadron Service 703 Naval Air Squadron

Notes
Intensive flying trials of the Sea Hawk are now taking place at RNAS Ford and it is intended to have two operational squadrons formed by mid-1953. Thereafter one squadron is to form every three months until nine are in service. The Sea Hawk will replace both the Attacker and Sea Fury in fighter squadrons but is regarded as an interim type, to be replaced itself by the N113 in due course. It is expected to be the last subsonic, straight-wing day fighter in RN service.

Sikorsky S-55 WHIRLWIND

Variants HAR 21
Role Assault helicopter
Engine 1 x Pratt & Whitney Wasp R-1340-40 developing 600hp
Rotor span 53ft **Length** 41ft 8½in **Height** 15ft 4½in **Max weight** 7,800lb
Max speed 90 knots **Crew** 1 or 2 pilots, 1 aircrewman
Equipment VHF radio, hydraulic winch
Armament Hand-held automatic weapons for crew
Squadron Service 848 Naval Air Squadron

Notes
10 Sikorsky S-55 helicopters to the US Marine Corps HRS-2 standard were recently delivered to the RN under MDAP arrangements and used to form 848 NAS, the first operational RN helicopter squadron. The unit is to be deployed to Singapore next year to prepare for operations in Malaya. A further 25 helicopters are to be delivered to HO4S-3 standard for dipping asdic evaluation.

Supermarine SEAFIRE

Variants F17, FR47
Role Fighter
Details for FR47
Engine 1 x Rolls Royce Griffon 85 developing 2,375hp
Span 36ft 11in **Length** 34ft 4in **Height** 12ft 9in **Max weight** 11,615lb
Max speed 400 knots **Crew** 1 pilot
Equipment VHF radio
Armament 4 x 20mm cannon in wings. 8 x 60lb rocket projectiles or 2 x 500lb bombs underwing; 1 x 500lb bomb on centreline. Provision underwing for 90 gallon drop-tanks.
Squadron Service 759, 1832(RNVR) Naval Air squadrons

Notes
Seafires have been superseded in operational squadrons by Sea Furies and Attackers but a few remain in use with conversion training and RNVR squadrons. They are to be replaced as more suitable aircraft become available. RNVR Seafires can embark when necessary to reinforce the front line.

Supermarine ATTACKER

Variants F1, FB1, FB2
Role Fighter, fighter-bomber
Engine 1 x Rolls Royce Nene 3 rated at 5,100lb thrust
Span 36ft 11in **Length** 37ft 6in **Height** 9ft 11in **Max weight** 11,500lb
Max speed 520 knots **Crew** 1 pilot
Equipment VHF radio
Armament 4 x 20mm Hispano cannon in wings. FB2 has provision for a 250 gallon drop tank under the belly and up to 8 x 60lb rocket projectiles or 2 x 1,000lb bombs under the wings.
Squadron Service 800, 803, 890,736, 787 Naval Air Squadrons

Notes
The first jet fighter to equip front line RN fighter squadrons, the Attacker is a conservative design and the only jet fighter yet developed with a tail-wheel undercarriage. 800 and 803 NAS`are serving in the new HMS EAGLE. Attackers are expected to be an interim operational type and Sea Hawks are to replace them once the Sea Fury units have been re-equipped.

Westland WYVERN

Variants TF2, TF4
Role Torpedo/strike-fighter
Engine 1 x Armstrong Siddeley Python ASP3 turboprop developing 4,110 ehp
Span 44ft (20ft folded) **Length** 42ft 3ft **Height** 15ft 9ft **Max weight** 24,500lb
Max speed 330 knots **Crew** 1 pilot
Equipment Torpedo attack recording camera, VHF radio
Armament 4 x 20mm Hispano cannon in wings; provision for a single Mark 15 or 17 torpedo or 1,000lb or 500lb bomb on centreline plus 16 x 2" or 8 x 3" rocket projectiles or 2 x 1,000lb or 2 x 500lb bombs under the wings
Squadron Service Due to enter service early in 1953

Notes
Despite having first flown in 1946, problems with the engine and propeller control unit in successive developed versions have delayed the Wyvern's entry into operational service. Although its usefulness as a torpedo aircraft is now questionable, it is still regarded as an important long-range strike aircraft and its entry into operational service is eagerly awaited. Some 20 aircraft to TF2 (with Rolls Clyde engines) and TF4 standard are undergoing development flying. The first squadron is due to form early in 1953.

Westland DRAGONFLY

Variants HR1, HR3
Role Plane-guard/air-sea-rescue helicopter
Engine 1 x Alvis Leonides 50 developing 550hp
Rotor span 49ft **Length** 55ft 4ft **Height** 12ft 11ft **Max weight** 5,870lb
Max speed 90 knots **Crew** 1 pilot + 1 aircrewman
Equipment Rescue winch, VHF radio
Armament Hand-held weapons for aircrew on Korean operations
Squadron Service 705 Naval Air Squadron, numerous carrier and air station air-sea-rescue flights.

Notes

RN name for the Sikorsky S-51 built under licence by Westland, the Dragonfly has nearly replaced the Sea Otter amphibian in air-sea-rescue flights in carriers and at air stations ashore and will have taken the task over completely by early next year. It has proved its value in the Korean conflict with the Commonwealth light fleet carriers on station being among the first to embark the type. The HR1 has wooden rotor blades, the improved HR3 has metal rotor blades and hydraulic servo controls. Although they are eventually to be replaced by Whirlwinds, Dragonflies remain in production for the RN.

FUTURE NAVAL AIRCRAFT

Vickers Supermarine N113D

Treasury approval has been given for the Admiralty to order 100 fighters to Specification N113D through the Ministry of Supply. The first prototype is expected to fly early in 1954 and the type is expected to enter service in 1956. The N113 is a swept-wing development of the twin-jet Type 508 which was demonstrated at Farnborough last year. The outstanding feature of this interceptor fighter is its rate of climb, expected to be in the region of 20,000 feet per minute. With a maximum speed of over 640 knots and a ceiling of 49,000', two 30mm Aden cannon and air-to-air guided missiles, this new aircraft will make interception from a deck-alert possible.

NA38

A revised Naval Staff requirement for a two-seat all-weather fighter has been accepted by the Ministry of Supply and issued to the de Havilland Aircraft Company. The Admiralty had hoped that it would be met by the DH 116, a comparatively small high-performance single-engined aircraft with re-heat which was in the design-study stage. It emerged, however, that the firm's design capacity was insufficient for the work and the project was abandoned. As an alternative the Ministry of Supply recommended that the DH110 be considered and an investigation into the possible application of this type to meet NA38 is now taking place. Preliminary appreciations of its suitability are encouraging. It actually takes less stowage space than a Sea Venom since it can be stowed nose under tail and its substantial load-carrying capability makes it suitable for adaptation as a strike aircraft. It is hoped to have a fighter version in service in about 1957.

NA39

A Naval Staff Requirement for a two-seat strike aircraft to replace the Wyvern has been placed with the Ministry of Supply. It calls for an aircraft capable of carrying a weapon load of 4,000lb over a radius of action of 500 nautical miles and further after a reduction in weapon load. Maximum speed at sea level is to be not less than 580 knots. It is hoped that this aircraft can enter service from 1959.

NA43

Calls for an anti-submarine and general purpose helicopter of about 15,000lb capable of carrying dipping asdic and an A/S homing weapon or the equivalent weight of depth charges. Early indications are that this requirement may be met by a version of the Bristol 173, the prototype of which is now flying.

Short M123D

Is a light anti-submarine aircraft which can be easily and economically produced in quantity if necessary and which is capable of operating in rough weather from small carriers. Shorts were awarded the contract and are producing an aircraft of robust yet simple construction capable of carrying limited search equipment or a weapon load. The first is expected to fly in 1953 and in the event of hostilities, quantity production will enable a rapid expansion of the RN's anti-submarine strength.

TBM-3E Avenger

100 Avengers are being supplied by the USN under the Mutual Defence Aid Plan (MDAP) to augment and replace Barracudas and Fireflies which are becoming obsolescent in the anti-submarine role to maintain operational capability until the Gannet fully enters service. They will be modified to RN equipment standards by Scottish Aviation at Prestwick. Avengers have already replaced Fireflies in the RCN.

USN Helicopters

25 HO4S-3 (S-55) helicopters are to be delivered to the RN from the USN under MDAP to allow early evaluation by the RN of dipping asdic tactics. The first squadron is scheduled to form in 1953. 20 Hiller helicopters are being delivered under MDAP to be used for pilot training duties.

OTHER NAVAL AIRCRAFT TYPES IN SERVICE

DAVID HOBBS COLLECTION

Airspeed OXFORD

Engines 2 x Armstrong Siddeley Cheetah X each delivering 370hp
Crew 1 or 2 pilots and up to 4 passengers

A few remain in service with 782 NAS used to give naval pilots conversion experience on twin-engined aircraft.

DAVID HOBBS COLLECTION

Avro ANSON

Engines 2 x Armstrong Siddeley Cheetah IX each delivering 350hp
Crew 1 or 2 pilots and up to 6 passengers

Used by 750 NAS for the observer school, 771 NAS fleet requirements unit and several station flights for a variety of training and second line tasks.

Beech EXPEDITOR

Engines 2 x Pratt & Whitney Wasp Junior each delivering 450hp
Crew 1 pilot an up to 8 passengers

80 were provided to the RN by the USN during the war under Lend/Lease arrangements for use as light transport aircraft worldwide. 2 remain with 728 NAS at RNAS Hal Far (Malta) to support the squadron's trials programme with passenger and freight movement. Others operate with 781 and 782 NAS on the southern and northern 'clipper' routes.

Boulton Paul BALLIOL

Engine 1 x Rolls Royce Merlin 35 delivering 1,280hp
Crew 2 pilots

The first prototype of this navalised version of the RAF Balliol flew in October. They are fully capable of deck landing, free take-off and catapult launching from aircraft carriers and 30 are being procured for a variety of second line and training tasks.

353

De Havilland TIGER MOTH

Engine 1 x de Havilland Gipsy Major delivering 130hp
Crew 1 or 2 pilots

Used for a variety of flying grading and air experience tasks at air stations.

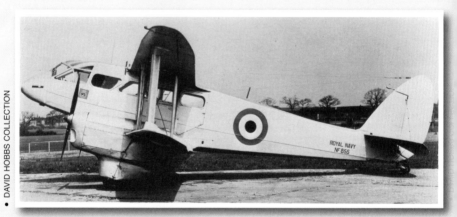

De Havilland DOMINIE

Engines 2 x de Havilland Gipsy 6 each delivering 200hp
Crew 1 pilot, 1 aircrewman and up to 9 passengers

A number of Dominies operate the RN southern and northern 'clipper' routes with 781 and 782 NAS carrying passengers and light freight between naval air stations on a daily basis.

De Havilland SEA MOSQUITO/MOSQUITO

Engines 2 x Rolls Royce Merlin 25 each delivering 1,640hp
Crew 1 pilot + 1 observer/winch operator

Mosquitoes were replaced in naval fleet requirements units by purpose-built aircraft earlier this year but a few, manned by civilian aircrew as part of target facility units, may still be seen flying near naval gunnery ranges.

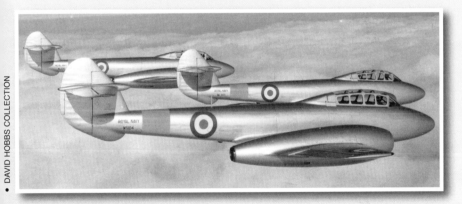

Gloster METEOR

Engines 2 x Rolls Royce Derwent 8 each rated at 3,600lb
Crew 2 pilots

A modified Meteor III fitted with an arrester-hook landed on HMS IMPLACABLE in 1948, the first British twin-jet aircraft to land on a carrier. T7 trainer versions have been procured by the RN for use converting experienced fighter pilots onto jets and for various fleet requirement tasks.

355

Hunting Percival SEA PRINCE

Engines 2 x Alvis Leonides 125 each delivering 550hp
Crew light transport 1 pilot + 8 passengers; Trainer 1 pilot + 1 staff observer +
3 student observers

42 Sea Prince T1s have been ordered to replace the variety of aircraft used by 750 NAS as part of the observer school at RNAS St Merryn. They are expected to enter service early in 1953; the 4 C1 versions are to be used by 781 NAS and air station flights in the light transport role.

Miles MARTINET

Engine 1 x Bristol Mercury XX delivering 870hp
Crew 1 pilot + 1 winch operator

Used extensively by the RN throughout the world during the war, only a handful of Martinet target-towing aircraft remain with 771 NAS at RNAS Ford for fleet requirements duties.

North American HARVARD

Engine 1 x Pratt & Whitney Wasp delivering 550hp
Crew 2 pilots

The number of Harvards in service has reduced but the type continues to serve as a utility trainer with 781 NAS and with 1830(RNVR), 1831(RNVR), 1832(RNVR), 1833 (RNVR) and 1840(RNVR) NAS.

Short STURGEON

Engines 2 x Rolls Royce Merlin 140S each delivering 1,660hp
Crew 1 pilot + 1 observer/aircrewman

Originally conceived as a carrier-borne strike aircraft, 23 Sturgeons have been procured for the RN as high-speed target aircraft capable of operating from carriers. Those with the Home Fleet were withdrawn earlier this year and they now serve only with 728 NAS at RNAS Hal Far in Malta in support of the Mediterranean Fleet. The elongated nose houses camera equipment to film firings.

357

Supermarine SEA OTTER

Engine 1 x Bristol Mercury XXX delivering 855hp
Crew 1 pilot + 1 observer and up to 2 passengers

Now almost completely replaced in the air-sea-rescue role by Dragonfly helicopters, a few Sea Otters may still be seen flying from air stations in the UK. The type is the last amphibian aircraft to be built by Supermarine, ending a long tradition.

OTHER AIRCRAFT YOU MAY ALSO SEE

Several air stations have retained in flying condition aircraft types that were used during the war and these may be seen from time to time. These include several Swordfish (above), a Hellcat and a Fulmar. Prototypes that are not necessarily intended for front line service such as the Hawker P1052 (below) are occasionally seen embarked in carriers for flying trials and at naval air stations. A number of other redundant old airframes can be seen concentrated at airfields awaiting disposal.

359

Index of Ship Names

363

364

369

371

372

OUR OTHER TITLES FOR YOUR BOOKSHELF...